European Modernity

Europe's Legacy in the Modern World

Series Editors: Martti Koskenniemi and Bo Stråth
(University of Helsinki, Finland)

The nineteenth century is often described as Europe's century. This series aims to explore the truth of this claim. It views Europe as a global actor and offers insights into its role in ordering the world, creating community and providing welfare in the nineteenth century and beyond. Volumes in the series investigate tensions between the national and the global, welfare and warfare, property and poverty. They look at how notions like democracy, populism and totalitarianism came to be intertwined and how this legacy persists in the present day world.

The series emphasizes the entanglements between the legal, the political and the economic, and employs techniques and methodologies from the history of legal, political and economic thought, the history of events, and structural history. The result is a collection of works that shed new light on the role that Europe's intellectual history has played in the development of the modern world.

Published:

Historical Teleologies in the Modern World, edited by Henning Trüper, Dipesh Chakrabarty and Sanjay Subrahmanyam

Europe's Utopias of Peace, Bo Stråth

Forthcoming:

Political Reform in the Ottoman and Russian Empires, Adrian Brisku

Social Difference in Nineteenth-Century Spanish America: An Intellectual History, Francisco A. Ortega

European Modernity

A Global Approach

Bo Stråth and Peter Wagner

Bloomsbury Academic
An imprint of Bloomsbury Publishing Plc

B L O O M S B U R Y
LONDON • OXFORD • NEW YORK • NEW DELHI • SYDNEY

Bloomsbury Academic
An imprint of Bloomsbury Publishing Plc

50 Bedford Square	1385 Broadway
London	New York
WC1B 3DP	NY 10018
UK	USA

www.bloomsbury.com

BLOOMSBURY and the Diana logo are trademarks of Bloomsbury Publishing Plc

First published 2017

© Bo Stråth and Peter Wagner, 2017

Bo Stråth and Peter Wagner have asserted their right under the Copyright, Designs and Patents Act, 1988, to be identified as Authors of this work.

All rights reserved. No part of this publication may be reproduced or transmitted in any form or by any means, electronic or mechanical, including photocopying, recording, or any information storage or retrieval system, without prior permission in writing from the publishers.

No responsibility for loss caused to any individual or organization acting on or refraining from action as a result of the material in this publication can be accepted by Bloomsbury or the authors.

British Library Cataloguing-in-Publication Data
A catalogue record for this book is available from the British Library.

ISBN: HB: 978-1-3500-0707-9
PB: 978-1-3500-0706-2
ePDF: 978-1-3500-0708-6
eBook: 978-1-3500-0709-3

Library of Congress Cataloging-in-Publication Data
A catalog record for this book is available from the Library of Congress.

Series: Europe's Legacy in the Modern World

Cover image © Emma Espejo/Getty Images

Typeset by RefineCatch Limited, Bungay, Suffolk

To find out more about our authors and books visit www.bloomsbury.com. Here you will find extracts, author interviews, details of forthcoming events and the option to sign up for our newsletters.

CONTENTS

Preface vii

1 Introduction: Europe – Modernity – European Modernity 1

Part One: Europe in Time and Space

2 An Origin and Goal of European History? The Long-term Perspective 25

3 What is Europe? 40

Part Two: European Interpretations of Modernity

4 Europe's Hesitations with Democracy 69

5 The Market-industrial Revolution in Global Perspective: Colonial Heritage and the Social Question 87

6 The Modern European and the Quest for Individual Autonomy 111

7 Religion and Modernity in Europe: The Christians and the Others – the Religious-political Entanglement 127

Part Three: The Great Transformations of European Modernity

8 The First Great Transformation: Organized Modernity for Welfare and Warfare (1870s–1960s) 147

9 The New Great Transformation: The Dismantling of Organized Modernity and the Search for New Forms of Social 'Self-defence' (1960s to the Present)   168

10 From Ambiguity to Disorientation: European Modernity Derailed   186

Notes   194
Bibliography   219
Index   234

PREFACE

At the beginning of this century, the authors of this book were both working at the European University Institute (EUI) in Florence, in the Departments of History and Civilization and of Political and Social Sciences respectively, organizing seminars and workshops on the modernity of Europe together with doctoral researchers and colleagues. It was a time of intense debate about the future shape of Europe with the introduction of the Euro as common currency, the drafting of a Constitution for the European Union and the accession of several East European countries to the EU. 'Europeanization' was a key sub-concept in the great globalization narrative that was then hegemonic. But it was disputed what Europeanization meant in relation to globalization. Did it signal that Europe was getting ready for a global self-propelling market society? Or was Europe trying to define a particular place within the transforming globe, a place in which and from which alternative courses of action could be developed? This was a moment for reflecting anew about the time-honoured theme of European modernity. The common view held that modernity originated in Europe and diffused from there across the globe. But in the early twenty-first century it seemed as if a global modernity had arisen that was to overwhelm any specificity of Europe.

Clearly, the way in which European modernity was embedded in a global context had to be rethought. On the one hand, Europe had to be provincialized, to use Dipesh Chakrabarty's felicitous term. But on the other hand, themes from the history of European modernity had to be retrieved to enable us to see the current global context as more than just a world market emancipated from any political agency. In one part of our work, we were looking for a perspective which emphasized the political embedding of the market and the political responsibility for the economy, as opposed to the standard view of the time in which a borderless market economy transcended political borders escaping control. With our colleague in the Law Department of EUI, Christian Joerges, we organized the research project *The Economy as a Polity*, funded by the Research Council of the Institute to organize workshops which gave us important impulses and resulted in a publication under the same title in which we argued for a new perspective on the connection between political and economic matters, questioning the prevailing hegemony of market autonomy. We are grateful to Christian Joerges and the participants in the workshops for our discussions on the economy as a polity. In parallel, we worked on numerous other aspects of European modernity and its transformations. References to the results of this work can be found throughout this book. At the same time, we had the ambition to elaborate a synthesis from these years of work in common. This is the background to this volume, of which we wrote a first outline almost ten years ago. But we did not then succeed in weaving together the numerous threads.

After our time at EUI, we continued our discussions and developed our thoughts and our research further within the framework of two European Research Council (ERC) Advanced Grant projects at the Universities of Helsinki (EReRe; grant no. 229700) and Barcelona (TRAMOD; grant no. 249438) respectively. We are grateful to ERC for the generous funding that made it possible for us to deepen our historical and sociological understanding of European modernity, in particular with regard to revisiting Europe's transformations during the nineteenth century, in the centre of EReRe, and with regard to comparing non-European and European varieties of modernity, in the centre of TRAMOD. We would also like to express our thanks to the members of the EReRe and TRAMOD research groups whose observations and comments have helped us to develop our analysis.

This second period of work fell into the time after the collapse of the global financial markets in 2008 and the subsequent fast erosion of the globalization narrative. An alternative view on the global context of European modernity, in contrast to the globalization rhetoric of the 1990s, became both more necessary and more plausible. Due to our parallel work on the ERC projects and due to the change in circumstances, our view on European modernity in historical perspective acquired a more distinct profile. We had always been critical of the influential perspective that sees modernity as the consequence of some intrinsic force within Europe, the combined effect of Enlightenment philosophy and the French and industrial revolutions accomplishing the modernization project as a model for the world. But now it became possible to spell out an alternative view in much more specific terms. Connecting to new research results and perspectives on Europe in the world by Kenneth Pomeranz, Christopher Bayly, Jürgen Osterhammel and others we discerned the European 'take-off' much more in terms of exploitation of global resources such as African slaves and American soil which provided possibilities for politics of both warfare and welfare. The shape of Europe's modernity came from without as much as from within and it was politically created for good and for evil, ambiguous and contradictory. 'Modernization' and 'globalization' then look very different than in the standard narrative, as we hope to demonstrate on the following pages.

We elaborated the ideas and conducted the research for this book in close co-operation during our common time in Florence and again in intense exchange over the past two years. All chapters have been jointly designed, developed and repeatedly discussed. But we also think that texts written by committees often lose the sense of engagement conveyable in personal writing. Thus, the reader will recognize two voices being in dialogue throughout this book, responding to each other and persistently generating new questions in the responses.

Torrita di Siena and Barcelona, July 2016
Bo Stråth   Peter Wagner

1

Introduction:

Europe – Modernity – European Modernity

Modernity is less European and Europe is less modern than we have for too long been used to thinking: this is what this book aims to show.

Two views about our recent history and present time are often taken for granted: that modernity emerged in Europe and diffused from there across the world; and that Europe has been the heartland of modernity during the nineteenth and twentieth centuries. These views are sustained from two distinct, but interrelated perspectives, a historico-philosophical and a historico-sociological one. In the former terms, modernity emerges with the philosophy of the Enlightenment. Modernity is here defined through the emphasis on the autonomy of the human being as a thinking and willing subject, and René Descartes is often seen as the crucial author. The perspective is extended in politico-philosophical terms by Thomas Hobbes and John Locke who grounded the modern polity on reason-endowed individuals and their capacity to enter into a social contract with one another. In historico-sociological terms, the Enlightenment marks a cultural-intellectual revolution that sparks off a political and an economic revolution: the French Revolution aimed to ground political power in popular sovereignty, and the market-industrial revolution expected increasing affluence and well-being from liberating the human 'propensity to truck, barter and trade' (Adam Smith) and from enrolling fossil fuels in the production of commodities. This double revolution, so the argument goes, set societies on an entirely new trajectory, combining the normative commitment to freedom with the functional superiority gained through an increasing mastery of nature. These are the core elements of the story of European modernity, which is a story of Europe because this is the space where the key events took place and from where their impact spread across the planet, and it is a story of modernity because of the rise to prominence of the principles of autonomy and mastery.

This story has often been told and often been criticized. Critique has accompanied modernity from its beginnings. There are problems in the reasoning, and there is too much historical counter-evidence for the account to be easily repeated any longer. But despite all criticism, the story always resurfaces. With the disastrous experiences of the first half of the European twentieth century, it seemed that this account was discredited once and for all. But after the end of the Second World War US-based modernization theory revived the story as a sociological account of modernization based on the institutionalization of freedom and functional differentiation. And at the end of the twentieth century, shortly after philosophers had talked about the end of all grand narratives of emancipation, the era of 'globalization' was announced as the one of 'human rights and democracy' and of the global realization of market society for the benefit of all. These revised stories have their core sites in North America or in an undifferentiated globe, respectively, but they trace their origins always back to Europe. Critiques of such accounts and alternative explanations often have much in their favour, but they fail to challenge the core of the persistent view to such an extent that it finally crumbles and fades away.

The reasons for this failure of critique lie in two errors of overemphasis. In more historico-sociologically oriented critique, the 'darker side of modernity' or the darkness of the European continent, paraphrasing Walter Mignolo and Mark Mazower respectively, is overemphasized to such an extent that whatever brightness there may also have been tends to become invisible. In more historico-philosophically oriented critiques, in turn, the normative promises of Enlightenment thinking are often recognized but they are considered as absolutely self-cancelling either because of conceptual flaws or because of their undermining in the attempt at historical realization. Theodor W. Adorno and Max Horkheimer's *Dialectic of Enlightenment* is the master account of such self-cancellation.[1] As none of these two critical views is entirely convincing – there is also brightness in European modernity, and it has never been absolutely cancelled out – the standard view that conflates the history of Europe with the realization of the promises of modernity keeps resurfacing. While it faces evident problems of persuasiveness itself, it serves too well the optimistic views, and the interests, of the agents who think they are driving history – may they be European national and colonial elites of the late nineteenth and early twentieth centuries; US political and economic strategists after the Second World War; or the global business elites of our present time, in each case including their intellectual fellow travellers.

To overcome this impasse, two movements are necessary. On the one hand, European history has to be placed in larger spatial contexts. It needs to be shown that what happened in Europe in 1800 or in 1900 is not 'European' in the sense of being specific to its place of occurrence, but has to be understood in its connectedness with larger spatial constellations. On the other hand, 'European modernity' should not be conceptualized as something that has been defined at one moment and then is being worked out in history, is either being realized or cancels itself out. Rather, the term modernity should be used to refer to a mode of world-interpretation that always demands specification in socio-historical situations, thus is never stable or devoid of ambiguity. Therefore, rather than identifying key features of 'European modernity' once and for all, a history of Europe needs to focus on socio-political transformations to identify the dynamics of modernity at work in challenges and in the responses to those challenges.[2]

Let us provide one illustration of our approach before going on. The standard view of European modernity, without using this term, arises during the nineteenth century. It connects the events of the late eighteenth century as mentioned above – Enlightenment, French Revolution, market-industrial revolution – with the fact of European world-domination achieved in the late nineteenth century. On a closer look, however, as we will argue, the rise of Europe to world-domination during the nineteenth century was not the result of accomplishments internal to an evolving project of 'European modernity'. Contrary to widespread belief, both scholarly and public, there was not that much in the intellectual, economic or political characteristics of Europe prior to the nineteenth century that can be seen as the seeds or sources from which modernity only needed to grow or spring. Rather, the so-called 'rise of Europe' was the regional consequence of a socio-political transformation of global dimensions. Most importantly, the triangular commercial relations across the Atlantic that had steadily grown over the preceding three centuries, using African labour and American soil under European military superiority, paved the way for freeing Western Europe from constraints to economic growth that it had shared with other world-regions up to this moment. At the same time, European elites succeeded in keeping relative peace among themselves while transferring conflicts to other parts of the world – her colonies, her former colonies, and the societies Europe was still trying to dominate by colonial or other means.

Thus, one cannot speak in any persuasive way of an antecedent European modernity that brought about the emerging European world-domination, namely because of its functional and normative superiority. And neither did such European world-domination mean the breakthrough of modernity. None of the features that have come to be seen as characteristic of modernity in scholarly debates over the past half-century can easily be detected in nineteenth-century Europe. Political modernity is today normally identified with the commitment to popular sovereignty expressed in the democratic nation-state. But by 1900, most European societies were not nation-states but colonial empires. They were not inclusive democracies either but oligarchies that operated with restricted suffrage. Economic modernity, in turn, is today often equated with liberating markets from state regulation and creating the free economic agent operating on markets. But even though industrial capitalism spread, market self-regulation had widely been found deficient and economic exchange remained highly regulated in Europe.

Economic growth occurred more through industrialization than through market exchange. Class-divided societies emerged instead of market societies in which producers met each other on equal terms. Thirdly, one tends to think of modernity as separating religion from politics, but in Europe the Christian churches mostly operated in close institutionalized alliance with the state. Finally, and maybe most importantly, we tend to think of modernity as committed to the idea of the autonomous individual, but in nineteenth- and much of twentieth-century Europe this idea remained largely limited to bourgeois and 'bohémien', entrepreneurial and artistic models of self-realization, thus to small groups in society, while 'the masses' were conceptualized as classes and nations, thus as collectivities with little scope for individuality.

This book re-examines the question of European modernity in the light of the above observations. It re-positions Europe in the global context of the nineteenth and twentieth centuries, without though giving up on the idea of a specificity of Europe and on the usefulness of the concept of modernity. Rather than erroneously equating the recent history of Europe with the rise of modernity, it treats the European nineteenth-century specificity that we have become used to calling 'modern' as the temporary crystallization of a socio-political formation within a global context, on the one hand. And, on the other, it shows that such a Europe can be seen as elaborating a particular interpretation of modernity, with its specific tensions around notions of class, nation, market and society, rather than a universal project of modernity of which Europe is the avant-garde and which everyone else needs to follow. In other words, we need to disentangle the concept of modernity from the history of Europe to be able to answer two questions that often arise, but are rarely adequately addressed: how far and in which sense can European societies and polities at certain moments indeed be called modern? And what does modernity mean once one distances oneself from the history of Europe during so-called early modern and modern times? The remainder of this introductory chapter will provisionally explore these questions further, starting with the former one, to prepare the ground for the more detailed analysis in the course of the book.

The historico-sociological notion of European modernity

At the end of the nineteenth century, the notion that European societies were in some way ahead of others was widespread. To have embarked on a steady trajectory of progress was part of the European self-understanding; and elites in other societies were often observing Europe with a view to identifying which aspects of them could and should be emulated to catch up with Europe. The European sense of superiority was expressed in distinctions between one's own social organization and the traditional or primitive ones, as employed in early sociology and anthropology. Conversely, the concepts of European sociology were translated into other languages, such as Chinese or Japanese, to enable their application in those contexts.[3] Searching for the roots of what he should call occidental rationalism, Max Weber would famously ask in the early twentieth century, 'what concatenation of circumstances has led to the fact that in the Occident, and here only, cultural phenomena have appeared which – as at least we like to imagine – lie in a direction of development of universal significance and validity?'

Thus, we have good reason to locate the emergence of some notion of European modernity in the nineteenth century, and to see early European sociology as a key intellectual site where such notion was forged. Certainly, the noun 'modernity' was not used, and few authors would identify their object of investigation strictly speaking as 'Europe'. But the view was widespread that some significant rupture with past socio-political organization had occurred, putting social life on new foundations, and that this had happened in a region of the planet that could be as small as a part of Northwestern Europe or as large as Western Europe and North America combined, but was often referred to as 'Europe' or 'the West'. As a first step, at least, we can therefore proceed to understand what 'European modernity' came to mean by looking at the thinking about social relations during the long European nineteenth century, which lasted from 1789 to 1914, referring to a range of scholars reaching from Henri de Saint-Simon and G.W.F. Hegel, Alexis de Tocqueville and Karl Marx to Émile Durkheim, Max Weber and Georg Simmel. Across all differences between them, these authors had in common that they identified a profound rupture in social life that had brought about, or was to bring about, a radically new form of social relations and social structure. Even though they chose different terms for characterizing the rupture and the ensuing social transformation, and varied in the identification of the events that they saw as most significant for the transformation (we come back to these issues below), they made the analysis of the emergent social formation their key concern, both because it was new and because it would mark the present and the future.

Modernity, in the sum of these authors' views, was characterized by a number of features that had been absent from the social world before the rupture or at least only of marginal importance. Modernity brought with itself a novel way of being-in-the-world and novel attitudes to the world as well as to other human beings, which were captured by terms such as abstract freedom, individual instrumental rationality ('egotistical calculation', in Marx and Engels's words), individualism, and occidental rationalism. The novel social constellation within which human beings found themselves and within which these attitudes grew, in turn, was captured by terms such as industry, division of labour, democracy, bourgeois society, working class and capitalism. Even though earlier developments are sometimes mentioned, all these authors claimed that these attitudes and constellations emerged, or arose to dominance, in Europe from the late eighteenth and early nineteenth century onwards.

It remains important to note, however, that, rather than developing an institutional analysis of 'modernity' as an established novel social configuration, these historically minded scholars aimed to grasp the meaning and consequences of the 'Great Transformation' (Karl Polanyi) that they had been witnessing and for which they were in need of new concepts. In other words, those scholars to whom we now refer as theorists of modernity tried to understand the European nineteenth century. But they were not entirely aware that it was this that they were doing, or maybe better: that doing this was possibly not the same as 'theorizing modernity'. And the canonization of sociology has forgotten about those scholars as persons, their intentions and the context of their writing. As a consequence, one has tended to conflate 'modernity' with the European nineteenth century. Before reflecting in more detail about the theoretical programmes of these authors, we shall therefore briefly explore the historical context that these authors were addressing.

The European nineteenth century

What was Europe in the nineteenth century? To answer this question, in due brevity in a preliminary way here, we will not directly investigate what these authors knew about their contemporary world, but will use the information we have at our hands today, most importantly contributions to the recently developed area of 'world-history'.[4]

In this current view, there was little difference in social and economic life between Europe and at least some other regions in the world, in particular in Asia, by 1800. By 1900, however, the world was dominated by European powers, in a combination of superior military force, actual colonial occupation and settlement of non-European territories, and by economic exchange – the conditions for which were often dictated by the Europeans. Partly as a consequence of this domination, furthermore, elites in non-European societies saw themselves as lagging behind and often considered the absence of European ideas and concepts as the cause for their weakness and slowness to change. As a remedy, thus, they aimed at importing and adopting European concepts for reordering their social life, including concepts from European sociology.

Today, we have good reasons to assume that 'the Great Divergence' (Kenneth Pomeranz) between Europe and other world-regions that emerged in the course of the nineteenth century was a contingent event. It was conditioned, as mentioned above, by the triangular commercial relations across the Atlantic that had slowly evolved over the preceding three centuries. In turn, current scholarship suggests, there was rather little in earlier intra-European history that prepared the ground for the European 'take-off' (Walt

Rostow). Neither legal regimes, in particular concerning property rights, nor technological advances emerging from the later so-called Scientific Revolution, nor the rise of universities in the early second millennium CE as autonomous sites for debate and exploration or of cities as sites for politico-economic organization, nor the power divide between pope and emperor mark such a difference between Europe and other world-regions that they could explain nineteenth-century developments. Whatever impact some of them may have had, this pales in comparison with the effects of the novel Atlantic trade regime.

Furthermore, it seems now less persuasive to see the 'cause' of the historical rupture in the combination of a socio-economic and an intellectual event, namely the rise of the bourgeoisie and the emergence of political economy and the associated idea of market freedom. Regardless of whether one sees the former as determining the latter or the latter as opening the path for the former, the transformative power of either has been exaggerated. In the early nineteenth century, the new economic possibilities created by the Atlantic connections came to be perceived. But no new world with new dominant actors arose. Rather, in response to the new possibilities, the old aristocratic elites gradually changed outlook and started building new alliances, containing any radical new visions as created in the French Revolution and in political economy and imposing their power in the novel constellation through violence at home and abroad. The period between the Vienna Congress of 1815 and the Versailles Peace Treaty of 1919 in Europe was neither as peaceful nor as revolutionary as has often been suggested. True, it witnessed the rise of industry, and with it, of wealth and power, both highly asymmetrically distributed. But the socio-political transformation that has often been seen to accompany the techno-economic transformation remained very limited.[5]

Thus, the fundamental change between 1800 and 1900 was the rise of Europe to world-domination, based on the exploitation of new techno-economic possibilities enabled by the emergence of the Atlantic division of labour. In principle, this was recognized by, for instance, Marx and Engels who, in their short and forceful account of recent social transformations in *The Communist Manifesto*, asserted that the 'discovery of America [and] the rounding of the Cape' gave an 'impulse never before known' to the revolutionary bourgeoisie. But even in their text this is an opening remark without consequences for the further analysis. Otherwise, scholars tended to see the changes in Europe as an 'endogenous' and self-propelled history either as determined by a logics of history, reaching from functional accomplishments and selection of superior solutions to the determined dynamics of class struggle, or at the least as producing inescapable results of a path once entered. In other words, by now we can say that nineteenth-century sociologists misconceived the causes of the European social transformations of the same period. What does this entail for their view of the modernity that they saw as being produced by those alleged causes?

Rethinking the historico-sociological notion of European modernity

Thus, we take a second brief look at the notion of modernity that emerged during the long nineteenth century. Two observations were crucial to the early European sociology of modernity: first, these scholars perceived a rather radical *rupture* in history, exemplified by the Industrial Revolution and the French Revolution – even though the relation between the two remained under-explored, and the latter under-theorized, with few exceptions such as de Tocqueville and to some extent Lorenz von Stein. Second, as alluded to above, they perceived a *dynamics* of history, which may not have been sociologically explicit in Hegel, but became evident from the middle of the nineteenth century onwards, with *The Communist Manifesto* of 1848 as a prime example. In connection of the two perceptions, the European sociology of modernity diagnosed a radical destruction of the existing fabric of social relations, which in turn unleashed an unprecedented dynamics.

As a consequence, the early European sociology of modernity provided predominantly an analysis of movement; it offered few 'portraits' of modernity. Émile Durkheim is the main European exception on which Talcott Parsons and the US-based sociology of 'modern society' should build after the Second World War. Such a claim may seem unfounded at first sight now that we have come to think of 'modernity' with the Parsonsian image of 'modern society' in mind. But we may interrogate its validity by briefly looking backward from Parsons's developed viewpoint. Parsons offered an institutional image of society as differentiated into subsystems with their own logics, including an economic system based on market exchange regulated by money and a political system underpinned by the formal, impersonal rules of rational administration. The image used elements of the European sociology of modernity, but it assembled them towards a coherence and stability that cannot be found in the original version, again with the partial exception of Durkheim. Following the political economists, Marx analysed money-regulated market exchange, but he insisted on the antagonism in the underlying social relations that would prevent any market from stabilizing into an economic system. Weber's 'dwelling-place of steel' (rather mistranslated as 'iron cage') is a 'portrait', indeed working with a visual metaphor to illustrate the outcome of rationalization, but Weber was sceptical about the stability of this construction, rather expecting it to be challenged and possibly dismantled because of its lack of desirability.

Why the European sociology of modernity emphasized tendencies rather than providing an institutional model of society can easily be understood against the background of the time. By 1900, as mentioned above, European societies did not look very modern at all, if one applies the post-Second World War view of 'modern society'. The resort to tendencies could make these empirical problems acceptable by projecting the full realization of modernity into an indefinite future. We may say that the European sociology of modernity engaged with the opening of the time-horizon effected by socio-political thought from the late eighteenth century onwards,[6] oscillating between more determinist, teleological projections of a future modernity on the one side, and indecisiveness and scepticism on the other. Sociologists certainly participated in the broadly evolutionist mode of thinking, triggered by the apparently unstoppable rise of Europe during the nineteenth century. Few of them, however, adopted a blunt linear view of progress across history, and of Europe as the territorial site of such progress. Let us just recall the tension in Marx's work between identification of the laws of class struggle and capitalist competition on the one hand, and the concern about the possible 'common ruin of the contending classes' on the other; and similarly Weber's analysis of the ongoing rationalization processes on the one side, as opposed to his conjecture about the return of old values or the rise of new prophets on the other. The observation of the novel social forms (structures) and novel human beings (rational individuals) constituted an agenda for thought and for action; it did not lead straight into a theory of modernity because the observed 'modernity' was too unstable and tension-ridden.

In the early years of the twentieth century, Weber being a key example, the tone of the self-diagnosis of modernity had indeed changed. The now so-called classical sociologists – such as Weber, Durkheim, Georg Simmel and Vilfredo Pareto – were struggling with a social transformation that we can now recognize as a first crisis of the kind of modernity that had emerged from nineteenth-century events, not least the development of capacities for collective action – by states, nations, classes – to counteract problematic consequences of trends set in motion.[7] These scholars were no longer, in their own view, writing at the dawn of a new era, as Saint-Simon, Hegel, de Tocqueville and even Marx had some reason to assume they were. They were looking back at a major transformation and were trying to assess its outcomes. Significantly, they were uncertain about both how such an assessment could proceed and what its results would be. The former uncertainty led to writings in the philosophy and methodology of the social sciences of often high sophistication; the latter to the ambivalence-ridden diagnoses that we have referred to above. The 'modernity' that the 'classical sociologists' were experiencing was everything but stable; and they knew so. Whether it would stabilize depended very much on how the future would look like, beyond the lifetime of these alleged founders of the European sociology of modernity.

To put it briefly, that future came to look bleak. The experience of the First World War, totalitarianism, the Great Depression and the Second World War shook any remaining optimistic expectations. Those who continued the critical historico-sociological investigations of the present time along the lines set out by earlier scholars could not fail to take these events into account. In 1935, Karl Mannheim published his book *Man and Society in an Age of Reconstruction*, which proposed to see 'fundamental democratization' as the key force in socio-political change of the time. He linked up to de Tocqueville's observation, a century earlier, that the democratic imaginary was so powerful in contemporary societies that inclusive-egalitarian participation had become the telos of politico-institutional change. At the same time, he recognized that this change could occur in such form and at such speed that democracy was at risk of self-cancellation.[8] A few years later, in 1944, Karl Polanyi's *The Great Transformation* provided a similar analysis focusing on the instability created by the dynamics of economic change. The idea of market self-regulation, the dominant economic ideology during the first half of the nineteenth century, entailed commodification, the tendency to turn goods into commodities even though they were not – and could not be – produced with the purpose of being exchanged, most importantly labour, land and money. Against such inappropriate commodification, which was destructive of social life, the 'self-defence of society' arose, and Polanyi analysed social transformations between the middle of the nineteenth and the middle of the twentieth century from this angle. His key concern was, having witnessed the rise of fascism and of Soviet socialism, in how far such necessary self-defence of society could be pursued without endangering freedom. Yet a few years later, after the end of the Second World War, in *The Origins of Totalitarianism* (1951) Hannah Arendt combined an analysis of an ever-expansive capitalism in the form of imperialism with an analysis of the nation-state that required a stable framework for political action to understand the tensions in European societies that, even though not necessarily so, had exploded and given rise to totalitarianism.

These authors provided powerful diagnoses of their time by employing selective elements from the earlier European sociology of modernity, but by simultaneously interrogating and questioning any previous assumptions about regularity and predictability of trends of modern evolution. Building on detailed historical reconstruction, they recognized the inherent tensions in, and the fragility of, modern socio-political arrangements and emphasized the contingency of historical outcomes, the ever-present possibility that things could have turned out otherwise had human beings acted differently at key moments in history.

The historico-philosophical notion of European modernity

Thus far, we have suggested that it was the specific position of Europe that has underpinned the historical and sociological debate over modernity for the last 150 years. Thus, a particular history was conflated with the – analytical and normative – theorization of society and politics. The critical debates in the middle of the twentieth century, based on experiences earlier in that century, seemed to spell an end to that conflation. European history, and the self-understanding of it, seemed to have returned to a 'normal' track, not different from 'pre-modern' times: 'World history may look like a chaos of chance events – in its entirety like the swirling waters of a whirlpool. It goes on and on, from one muddle to another, from one disaster to another, with brief flashes of happiness, with islands that remain for a short time protected from the flood, till they too are submerged', as Karl Jaspers put it in *The Origin and Goal of History* in 1949 (we come back to Jaspers's diagnosis in Chapter 2). At a closer look, we can see that this scepticism gave way to a new optimism, with its base in the USA and exemplified by the view that modern society had been realized there and was to occur through processes of 'modernization and development' elsewhere. But this new optimism proved short-lived, and by the closing decades of the twentieth century we witness a rapid alternation between declarations of the end of modernity, returning fragility and uncertainty to centre-stage, and those of the end of history, reweaving the thread of grand narratives as if nothing had happened in-between.

But in the light of these fluctuations, what has happened to the normative promises that modernity also entailed? Until now, we have contextualized the European self-praise as modern by relating it to actual European world-domination. But the view, widespread at around 1900, that Europe seemed to be 'ahead' of other societies was not only due to the impression that power leaves on its holders and on those over whom it is exercised. This view demands further reflections on the temporality of modernity, on the question of how far the supposed arrival of modernity in one place, Europe, alters the ways in which human beings situate themselves in time and history worldwide. Analytically speaking, this is the question about a direction of history, which was central to philosophies of history up to the nineteenth century. This genre has largely been abandoned since, at least in academia, leaving the question not only without an answer but even without a fruitful way of posing it – although it does not go away either. In normative terms, this is the question about progress in human history, about modernity as a progressive project that endows itself with the means for its own realization, as expressed in some of the hopes and promises of the Enlightenment.[9]

Our proposal should not be misunderstood as replacing the normative concerns of the philosophy of history with the sober, 'realistic', empirically-based insights of historical-comparative sociology (the relation between the two perspectives is discussed in Chapter 2). Rather, the task is to understand, beyond the strong assumptions in the tradition of philosophy of history, how normative concerns and commitments become forces of historical change by virtue of the fact of being held and shared by historical actors. We shall start the exploration of such an agenda with a brief look at recent debates.

Within the philosophical debates on modernity, the entangling of history and theory has often taken the form of claiming the historical existence of a normative project of modernity that held out promises for humankind on the one hand, and stating that these promises have not – or, not yet – been fulfilled on the other. This theme has been discussed in numerous ways. Most interpretations focus – implicitly or explicitly – on the European experience; within those, two perspectives have been dominant. On the one side, scholars have suggested that modernity's promises have indeed been translated into modern institutions, but that the process is incomplete and that further claims for freedom and justice keep arising and need to be addressed (Jürgen Habermas and Axel Honneth among others). On the other side, authors have emphasized that new forms of domination and oppression have arisen with modernity, and thus that the rise of modernity should be seen as a transformation in the form of domination and oppression rather than the advent of emancipation and liberation (Michel Foucault and Zygmunt Bauman among others).

Although this latter reasoning had originally been developed with the European situation in mind, it is most compelling when associating colonial domination with the history of modernity. Investigating the history of Africa, America and large parts of Asia, the era that in Europe is considered to mark the rise of modernity is clearly one of new forms of oppression originating with the European colonizers. In parts of the globe, therefore, this period does not signal the overcoming of the oppression in an un-Enlightened past, as a traditional European view suggested. Rather, modernity itself, so it seems, inaugurated a history of oppression. At the same time, the observation that modernity held out the prospect of liberation and emancipation is not refuted by this change of perspective. Movements for liberation in the colonized world often, though not always, appealed to the normative claims made in modern European reasoning and led their struggles against European domination in the name of these claims, from the Haitian Revolution to the African National Congress. Thus, the horizon of future freedom and justice, as opened in a novel way during the European Enlightenment, was and remains a point of orientation in the history and present of modernity.

This insight into the deep ambivalence of modernity – inaugurating a history of oppression while at the same time serving as a reference-point for resistance to oppression and struggle for justice – translates into a need for revising the standard temporality of modernity. It is no longer straightforwardly possible to assume that the onset of modernity means exit (nor even the first step of exit) from oppression and injustice on the long but linear way to reaching freedom and justice. If the reference to modernity, depending on the context, can lead to either an increase of freedom and justice or increase of oppression and injustice, or even both, but for different groups or in different places, then modernity needs to be understood in a radically different way than the one maintained by standard historiography, sociology and philosophy.

Contextualizing the historico-philosophical notion of modernity

Developing such a new understanding, we may well preserve the historical reference to the Enlightenment and the subsequent revolutionary transformations; it would be difficult to write world-history or theorize modernity without it. However, these events should no longer be seen as having the clear and indissoluble double meaning that has been taken for granted: namely, being at the same time a breakthrough in normative philosophy, on the higher plane of reason, and, in the this-worldly realm of power and interest, opening the way for a progressive transformation of society and politics. Instead, the philosophical proposals should be seen contextually as responses to socio-political problems that had emerged earlier. Among those are, most importantly: the question of common humanity after the encounter with absolutely unknown and unexpected others in America and the consequences of any recognition of the others for the relation to the 'discovered' territories; the challenge to the presumed certainty of revelation after the scission within Christianity and its impact on the view of the knowledge-seeking subject; and the lack of justification for power in the absence of a common cosmology and in the presence of multiple states with claims to sovereignty.[10] And even though socio-political transformations occurred in the wake of the new philosophy and partly inspired by the new philosophy, these transformations should not be seen as the straightforward implementation of philosophical maxims but as interpretations of such philosophy that were open to contestation on conceptual grounds, as well as related to mobilizations on grounds of power and interest.

In other words, rather than accepting the claims of the European philosophy of modernity to supra-historical validity, we should see its propositions as the outcome of the human faculty of imagination applied to the particular problems of the sixteenth to nineteenth centuries, as perceived by Europeans. Saying this is not to deny specificity to European thought from Las Casas, Descartes and Hobbes to Kant and Hegel. To the contrary, reading these authors in context suggests that the problems they were addressing – need for forms of recognition of the other, search for epistemic certainty, lack of ultimate sources for justification – were seen to be of such a kind that they required the *radical criticism* of prevailing views on otherness, certainty and justification that were found wanting. And, subsequently, the response to the shortcomings of earlier thinking was the *explicit construction* of alternative routes to recognition, certainty and justification that were less reliant on unsustainable presuppositions, and thus showed less need for external support while requiring greater internal coherence. Radicality and explicitness are key features of at least the 'canonical' authors of the European philosophy of modernity.

One may suggest that such radicality and explicitness are constitutive features of all modernity; that they are what makes modernity *one*.[11] This would be consonant with the denial of external and stable sources for certainty, such as in Immanuel Kant's *sapere aude* but also already in Socrates, and also with the commitment of modernity to autonomy, to self-determination and self-alteration, as emphasized by Cornelius Castoriadis.[12] But none of these features make the substantive results that such a questioning philosophy arrives at 'correct', neither in the sense of providing adequate solutions to the existing problems nor in the sense of obtaining universal validity. To give one key example (to which we return in detail in Chapter 6): the European philosophy of modernity created the concept of the rational subject as an atomistic individual. It did so in response to the quest for certainty under conditions of high uncertainty. But while it is making universal claims, an atomist social ontology is not very compelling, and the individualist political theory that is derived from it has shown to carry deep normative ambiguities. Accordingly, this philosophy has never been as widely accepted in European intellectual and political history as both its followers and its postcolonial critics have later often claimed. Every single proposition of Enlightenment thought has been criticized at its time, and not merely in ways that can be denounced as rejecting the 'modernity' that was upcoming with this new thinking, but also by showing flaws – inconsistencies, ambivalences, paradoxes – in the reasoning.

Conceptuality and historicity

These flaws are one reason why the philosophy of modernity has not been – could not be – straightforwardly implemented in the further course of European and world-history, not even slowly or incompletely. The other reason is resistance by those who were likely to lose in the ensuing socio-political transformations, such as those who made unquestioned claims to certainty or unjustifiable claims to power. The critical debate about modernity has suffered from the common assumption that, once such resistance was overcome, which was seen as merely a matter of time, an unambiguously modern socio-political order could and would be created. However, the relation between concepts and history is more complicated than this. We have to briefly explain how we are going to address it.

Human beings are 'self-interpreting animals' (Charles Taylor). The ways in which they interpret the world impacts how the world is shaped. But interpretative devices such as socio-political concepts are not of the kind that they can be 'realized' in the form of a straightforward transfer into a practice or an institution. In turn, practices and institutions may well be informed by concepts, even created and sustained by them, and as such they should be analysed. But they are not the unequivocal realization of any concept. One can say, to give an example, that the concept of liberty informed many institutional innovations in post-revolutionary France. But it would be wrong to say that the concept of liberty was realized in the institutions of post-revolutionary France.

The main reason why this is so resides in the inherent ambivalence of many socio-political concepts. Philosophers referred to such concepts as 'essentially contested' (W.B. Gallie), but we do not need to retrieve the whole debate that this term triggered. The key point is that concepts show an openness to interpretation, and more specifically, that there is a requirement for a particular interpretation once a concept is to be 'applied' in practice. To continue with the above example, post-revolutionary France witnessed the application of a concept of liberty that was unequal – it did not give the same rights to freedom to everyone – and favoured certain freedoms over others – the freedom of commerce over the freedom of association, to mention just one aspect.[13]

This openness to interpretation becomes furthermore significant in the face of the recalcitrance of the world when submitted to the application of concepts. During the first half of the nineteenth century, undesired consequences of the specific application of the concept of liberty were recognized and movements for reinterpretation began that insisted on equal freedom and on the need to tie the concept of liberty with that of solidarity.[14] In other words, the experience with the application of a specific concept leads to processes of reinterpretation. Socio-political change is not least based on conceptual reinterpretation.

Modernity in history

Let us turn from this general reflection about conceptuality and historicity back to modernity. There is widespread agreement that the key commitments of modernity – its 'imaginary signification' (Cornelius Castoriadis) – are to freedom and reason, in philosophical terminology, or to subjectivation and rationalization,[15] or to autonomy and mastery, in more sociological terminology.[16] There is still too little recognition, though, of the degree to which the conceptual elements of this signification entertain tensions with each other, or, to phrase the issue more widely: too little reflection about the relation between these conceptual elements. Autonomy means giving oneself one's own law. Arguably, therefore, the idea of autonomy already contains a reference to mastery, namely to establish the law that henceforth is to guide one's own action. In the same move, a tension is created: once there is a law to be followed, there is a limit to autonomy, to freedom. The temporality of human action is at the core of the matter; we may have freely established the law to follow at one moment, but at the next moment this law turns into a constraint. Cornelius Castoriadis referred to this tension as the relation between the instituting moment of social life, giving the law, and the instituted moment, facing the law that already exists. At that later moment, though, the self may no longer be the same as the one that gave the law. That is why every institution needs to be open to re-instituting – under conditions of modernity, that is, of autonomy.

Furthermore, the commitment of modernity to autonomy is insufficiently specific to suggest any institutional model of modernity. The concept of autonomy contains within itself the tension between individual and collective autonomy; the concept of mastery begs the questions about the object of mastery – oneself, others, or nature – and about the mode of mastery – instrumental control or hermeneutic understanding, to suggest only two such modes. These tensions and the lack of specificity cannot be overcome by conceptual reasoning alone, as much as social and political philosophy have tried over the past two centuries and more. The ways in which these tensions are being addressed in practice, in turn, lead to a great variety of different interpretations of modernity, as specifications of the basic imaginary signification. Rather than implementing unambiguous principles, therefore, the history of modernity should be seen as the work of interpreting the imaginary signification of modernity with a view to sedimenting them in institutions, and to re-interpret modernity in the light of experiences made with modern institutions and of the critique of their falling short of expectations.

These observations give us a first and still very general clue to understanding the dichotomous views of modernity, mentioned above – as realizing freedom and justice on the one side, and as generating new forms of oppression and injustice on the other. In historical reality, namely, freedom had by far not been achieved by all after the so-called onset of modernity in Europe around 1800. Rather, a minority of free human beings exercised their autonomy with a view to dominating nature, others outside their own society, and the unfree majority in their own society. And this domination, in turn, was increasingly resisted by this unfree majority, by the dominated others elsewhere and also by nature. Much of the transformation of the human condition over the two centuries since then, therefore, was not due to the interaction between autonomous human beings, but resulted from domination and the resistance to domination.

Intellectually, clearly, the European nineteenth century stood in the shadow of the Enlightenment and its commitment to autonomy. But in terms of practices and institutions much less so. With the Vienna Congress of 1815, the revolutionary period was over for the time being. The revolutionary moments of 1830, 1848 and 1871 signal that the imaginary of autonomy was alive in Europe. But their occurrence and their suppression also demonstrate that European societies had not at all yet been transformed in the light of this imaginary. For reasons of this discrepancy between intellectual change and socio-political change, observers have misinterpreted the European nineteenth century as a history of normative advances based on autonomy and, accordingly, have exaggerated the consequences of autonomy. Critical theorists from Marx to Weber to Adorno, with an echo in Jean-François Lyotard, have assumed that the nineteenth and early twentieth centuries witnessed the undermining of autonomy in the process of its realization. Actual historical practice, however, was not shaped by generalized autonomy, but rather by the combination of an increase of autonomy of the European elites with domination over nature, over the majority of the European population and with colonial domination. From the elites' point of view, this combination generated progress in modernity. From the point of view of critical theorists, it did not, but these theorists failed to recognize how progress had been derailed: not by the consequences of autonomy as such, but by the limited exercise of autonomy in combination with domination.

The agenda: modernity in Europe

Against the background of the preceding reflections, our reasoning will proceed as follows. In the following section (Part One), we will first try to circumscribe the object of our considerations, 'Europe', in time and space. 'Europe' is the designation for a relatively clearly delimited space on the earth, even if its usage is somewhat variable as a geographical term: from Scandinavia or the British Isles one can 'go to Europe', and in ancient Greek usage, too, Europe was elsewhere, further northwest. But despite this variation, the geographical meaning is rather clear compared to the cultural-historical meaning of Europe. The answer to the question of whether Russia or Turkey are European societies does not depend on whether the Ural or the Bosporus marks the borders of Europe. The use of the term 'Europe' itself is part of an act of world-interpretation. For this reason, we will devote two chapters to explore how 'Europe' was seen as emerging from and moving through history (Chapter 2) and how Europe and the Europeans were identified by matching a geographical space with a socio-cultural place (Chapter 3).

Chapter 2 takes a long view at European history. Rather than considering the triple revolutionary period around 1800 as the onset of modernity, it goes back to what European historians call antiquity to widen the perspective. This move is significant in two respects. First, it permits a wider reconsideration of the notion that the 'seeds' of European modernity were sown during Greek and Roman antiquity (a question that will be addressed in specifically political terms, with regard to the origins of democracy, in Chapter 4). Thus, we can open up to further scrutiny the question whether history has 'origins and goals', an issue that continues to underlie much reasoning about modernity. Second, it also allows us to pose the question whether the so-called Axial Age transformations, during the period between the eighth and the second century BCE, across Eurasia are a fruitful starting-point for pluralizing the notion of modernity. In elaborating the idea of 'multiple modernities', Shmuel N. Eisenstadt had suggested that the Axial Age could be seen as a period of crystallization of cultural programmes, the encounter of which with European modernity would lead to the multiplication of forms of modernity.

As a second step of this exploration of 'Europe' as a mode of world-interpretation, we circumscribe the changing meanings of Europe, in Chapter 3, guided by three main ideas. First of all, we discuss when and under which circumstances 'Europe' is seen to exist, as something more than merely the geographically westernmost extension of Eurasia and as something distinct both from the component parts of Europe, such as a plurality of nations and states, and from something larger than Europe in the form of 'Christianity' or 'the West'. Secondly, this 'Europe' will be discussed in its relation to other parts of the world, in particular to the areas of European colonial domination, to Africa, America and Asia. And thirdly, we will analyse how far such notions of Europe address, more or less explicitly, components of modernity as supposedly being embodied by Europe.

The subsequent section (Part Two) will interrogate in more detail the four core European claims to generating the supposed model of modern society: politically democratic; economically based on market coordination; considering individual autonomy as one of the highest values; and separating religion from politics. Our interrogation will proceed step by step, all the while integrating the findings of the earlier explorations into the later ones.

Chapter 4 discusses the tenuous nature of the connection between supposed European modernity and democracy. It goes back to the claim that ancient Greece provided the seeds for democracy that then started to blossom in late eighteenth-century Europe (and America), but turns the argument around: political debate around 1800 explicitly discussed the Greek experience with democracy but rejected it for Europe. Since then, Europe experienced a marked discrepancy between a democratic political imaginary that remained alive on the one, and a strong suspicion about the viability and desirability of democracy and on the other, that kept informing the dominant political practices up to at least the 1960s, if not the present day.

Arguably, the key – largely unacknowledged – tension in political practices is the one between political equality and socio-economic inequality, even dependence. This tension is discussed in the concluding section of Chapter 4 and it informs the reasoning in Chapter 5, which is devoted to interrogating the economic modernity of Europe, supposedly based on the combined effects of the Industrial Revolution and the unleashing of market forces. In contrast to this prevailing assumption, it is shown here that the Industrial Revolution is not an endogenous European event, but rather dependent on a 'new international division of labour' that gained shape before 1800 but reaped full fruit for Europe in the nineteenth century. The effects of this Atlantic economic embeddedness notwithstanding, European societies needed to face the emerging 'social question', the impoverishment of large segments of the population in the course of capitalist industrialization, to be answered by a combination of exporting surplus labour to the colonies and former colonies, by way of large-scale migration, and of developing social-policy measures in Europe. The chapter prepares the ground for showing, in Chapter 8, how the transformation of European modernity in response to these challenges made welfare go in tandem with warfare.

While Chapters 4 and 5 focus on what is mostly seen as the institutional pillars of modernity, markets and democratic states, Chapters 6 and 7 explore the underlying cultural commitments, the pillars of modern world-interpretation, as one might say. The core of the currently dominant view of modernity is certainly the commitment to individual autonomy, the rise of which will be traced in Chapter 6. But ways of world-interpretation are not individual affairs; they are co-created and to a certain extent shared within collectivities. The relation to religion stood at the historical centre of the rise of modernity,[17] be it as a source for the modern world-interpretation, as proponents of the notion of a Christian modern Europe hold, or as a heteronomous world-interpretation against which the modern commitment to human autonomy would need to assert itself, in the *laique* view of Europe in the radical Enlightenment.

Chapter 6 reviews the idea that the commitment to individual autonomy is both an outstanding normative particularity of Europe and one of the main reasons behind its historical rise to world-domination. It will do so by critically analysing the three main components of this idea: the claim that the commitment to human rights can be traced to early Christianity; the claim that the focus on the individual human being as the starting ontological assumption of much of Enlightenment philosophy indeed provides the foundations of modern European polities; and the claim that individualization is the dominant trend of social transformations over the past two centuries.

Chapter 7 takes its point of departure in the observation that historically religion was early on a legitimizing part of politics with strong entanglements of state and church. These entanglements emerged in solution to violent confessional conflicts in the sixteenth and seventeenth centuries culminating in the Thirty Years War (1618–1648) and the English Civil War (1642–1651). No need to say that religion was instrumentalized in these conflicts which dealt with much more than religion. The Augsburg Settlement (1555) and the social contract theory of Thomas Hobbes (*Leviathan*, 1651) were attempts to settle these conflicts. From the perspective of the modernity of Europe, the remarkable point is that these conflicts were exclusively intra-Christian. After outlining this historical background, the chapter deals with the long-term marginalization and exclusion respectively of the practitioners of Mosaic and Muslim confessions. They have been the Others of the Christians. There is historically a colonial dimension in the view on the Muslims as the Other, visible today in the ghettoization of Islamic immigrants in the cities of Europe. The chapter confronts the thesis of modernity as continuous secularization.

After this critical review of the supposed pillars of European modernity, a new question arises: if democracy, industry, markets, secularization and individual freedom are not in the conventional sense the core characteristics of modernity in Europe, how else should we read European history and in what ways can it be seen to be modern? The concluding section of this volume (Part Three) will try to answer this question by changing the perspective: rather than searching for key features of European modernity we will analyse major socio-historical transformations in Europe with a view to identifying what were seen as the core problems that European societies had to face and what resources were mobilized to address these problems.

For this analysis we start out from the period around 1800, which for reasons given in Chapter 2 can be seen as such a major moment of social transformation, a moment of instituting society, as Cornelius Castoriadis put it. In Chapter 8, we return to this period but do not look at it as the beginning of a new, coherent institutional order of society, both normatively and functionally superior to others. Rather, we view it from the angle of the new problems that it created and, accordingly, to the dynamics of socio-political transformations that it generated. We employ here Karl Polanyi's fruitful notion of 'Great Transformation', adapting it for our purposes. Writing more than half a century after Polanyi, importantly, we no longer see this as a singular Great Transformation, but as one that, for reasons of the ambivalences of the responses it developed, triggered further needs for transformation.

Chapter 8 connects to Chapter 5 on the Industrial Revolution and the long economic stagnation that followed on a bursting speculation bubble in the early 1870s which brought the prevailing interpretative framework of economic liberalism into a lengthy state of crisis, the Great Depression as the stagnation period was called at the time. The response to the crisis reflected in terms of stagnating wages and profits was hierarchical organization of interests with the aim to mobilize and coordinate resources for the struggle with conflicting interests. The long-term outcome of this trial of strength was not more conflicts, however. Since more resources were at stake in the conflicts the propensity for compromises between the conflicting interests grew. The governments and the state administrations got involved in these conflicts and search for compromises. Social policies and welfare programmes became a mitigating instrument promoting social integration and social peace. Hierarchical tripartite bargaining structures emerged. The era of the world wars, the Second European Thirty Years War (1914–1945), reinforced these corporatist structures and brought the masses much more into politics than earlier. Mass politics was not only the expression of the popular will but also the manipulation of mass opinions. The era of the world wars, not the Enlightenment philosophy, brought democracy to Europe. With this argument the chapter reinforces and enhances the conclusion in Chapter 4 of European hesitations with regard to democracy. Not only the later breakthrough of democracy as a consequence of the mobilization of the masses for the two world wars reinforce the conclusion of Chapter 4, but also the fact that the era of mass politics in Europe did not only result in democracy but also in totalitarianism, populism and authoritarianism. The culmination of the era of organized modernity initiated in the 1870s was the neo-corporatist organization of society in the 1960s under legitimization by the political management of Keynesian economies of growth.

After the upheavals and catastrophes of the first half of the twentieth century, an 'organized modernity' seemed to stabilize in Western Europe (and in a different way in socialist Eastern Europe).[18] But today we can identify the shakiness of the foundations of this mode of socio-political organization, its ambivalences and incoherencies as well as its untenable hierarchical positioning in the global context. Thus, Chapter 9 will analyse the dismantling of this organized modernity as another 'Great Transformation'. For some time, the dynamics of this transformation was simply described as a double linear tendency of 'globalization' and 'individualization'. However, now we can recognize that the erasure of historical time and lived space that this programmatic tendency entailed, encounters forms of 'self-defence of society' analogous to, though not identical with, those identified by Karl Polanyi. In particular, demands for dealing with historical injustice and claims for effective collective self-determination are characteristic of today's 'self-defence'.

Europe is in a whirlwind of crises at this very moment: the economic-fiscal crisis after 2008; the inability to deal with cross-Mediterranean immigration; the lack of criteria for dealing with international conflicts at its borders as well as within; the current refugee crisis. None of these crises is entirely made in Europe, but past European action has contributed in large part to their creation. Furthermore, 'European modernity' has widely been assumed, implicitly and explicitly, to have the criteria, the will and the force to deal with such crises in both an effective and normatively acceptable way. Our reconsideration of modernity in Europe can help understanding why this is not at all the case. In the form of an epilogue, Chapter 10 will go beyond this diagnosis and offer some reflections as to the tasks that need to be confronted today.

PART ONE

Europe in Time and Space

2

An Origin and Goal of European History?

The Long-term Perspective

Origins and goals

Every historical account will need to start at some moment in time, and its authors will be tempted, but also asked, to give reasons why the account starts there. The most common reason is to suggest that this moment was a moment of major transformation during which something new was created. We may even call this the minimum conceptual reason for setting a starting-point of a historical account. In numerous cases, though, the justification goes beyond this minimum, and in particular with regard to the history of Europe. One significant additional reason is to hold that at the selected moment something new was created that from then on existed with a considerable degree of continuity. The starting-point then turns into the origins of a lasting phenomenon, often the origins of the present. Furthermore, it may even be suggested that from the starting moment onwards history evolves towards the present. Then this moment also determines the goal towards which history moved from then onwards. When applied to the history of one world-region, typically Europe but not exclusively so,[1] such reasoning also includes the notion that the new that is created is superior to that which already existed so that the creating region determines the course of history from then on. In the twentieth century, critical thinking about the course of history often reflected upon those very notions of 'origins' and 'goal', which we borrowed here from the philosopher Karl Jaspers.[2] Jaspers wrote after the end of the Second World War and of Nazism, under the urge of rethinking the course of history in this moment of deep crisis in Europe. He used the notion of the Axial Age to mark the supposed turning-point, the axis, after which human history unfolded in some direction. The sociologist Shmuel N. Eisenstadt returned to this notion almost half a century later to grasp the modern human condition in the plurality of its forms.

Now one may want to argue that such remnants of philosophy of history have long ceased to be persuasive. Despite compelling conceptual and methodological criticism, however, this is by far not the case. For the history of Europe, two alternative starting moments keep being proposed, and they are both associated with notions of origins and goal: either antiquity or the age of revolutions around 1800. The former choice was motivated by a search for the 'seed-beds' (Talcott Parsons) of later evolution or the 'needle's eye' (Christian Meier) through which world-history passed. The latter, in turn, as presented in the preceding chapter, was motivated by the argument that this is the moment when everything changes, the moment at which an already extended world-history is set on a different track, the onset of modernity.

The argument about the roots of Europe in antiquity was considered to be sufficient for a world-history because the rest of the world supposedly transformed under the influence of 'Europe', the 'West' or 'modernity' from a certain point in time onwards. In substance, alleged features of the West such as democracy, codified law and rights, individualism, and universal ethics were traced to ancient Greece, Rome, Judaism or Christianity. However, the reasoning cannot be sustained in its two main claims: the line of continuity from antiquity to the present, and the diffusion from one world-region to all others (we discuss democracy and individualism in detail below in Chapters 4 and 7). The Axial Age hypothesis, which suggests that parallel cultural transformations occurred in different regions of Eurasia between 800 and 200 BCE, bringing about new cosmologies around which the major world-civilizations crystallize, introduces an interesting variation into this reasoning.[3] This hypothesis maintains the search for origins in time but suggests a plurality of origins in space, allowing for the later elaboration of the idea of 'multiple modernities'. It thus abandons diffusionism, but maintains the idea of long-term continuity, now captured with the metaphor of 'crystallization'.

The main alternative way to mark the starting-point of European modernity is to focus on the revolutionary period of the late eighteenth and early nineteenth centuries. In the standard view of the sociology of 'modern societies', the combined effects of scientific revolution and Enlightenment, democratic revolution and industrial revolution bring about a functionally differentiated society that is superior to all preceding forms of socio-political organization and can itself not be superseded by any future such form.[4] The assumption of a radical rupture permits a way of looking at 'origins' without having to go deeply into human history: the transformation allegedly marks the origins of modernity, and all preceding societies look similar from the vantage point of this transformation: they are 'traditional' or 'primitive' societies, to be analysed by different conceptual means than the contemporary Western, 'modern' ones. At the same time, this account provided 'modernity' with spatial origins, namely Western Europe, from which it later supposedly diffused across the world.

Although widely criticized by now, this perspective still marks much of sociological debate – as well as much of publicly voiced Western self-understanding. At this point, it may suffice to mention two main objections, already alluded to in the preceding chapter (Chapter 1). By 1800, regions of the globe were far too interconnected to consider any event – such as the French Revolution or the Industrial Revolution – as being predominantly endogenously shaped by its close socio-political context – such as the state of France or British capitalism. Thus, if there is an 'onset of modernity' around 1800, it cannot unproblematically be qualified as 'European'. Furthermore, one also needs to qualify the meaning of 'onset of modernity'. True, one can identify a set of arguments being forcefully made during the eighteenth century that add up to an image of modernity that became widespread: such as arguments about rational and independent generation of new knowledge, about extending commerce on the basis of self-regulation of markets, and about equal-suffrage democracy. Looking at changes in socio-political practices, however, one will recognize that this imagery was not transformed into reality in any region of the globe.

However, these objections to both ways of 'starting' European history, valid as they are, have until now not been sufficient to remove these ways of writing the history of Europe. Thus, these accounts must express and satisfy some particular need in understanding history that the critiques fail to address. For this reason, this chapter will discuss European history in long-term perspective, beginning with antiquity and the Axial Age hypothesis and then placing the argument about the onset of modernity at around 1800 in long-term historical context.[5]

The Axial Age hypothesis

A review of the debate about the so-called 'Axial Age', inaugurated by Max and Alfred Weber and Karl Jaspers and continued by Eric Voegelin and Shmuel Eisenstadt, lends itself to our purpose for at least two reasons. First, it increases the spatio-temporal scope in the discussion about modernity so considerably that it underpins a world-historical perspective, dearly needed in an era of alleged globalization. Second, one of the major contributors to the recent debate on 'multiple modernities', Shmuel Eisenstadt, derives his own perspective on the plurality of forms of modernity rather directly from the Axial Age debate.[6] In brief, the Axial Age thesis holds that the European revolutions towards modernity were neither entirely unprecedented in European history nor specific to that region of the world. Rather, a set of major socio-cultural transformations had occurred in various regions of Eurasia in a roughly parallel way between the eighth and second centuries BCE. While there is quite some debate about the nature and lasting effects of these transformations, as we will discuss below, two claims give particular significance to the idea of an Axial Age. First, some authors come close to saying that these transformations are the true key to understanding world-history. In its original formula, the term 'Axial Age' suggested that this period is the axis around which history revolves, distinguishing a pre-history from the conscious appropriation of the world through human beings in the aftermath of these transformations. While nobody would nowadays sustain this view, the axial transformations remain associated with the emergence of an agential and reflexive understanding of the human being-in-the-world and a conscious human self-positioning within a frame of historical change. As such, the argument bears resemblance with the claims about the coming of modernity much later in European history. Second, the axial transformations are sometimes associated with the idea that basic socio-cultural commitments crystallized during that period and were sustained in a lasting way. In this view, contemporary civilizations such as the Judaic, Chinese or Greco-European ones were basically formed during the Axial Age. Contemporary multiple modernities often draw on the cultural resources provided in that period, according to Eisenstadt.[7]

In the following, we shall start by analysing the Axial Age debate with a view to the European nature of the debate itself, which has in many respects been a vehicle for understanding the fate of European modernity in the twentieth century. Subsequently, we shall try to identify the major questions raised in this debate and to separate those that are of relevance for our purposes from some other questions that have shaped the debate, but are both difficult to answer and less significant for us. These considerations lead us finally to three key aspects: the alleged crystallizing impact of the Axial Age transformations; the connection between the axial transformations and later European history; and finally the significance of the axial transformations for our understanding of modernity.

The Axial Age debate: a European twentieth-century quest

In the light of our concerns, two rather simple observations can be made about the Axial Age debate. First, the debate can be described as moving between two quite different genres of investigation, or as trying to connect those two genres, namely historical sociology and philosophy of history. The former aims at understanding historical processes by comparing them with one another by means of sociological categories. The latter tries to understand the relation of ourselves in the present to the past by means of conjecturing about the meaning and direction of history, as mentioned above. Within the Axial Age debate, even though neat distinctions are impossible, as we will argue in a moment, the Weber brothers at its beginnings and Eisenstadt much more recently stand close to the socio-historical pole, whereas Jaspers and Voegelin in-between are close to the philosophical one. In our time, one may easily be tempted to permanently abandon the latter approach and to concentrate on minute socio-historical reconstruction and conceptual clarification to finally determine clearly which aspect of the Axial Age hypothesis can be sustained and which cannot. True, the contributions with a strong philosophical emphasis can easily be criticized, and often discarded, because of unsustainability in the light of historical evidence and/or untenability of some of their normative assumptions. Once one moves determinedly to the socio-historical mode of investigation, however, the entire hypothesis will dissolve in a welter of divergent observations. One starts to wonder whether there was any question at all. The transformations certain Eurasian social configurations underwent between the eighth and second centuries BCE were of a great variety of origins, forms and outcomes. And these transformations can only be held together by a question that we have to pose and that relates us to those transformations – this question, thus, will inevitably be posed in cultural-philosophical terms, as Max Weber, not a purist socio-historical mind at all, was always ready to grant. In other words, the link between the two genres can be provided if the historical sociology employed demonstrates a strong cultural and hermeneutic sensitivity and if the philosophy of history pays attention to historiographical insight. Under these circumstances, the Axial Age hypothesis was and remains an important heuristic device for both understanding the past and situating ourselves in the present.

At this point, a look at the context of the debate is not only legitimate, but necessary – this leads to our second observation about the debate. The Axial Age hypothesis is a product of the short European twentieth century. Even though a similar general idea was connected with the construction of world-history as consisting of a variety of 'high civilizations' in the eighteenth and nineteenth centuries, it gains more temporal precision with observations by Max Weber during the First World War.[8] It arrives at its most forceful expression after the end of Nazism and the Second World War – and is clearly related to both – with the works by Jaspers and Voegelin; and it regains momentum with Shmuel Eisenstadt's comparative research programme after the strong critique of Western modernity in the late 1970s and during the declining period of Soviet socialism.

Even though this short century is rich in historical turns, it becomes immediately evident that the debate about the Axial Age is work at self-understanding within a civilization, work at self-positioning at certain historical moments by reconstructing the long-term trajectory that led to these moments. The emphasis on the achievement of a reflexive relation to one's own history during the Axial Age is thus mirrored in the fact that this very debate has been an exercise in historical reflexivity. With all due caution against the ever-present risk of oversimplification, one may even trace the stages of the debate as an exercise in reflexivity that changes with the abrupt turns of European history during the twentieth century.

Max Weber's interrogation of the specificity of the West still harbours a sense of radical Western exceptionalism, understood by contrasting the West with other world-regions, even though Weber's work marks a strong break with the historiography of evolutionary progress that had dominated much of the nineteenth century. With Jaspers and Voegelin, after the disasters of mid-century, a more self-critical look emerged. One way of gaining distance from the Roman-Christian core of the mostly self-congratulatory self-understanding that had – implicitly or explicitly – long dominated was the recourse to the 'extra-European' sources of that self-understanding, namely Judaism and Greek philosophy.[9] This – at first sight, apparently minor – shift in emphasis entailed a significant conceptual step away from even Weber's sociology of world-religions. By focusing on world-views that had informed the rise and formation of Europe, but were only in an ambivalent way a central part of Europe, it allowed the move beyond the opposition between a rationalizing Occident and other civilizations that lacked this potential. Thus, it permitted a more open-minded view of the plurality of world-views and a more profoundly self-critical view of Europe and of the West. Thus, the birth of the fully developed Axial Age hypothesis needs to be seen as a discourse of crisis and as a contribution to reorientation.

To understand the subsequent round of debate, one needs to remember that the Axial Age hypothesis was not widely discussed during the 'thirty glorious years' ('les trente glorieuses', in Jean Fourastié's expression) after the West's recovery from the doubt-ridden immediate aftermath of the Second World War, neither in Jaspers's nor in Voegelin's version. Despite the Cold War, optimism about evolutionary progress and the superior mode of societal rationalization in the West regained intellectual predominance, with sociological modernization theory now becoming a full substitute to earlier modes of philosophy of history (as well as the alternative to historical materialism). Eisenstadt's reappraisal of the Axial Age hypothesis is then fully informed by the enormously developed work in comparative-historical sociology during the 1960s and 1970s. On this basis, Eisenstadt breaks with the linear evolutionism of modernization theory and any idea of convergence and uses the recourse to the Axial Age debates as a cornerstone for a theorization of multiple modernities, as the contemporary expression, namely, of the variety of cultural programmes into which modernity can be, and historically has been, inscribed. While Eisenstadt's work can thus be described as an intellectual innovation inside a sociological research programme, namely the comparative study of modern society, its significance would not be fully grasped without a look at its socio-political context. Short of a full analysis along these lines, on which more detail later, the most important contextual occurrences to note are the rise of non-Western societies, first of all Japan, to full economic competitiveness; the process of decolonization that is accompanied by expressions of cultural-symbolic assertiveness against the Western model; the Iranian Revolution with its explicit break with a programme of Westernization; and the rising internal criticism of Western modernity, much of which has been captured under the name of postmodernism. In this sense, the reappraisal of the Axial Age question as the underpinning for the conceptualization of the diversity of forms of modernity is again a contribution to a critical reorientation of the, broadly understood, Western self-understanding at a moment of crisis and, possibly, of a historical turning-point.

The central questions of the Axial Age debate

This brief attempt at reconstructing a contextual history of the Axial Age debate served one main objective: to demonstrate how the tension between the historical sociology and the philosophy of history of the Axial Age can be understood and, in the end, appreciated as an inevitable, and not necessarily unacceptable, combined employment of different genres of inquiry for a given purpose, the purpose of understanding the contemporary condition of European modernity. The results of further investigations into the Axial Age thus have to withstand a double test: they have to be sustainable in the light of the best available historical evidence, and they have to give answers to the questions we pose to the past from the point of view of the present. Rather than making the debate more complicated, though, this double requirement may make the assessment of the findings easier. That is, some of the issues that are contested or remain unanswerable from the point of view of historical sociology, do not necessarily need an answer from the point of view of philosophy of history.

This maxim requires of us first of all a clarification of the question to which end we keep investigating the Axial Age, after we have become sceptical about facile assertions on the 'origins' and 'goals' of history. Abstracting across the various layers of the Axial Age debate, two questions appear to possess central and persistent significance: we are interested in the conditions under which, and the ways in which, human beings relate reflexively to their being-in-the-world; and we aim to assess the possibility of human beings to collectively employ their capacity for reflexivity such that they can critically relate to their history and give themselves new orientations in the present.[10] A third question possibly can be added: we would like to know how far our contemporary location as members of certain societies or civilizations – for instance, as Europeans – rather than others provides us with specific cultural resources and constraints from the past. But this third question will be addressed only later in this chapter.

The continuous deepening of scholarship on the Axial Age as well as its widening in terms of an extension of the Axial Age *problématique* to regions and periods outside of the original core area of interest,[11] has led to two rather clear-cut results. First, in the absence of the above questions, it becomes difficult to identify an Axial Age at all. The refinement of knowledge has led to a gradual disappearance of the view that there is a relatively limited period in time during which a number of contiguous Eurasian civilizations underwent major transformations that were highly specific in world-history and, at the same time, so similar in kind that they can be grasped with a very limited number of key concepts. Second, however, when we connect the above questions to the historical findings, we receive a rather strong and – normatively speaking – highly encouraging answer. There are more instances than initially expected of plausible evidence of reflexive engagement of human beings with their situation, and there are also more cases in which such engagements aspired towards, and sometimes achieved, a re-direction of collective self-understandings. If one permits a loose way of speaking for a moment, one may say that the Axial Age keeps expanding with the growth of knowledge about the past.

It is not merely better evidence that is responsible for this enlargement of the Axial Age. There seem to be at least two other reasons. First, compared to Jaspers's' time, scepticism in the human and social sciences has grown about the tenability of any firm demarcation line between our time, however defined, and the times preceding it. The critical scrutiny of the use of asymmetric counter-concepts, such as both 'history' and 'pre-history' and 'modernity' and 'tradition', as pioneered in the historiography of concepts, has had an impact across all fields of scholarship and has redirected the empirical gaze.[12] Second, our understanding of the key concepts in use in the Axial Age debate – reflexivity, historicity, agentiality – has been significantly broadened beyond the interpretations they have received in European intellectual history of the past two centuries, not least due to work in anthropology and postcolonial studies.[13]

The issue gets considerably more complicated when we look at the collective outcomes of the reflexive engagement of human beings with their world. The very least we can say, though, is that the results give evidence of the diversity of 'ways of world-making'[14] that has been created and sustained by human beings. Research on the Axial Age has thus provided empirical underpinnings for theses, such as the one offered by Cornelius Castoriadis, about the existence of a wide range of 'imaginary significations of society' in human history. Castoriadis indeed connects that observation to the view that these imaginary significations cannot but be seen as human creations, thus providing evidence for the human capacity for radical imagination.[15] And maybe this is all we need to know, at least in the first instance. However, one immediately gets the sense that a shift of interest from human capacities to the outcomes of the use of these capacities makes the Axial Age, and the interest in it, more contested. To advance the reasoning further, it may be useful to first identify the questions we do not need to answer.

Questions we need neither ask nor answer

For several – probably most – contributors to the Axial Age debate, it was important to argue that the age brought radical novelty into human history, for some even it meant the beginning of human history in the stricter sense of the term. It is quite clear, though, that this reasoning cannot be sustained in general terms. On the one hand, the 'expansion' of the Axial Age through further research also took place 'backwards' into earlier history, as is most convincingly argued by Jan Assmann, who detects axial features in 'pre-axial' Egypt.[16] On the other hand, as the same author cautions in other places, we just do not know enough about earlier social configurations to make a strong statement about the radical rupture that axial transformations allegedly marked.[17] The Axial Age has long marked the limit of our at least relatively certain knowledge about the ancient world, because of the availability of written and readable sources, and it has been given priority of interpretation for that very reason, not because it necessarily stood out from history.

But then again, the Axial Age need not mark history's beginning, or even stand out from history, to offer satisfactory answers to the questions we pose. Research and speculation on the Axial Age provided early answers to these questions. But there is no good reason why acceptable answers should not emerge from elsewhere in human history. Viewed in detail, though, the strong claim for specificity of the period rests on yet another hypothesis that we need to briefly discuss. It is argued that the axial transformations created civilizational forms that could be durably *institutionalized* and proved, thus, more sustainable than other assertions of reflexivity in human history.[18] This claim is based on assumptions about crucial occurrences during the period, namely the elaboration of cosmologies based on a separation of a transcendental from a mundane sphere and the codification of these cosmologies in textual form and their diffusion by intellectual elites. We will first argue that these assumptions again lead to discussions not necessary to answer our questions, and then assess the empirical-historical claim that the civilizational forms created during the Axial Age gave lasting shape to world-history.

The main problem with these further assumptions is that they are far too specific. They tend to 'shrink' the Axial Age, whereas the tendency of recent research was to 'expand' it, as discussed above. And as a consequence of their overspecificity, they reduce the understanding of more general phenomena and limit comparative investigations instead of enhancing them. While it is overall plausible to assume that the preservation in writing of basic texts that ground the key commitments of a group of human beings alters *something* compared with transmission via oral speech, what it precisely alters is much more difficult to say. On the one hand, it can be argued that the availability in writing of central texts supports both a broader diffusion of a given cosmology through a social configuration and a greater consistency and homogeneity of the 'message' that is conveyed. On the other hand, however, one may insist on the infinity of interpretations that is possible with any text, and the availability of a central text may precisely have instigated the pluralization of interpretations. With this basic question being undecided, the close association of axiality with the written risks giving undue weight to the 'religions of the book' in the narrative of world-history – a note on 'Greek exceptionalism' will be added below.[19]

This suspicion is confirmed by a consideration of the argument about the separation of the transcendental and mundane, since a codification of that separation is central for the understanding of monotheistic religions. A closer, more contextual look at the axial transformations suggests a different, broader interpretation.[20] Given that these transformations occur in contexts of political crisis, often of deep dissatisfaction with the existing political regime, the recourse to the 'transcendental' most broadly refers to the conviction that, to use a slogan of our much more recent past, 'another world is possible'.[21] This conviction may be codified in terms of a distinction between religion and politics (on which see Chapter 7 below), then often assuming that the 'other world' is already there, only 'elsewhere', or that it will be there with certainty, but is 'always yet to come', at the end of times. And the certainty of that other world may then be revealed in a book. But rather than any certainty, its possibility may find expression also quite differently, as Kurt Raaflaub rightly argues for ancient Greece, after all a core case for the Axial Age hypothesis: the possibility and availability of another world may be debated – orally and textually – and contended in philosophy and in political action.[22]

The 'classical' model of the Axial Age hypothesis appears to make a strong projection upon the past, roughly as follows: the core features of reflexivity, historicity and agentiality are actualized by reference to a central text that provides the basis for the transcendental perspective and is interpreted by a specialized class of readers who under certain conditions can convey their reading in such a way so as to initiate and support a major social transformation. This is rather precisely the model of revolutionary activity by intellectuals based on insight into the essence of the world, as it formed in nineteenth-century Europe in an amalgamation of idealism, class struggle and the formation of an *avant-garde*. Our understanding of world-history would be helped if we were to abandon the attempt to generalize such a model, and rather take from the observation of the Axial Age the broader insights that the faculty of imagination allows human beings to consider states of the world as possible that differ from the actual one; and that the communication about such different possible states may support collective action to bring such states about.

Axiality and civilizational patterns

However, the resonance between the nineteenth-century European situation and the interpretation of the Axial Age, rather than a matter of perspective, could also have its basis in the fact, if it were so, that the transformations of the axial period brought about the basic structure of the world as we still know it today. This is what is also argued in the Axial Age hypothesis, and maybe it is its most significant claim: during the axial transformation, a plurality of civilizational forms was created and institutionalized. These developed across varied civilizational trajectories to be still recognizable in the plurality of contemporary civilizational forms. (Here we return to the third question that was mentioned above but postponed.) With this emphasis, the Axial Age hypothesis lays the ground not only for the claim that there has been, as suggested above, a plurality of possible *'mises en forme du monde'*, but also for reasons to sustain the current existence of multiple forms of modernity, which namely can be traced to the persistence, while undergoing changes and reinterpretations, of those once-instituted forms.

Again, we want to suggest that we can retain the main insight from this conceptualization while shedding some of its more problematic, sometimes outright unsustainable, implications without relinquishing our capacity to answer the questions we ask of world-history. There is little doubt that some of the socio-cultural configurations described by the Axial Age hypothesis indeed underwent a major social transformation during the period in question. What, however, are our means to assert whether these transformations gave rise to 'axial civilizations' of a certain durability and world-historical specificity? The prima facie case for the assertion is the presence in the contemporary world of Greek philosophy and political thought and of Judaism, going back to the core cases of the Axial Age hypothesis, as well as of Confucianism, Christianity, Islam, and, furthermore, the fact that these modes of thinking exist in some affinity to territorially defined polities in the current world.

However, it seems right to underline, with Aleida and Jan Assmann, first, that this presence is the result of the creation of a tradition that started in the Axial Age but needed to be steadily pursued through 'social labour' across the centuries, which indeed were also marked by temporary losses, re-appropriations and reinterpretations. Following up the earlier reasoning about the lack of knowledge about pre-axial times, one needs to insist that the fact that other cosmologies were not preserved and universalized does not entail that they were not preservable and universalizable. All we can say positively is that those texts that are still present have been preserved, and to understand how that was possible we need a 'sociology of tradition' that barely exists.[23] Secondly, the precise nature of the affinity between a cosmology and a territorially defined polity also needs further exploration. While it is true that the Axial Age debate does not consistently make a strong assumption about a tendency towards correspondence between 'culture' and 'politics' in the post-axial world, it does suggest that common interpretations of the world have led to the creation of 'civilizations' that provide underpinnings for political formations.[24]

Our current thinking about this question is strongly informed by the European experience of building national polities on the assumption of the need for a homogeneous cultural-linguistic underpinning, and one may have the suspicion that too much of this contemporary thinking also inspired the interpretation of the Axial Age. In such view, polities are seen as the institutional expression of a collective identity based on shared norms and values. While there may be some – insufficient, anyway – grounds for such reasoning if it refers to consolidated democratic polities constituted by some form of expression of opinion and will by its members,[25] it needs heavy qualification for all other political configurations. One of the assumptions in the idea of such correspondence needs to be explicitly problematized here:[26] polities often indeed have clear boundaries that are more or less well guarded by military, police and administrative officials. If 'cultures', however, are to correspond to polities, then norms, values, and cosmologies need to be shared by precisely the same group of people, the members of the polity. Cultures are then seen as distinct units of social life, internally coherent and closed towards other cultures. But there is no reason to assume that values and beliefs should not have other patterns of distribution among human beings, patterns not related to the boundaries of instituted polities. In the version offered by the Axial Age debate, civilizations tend to become cultures writ large, and there is a distinct risk that the analysis of multiple modernities, if based on the Axial Age debate, succumbs to the temptation of repeating the error of European social theory of much of the nineteenth and twentieth century, namely to inscribe the forms of modernity into compact and stable units similar to the national societies of former theorizing. The variety of contemporary modernity, however, can find expression in a range of ways, only some of which may overlap with constituted polities. If one looks at contemporary polities and their members, it seems very clear that it is most often highly difficult – and at the very least a highly complex exercise – to trace the cosmologies to which they may be committed to the axial transformations. For East Asian societies, one can show that the common reference to Confucianism can be more misleading than helpful.[27] In the following, we will briefly discuss Europe's relation to the axial transformation in this light.

Axiality and Europe

The Axial Age debate has been a significant means of broadening the debate about modernity, of making it less Eurocentric. A discussion about the relation between axiality and Europe is thus necessarily a discussion about modernity insofar as the latter is understood as a spatio-temporal phenomenon.[28] What makes this discussion difficult and complex, however, is the fact that 'Europe' was hardly present in the Axial Age[29] and that the relation between the Axial Age and the existing forms of Europe at later points in history can be constructed in different ways and, indeed, have been constructed in a number of highly different ways.[30]

The topical significance of the question becomes evident when one looks at current discussions about the sense in which contemporary Europe is 'Christian'. While, as noted before, there are some good reasons to assume that Europe was born historically in the declining phase of the Catholic-Christian Western Roman Empire, it is important to note at the same time that this 'identity' of Europe is 'eccentric', because it relies on at least two major sources of inspiration outside of Europe, Judaism and Greek philosophy.[31] 'European identity' is in this sense 'secondary' to the Axial Age and indebted to it, but the long-used term 'secondary breakthrough' suggests both too much a line of continuity and too much a line of evolution. In Rémi Brague's view, it is rather the creation of such an 'eccentric identity' that marks a breakthrough that explains the later rise of European modernity.

Brague's view, which is strong as a qualification of the standard accounts of axiality, is as contestable as the latter when it is read as a claim to ground a specific continuity of Europe. Following on from Brague's 'Roman way', we can identify at least four later major historical transformations, which cannot be derived in any convincing way from either axial origins or from a Roman-instituted restlessness:[32] the 'first European revolution' early in the second millennium,[33] which already caught Max Weber's attention; the Renaissance, indeed a crisis-born attempt at giving oneself a new orientation by looking backwards towards antiquity; the Reformation and the religious wars; and the period around the French Revolution, often referred to as the onset of political modernity.

The mere listing of these further transformations in their diversity should intuitively suggest that it is difficult to speak of a European trajectory from axiality to modernity in which earlier stages determine, although not the precise outcome, the path that could be taken.[34] In contrast, these ruptures are arguably more adequately interpreted as breaking open a prior configuration through human creativity based on the faculty of imagination. Elements of the cosmologies that have defined earlier configurations are resources available to interpret and resolve a situation conceived as problematic, rather than determinants of the outcome of a transformation. The actual outcome then becomes something that is neither necessary nor impossible; these transformative situations are moments of experienced historical contingency.

Secondly, a look at 'post-axial' Europe is also of particular relevance in this context because the Axial Age debate is predominantly a European debate, in particular in its more philosophical forms.[35] As proposed earlier, it can be interpreted as a debate about a crisis and a search for reorientation. The features that are highlighted in the Axial Age – reflexivity, historicity, agentiality, but also the more problematic ones about an other, possible world and the textual guidance towards it – are precisely those that are seen as lost, indeed repeatedly lost in European history. Very schematically, the losses can be associated with the resolutions of the critical transformative situations: the establishment of a Christian Roman Empire; the building of what is often called the modern state system after the Treaty of Westphalia; the establishment of nation-states after the Revolution. After the high-points of reflexivity, historicity and agentiality achieved during the Greek era of the *polis*; during early modern Europe culminating in Renaissance humanism and republicanism; and during the era of the Enlightenment culminating in the democratic revolutions, each time these consolidated political forms marked a step away from the salient features of axiality. This observation leads to the final point of our discussion, the relation between axiality and the concept of modernity.

Axiality and modernity

Our suggestion is that one can well observe spatio-temporal constellations at various points in world-history that are marked by the features of axiality. Such constellations may also cluster at certain times, among others the Eurasian Axial Age, but they occur in a wide range of times and spaces. Rather than indicating the rise of a novel historical stage of a civilization, they are specific of periods of major societal transformation. Thus, we prefer to speak about 'axial transformations', which are then marked by these features, rather than about an 'Axial Age', in which these features become institutionalized and, thus, turn into a common accomplishment, an *acquis* of variously 'modernizing' civilizations. In other words, it seems erroneous to assume that reflexivity, historicity and agentiality are being institutionalized during those transformations. Even and especially for the core area of the Axial Age debate, that of the monotheistic religions, we see the consolidation and codification of those religious doctrines as a relative loss of a sense of reflexivity, historicity and agentiality, or maybe better: as a channelling of these modes of consciousness into tightly circumscribed forms.[36] This is not to say necessarily that there has been no 'historical learning' at all.[37] However, at no time and no place have reflexivity, historicity and agentiality been securely gained – in a truly 'modern' reading, they open up the issue of contingency, and societal consolidation seems to have been always about, among other things, the limitation of contingency.[38]

There is no other direction in history than those that can be discerned in retrospective reflection. Historicity and agentiality in terms of the capacity to identify a past and a future that was and can be made different through human agency provoked attempts to change the world of the present as well as attempts to maintain it as it was. The outcome of the struggle between the adherents of change and of preservation was at the end a matter of social power relationships. There was no teleology built into these processes. There is possibly no better illustration of the open outcome of the struggle for the future between forces for change and for preservation than the European nineteenth century during which radical ideas flourished in the wake of the French Revolution and the Enlightenment proposals but during which the conservative resistance remained successful up to the First World War.[39]

This is where the Axial Age debate is related to the conventional reading of the 'onset of modernity', the late eighteenth and early nineteenth century.

The era of the Enlightenment was centrally concerned with reflexivity, historicity, agentiality and with reasons for assuming that other worlds are possible. It culminates in the revolutions, whereas, in contrast, the European experience after the revolutions should be read as being preoccupied with finding means to cope with contingency, already from the Vienna Congress onwards. The rise of the social sciences as well as the rise of the political ideologies of the nineteenth century indicate attempts at building safely compartmentalized tracks across the suddenly emerging – and initially empty – space towards the 'open horizon of the future', to paraphrase Reinhart Koselleck. Europe around 1800 can thus be described in terms of an 'axial transformation', and that transformation ushers in new institutional forms of polities. The process mirrors rather precisely the description of the Axial Age and its aftermath, according to the Axial Age hypothesis.

If that is so, then we learn from studying the 'axial' period first of all about the character of major societal transformations. To say that reflexivity, historicity and agentiality are key components of all – or most of – those historical events that in their aftermath can be described as major social transformations is, however, almost a truism – unless social transformations are more endured than enacted, if provoked by natural catastrophe or by invasion and colonization, for instance, even though there is hardly ever mere endurance. Nevertheless, the fact that the Axial Age has been described in precisely these terms, and that such description has been proposed in our own age of 'modernity', which is allegedly marked by a particularly pronounced availability of these beliefs, is significant. In this light, the Axial Age hypothesis is at its core a 'modern' interpretation of social transformations in apparent gradual preparation of modernity, an interpretation, thus, which endows modernity with suitable 'origins'. Such a statement, valid as it may appear, creates an interpretive circle from which it is impossible to escape.

These observations raise other questions about modernity. Contrary to a standard narrative about modernity, our observations suggest that any strong belief in, or commitment to, reflexivity, historicity, agentiality and the possibility of different worlds tends to be transitory, a feature of a liminal situation, as one may want to say, and has never been truly institutionalized. Enlightenment, to paraphrase both Immanuel Kant and Michel Foucault,[40] marks an 'exit' from a state of serfdom by means of an ethos of interrogation of the world, but it does not indicate the entry into a safely established world of modernity. Thus, what is often called the onset of modernity, if this is meant to be a historical term to signal the beginning of an era, is not very well described and conceptualized. The current debate about multiple modernities may have the potential to correct this error of conceptualization. It will live up to that potential, though, only if it is seen as a debate about crisis and a search for reorientation rather than the ultimate concept with which to finally grasp the eternal nature of modernity.

3

What is Europe?

Beyond the myth of origins

The search for an understanding of what Europe is has not always taken historicity very seriously. Those who claim to have found the origins of Europe in Greek and Roman antiquity have rarely addressed the question of how those 'origins' are supposed to have continued to shape Europe over more than two millennia, as we discussed in the preceding chapter. Even less have they reflected on their own position in history. Let us briefly reconsider this case in more historical-contextual terms. Philhellenism became a European movement in the eighteenth- and early nineteenth-century intellectual search for the origin of Europe influenced by the French Revolution and in response to its Napoleonic consequences. Winckelmann, Schinkel, Schliemann, Evans and others built a memory temple where Homer's outline of the war of the Mycenaeans at Troy in 'Minor Asia', and Herodotus's narrative about the Greek battle against Persia in Marathon and the Spartan struggle at Thermopylae constituted the foundation stones. Philhellenism constituted a crucial experience and point of reference when Karl Jaspers after 1945 again put the question of the origin and meaning of Europe as we saw in Chapter 2.

This nineteenth-century Hellenism was often associated with Germany and England. In Germany, the preeminent figure in the movement was Johann Joachim Winckelmann, the art historian and aesthetic theoretician who first articulated what would come to be the orthodoxy of the Greek ideal in sculpture (though he only examined Roman copies of Greek statues, and was murdered before setting foot in Greece). In England, the so-called 'second generation' of Romantic poets, especially John Keats, Percy Bysshe Shelley and Lord Byron, were protagonists of Hellenism. Drawing on Winckelmann, they turned to Greece as a model of ideal beauty, transcendent philosophy, democratic politics and homosexuality, the latter aspect later to be developed in particular by Michel Foucault.

One hundred and fifty years after the initial philhellenism a new wave of academic interest in ancient Greece emerged. This wave, which during the 1970s and 1980s involved many more than Foucault, focused on the universal implications of the Greek achievements. Johann Arnason and Peter Murphy emphasized the importance of the Greek *polis*, something that went beyond the concept of the city-state. They explored political structures more open to conflict, debate and reasoning than in regimes based on kingship and priesthood.[1] Christian Meier, as we mentioned earlier, referred in this vein to the Greek legacy as a political revolution of world-history.[2]

The new interest in the Greek origin of European culture was a transformation of the nineteenth-century Greek cult in romanticism and humanism, although it had a much more critical thrust and focused on philosophy much more than on archaeology and philology. It did not at all have the corresponding aestheticizing core as the eighteenth- and nineteenth-century neo-classicism.[3]

This older neo-classicist myth about the origin of Europe, subject to critique from the 1970s onwards, is still to a certain degree alive, however, although in popular imagination rather than in academic reflection. The palace of King Minos at Knossos, with the labyrinth of the Minotaur, is seen as a cradle and *lieu de mémoire* of Europe. From there the European road went to Mycenae, from where Agamemnon made war on Troy as the commander of a Greek multi-city-state army. Homer stylized this struggle between West and East, which became an intellectual prototype of the Persian Wars where Europe defeated Asia and Marathon became another European *lieu de mémoire*.[4] Such imagination aims at defining Europe through reference to key past events and to locate Europe firmly in socio-historical space.

A somewhat different attempt to reflect on current Europe's sources in the past was undertaken by Rémi Brague who we met in the previous chapter.[5] His thesis is that European culture is essentially Roman because the Romans did something more than just pass on the Jewish and Greek cultures. They adopted them while at the same time transforming them. The importance of Roman mediation and transmission was that they deliberately assumed secondarity to the Jewish and Greek legacies. For Karl Jaspers, Socrates and Jesus were the main figures of the legacy on which Europe was built. For Martin Heidegger it was the Greek idea of rational man and the Christian idea of man as the imitation of God, and according to him both had to be overcome.

Brague's reinterpretation of such reference to antiquity was to see the Romans as accepting their inferiority to Greece and Christianity and to transform the legacies by learning. The Roman way of Europe means that Europe began in what is seen as outside itself with an Asian foundation myth (Europa and the Bull) and an Asian religion. The European greatness was the incorporation of this religion under continuous adjustment and adaptation. Secondarity, which is a key concept in his argument, means for Brague a willingness to learn. The Roman way implied acceptance of inferiority to Judaism, Greece and Christianity, and transforming these cultures rather than copying them. The Romans did not invent anything. They learnt, transformed and adopted.[6]

Secondarity means critical self-reflection and a capacity to step out of oneself. The roots of Europe are not in Europe but in Jerusalem and the Eurasian East Mediterranean. European culture takes its bearing from references that are not in Europe but externally located. Europe is eccentric. The Romans recognized their own imperfection and the benefits by borrowing and learning from what went before. The Roman character of the Eastern legacy is, in the view of Brague, particularly strong in the Christian, especially the Catholic embodiment of the Eastern impulses. The Romans knew that Greek culture was an ideal to strive for and that the risk of not doing so was to fall into its opposite, barbarian decay. Christians recognized their secondarity to the Jews, and this insight prevented all European cultures inherited from Christianity from considering themselves as its own source.[7] Brague's particular search for origins avoids locating those origins in a firmly defined place and thus marks a step towards abandoning the search for origins. Even though he does give an answer – the origins are in Roman antiquity – that answer refers to a displacement rather than a place. As such, it invites further historicization.

Brague contrasted the Christian/Roman secondarity with the Byzantine and Islamic approaches to Greek culture. The Byzantines took Greek culture for theirs. The Muslims often translated and then discarded the original texts, 'throw[ing] away the empty shell', as Brague phrased it. With these differences to Rome, neither of these cultures could develop the dynamics of Europe, which again and again regenerated by looking to a past that they located outside themselves. The consequence was a series of European renaissances, the 'axial transformations' that we underlined in the previous chapter instead of an 'Axial Age' that marks origins and defines an identity. The restless European cultures always on the move did not rest on their laurels. The content of Europe is an attitude to be a container, open to the universal. Brague's theory about a European eccentrism means that he takes issue with the term Eurocentrism.[8]

Brague's 'Roman way' is a universalism without ethnic demarcations. His universalism does not say anything about social hierarchies like, for instance, the place of women and of slaves in Greece. The Roman egalitarianism under the motto *romanus sum* is a matter of form more than substance. In the final chapter of *Eccentric Culture*, Brague refers to the European modernity that followed with Enlightenment, where many negative aspects surfaced such as Eurocentric imperialism and arrogance, the self-understanding of European culture as civilized, as opposed to other cultures as savage, the negative sides of technical developments, and the negative sides of economic expansion with new forms of exploitation.

Brague seems to refer this development to the confrontation between Enlightenment and Christianity. He denotes the technical and cultural Marcionism. The heretic Marcion sought in the second century to eliminate the Old Testament. Marcionism thus refers to the hubristic attempts to cut off traditions. Saint Irenaeus fought successfully against the heresy of Marcion laying down the connection between the God of the Old Testament and the God of the New Testament. Thereby he became not only one of the Church Fathers but also one of the Fathers of Europe. Saint Irenaeus laid the ground of the successful secondarity. The arrogant Enlightenment rupture with that principle explains the negative sides of modernity.

Brague is a philosopher not a historian. The Roman way represents a kind of Hegelian movement of the torch of history through distinctions, separations, ruptures: Judaism-Christianity, Christianity-Islam, East Rome-West Rome, Catholicism-Protestantism with the Catholic church in the centre of the village at the end. The eccentric definition of Europe, as Rémi Brague develops it, through continuous alienation from its own Asian origins, at the end becomes centric when, after the discovery of America, the look backward and eastward changed in the direction of forward and westward. The crusades were an important step in this process. The rupture between Enlightenment and Christianity is developed much less in his theory. In a certain sense Brague's argument seems to stop with modernity. Brague's Eurocentrism becomes Euroeccentrism at this point. Furthermore, there is much less place for institutions than for thoughts in his narrative. His philosophy is persuasive but the questions of practices and of power are left out.

In a recent book, Garth Fowden takes up the question of how to get Islam into the genealogy of Europe.[9] He argues for a history which does not move from Asia to Europe and at the end makes Europe the centre of the world. He suggests a new periodization, during which the ancient world was gradually transformed and there came into being, across Europe and West Asia, a triad of sibling civilizations, successors of Rome, whose commitment to revealed monotheism either Biblical in Greek and Latin Christendom, or Qur'anic in the Muslim world, was to varying degrees tempered by the rational principles derived from Greek and Roman antiquity. Fowden undertakes a re-contextualization of Late Antiquity in time as well as space. In the dimension of space, the conventional Mediterranean framework of late antique history is superseded by the triptych of the Iranian plateau and the Eastern Mediterranean basin flanking the 'Mountain Area', the area embraced by the Amanus, Taurus and Zagros Mountains, the highlands of South Arabia and Ethiopia's rugged plateau in the south, and to the west the mountains flanking the Red Sea and backing the Eastern Mediterranean littoral. Fowden challenges the idea of Europe as the centre of modernity and looks for a more entangled Eurasianafrican understanding where the role of Islam is seen as not less important than Christianity, rather more important.

Fowden's cosmopolitan understanding of the origin of Europe provides important suggestions for a genealogy that emphasizes entanglement and plays down essence.

The impossible definition of Europe: unification and division

Friedrich Nietzsche once wrote that what can be defined has no history. By this he meant that definability requires general agreement and history is lived disagreement. Definitions are based on consensual understandings. History is not consensus but contention.[10]

Europe indeed has a history and exactly therefore it cannot be defined in terms of extent, content, substance or form. Europe is a discourse, a narrative, an ideology with not one but many meanings, a continuous work at self-interpretation marked by contestation through new proposals and counter-proposals.[11] At times some of these meanings have had more or less hegemonic proportions, but there have always been alternative interpretations, although often less present in the debate. Europe is a concept full of contentious meanings. Each of these meanings may have the pretence to define Europe. The ongoing contestations show, however, that they do not invalidate Nietzsche's statement since there is no final definition, no neutral point from which it can be unambiguously outlined.

Modernity has meant a continuous and contentious search for the definition of Europe. The search has had various targets: Europe as a value community, as a normative centre, as a political community for peace and stability, as an economic community for wealth, for instance, a variety of targets, overlapping or exclusive.

Europe was never one and undivided, but split in shifting patterns where some dividing lines have been more strongly drawn and more difficult to move again than others. The Northwestern part of Europe and Britain should not be confused with Eastern and Southeastern Europe. However, the economic, political and cultural divisions between West and East, Northwest and Southeast did not exclude similarities across the dividing lines. The industrialization of Europe was generally faster, more permeating and more solid in Western and Northern than in Eastern and Southern Europe where feudal agricultural structures prevailed longer. However, the conventional imagery of industrial capitalism spreading like ripples on water from its British origin eastwards and southwards is too simplistic. Early on in the nineteenth century industrial regions emerged also in Eastern and Southern Europe, and considerable parts of Western Europe were still at the beginning of the twentieth century mainly agricultural. In terms of political modernity the conventional view depicts Western Europe progressing steadily towards democracy compared with backward Eastern Europe with its authoritarian or reactionary political institutions. Political modernity in the West reflected liberalism and parliamentarianism and in the East conservative or reactionary paternalism and authoritarianism. This conventional view ignores the fact that most of Europe on the eve of the First World War was conservative and authoritarian. There was no parliamentarian democracy in our understanding of the term but imperial and monarchic rule. Liberal and socialist ideas certainly since long challenged the conservative establishments, and they were articulated also in Eastern and Southern Europe, but before 1914 they did not really break through anywhere in Europe with the exception of Norway. In terms of political modernity there were more similarities than differences across Europe before 1914. The Enlightenment imagery of progress, driven by liberal and socialist ideologies, did not only provoke claims for change but promoted also opposition from conservative defenders of the existing order, forces against change arguing for restoration and preservation. These forces wielded power still in 1914.

Democracy broke through as a consequence of the mass mobilization for the world wars, but not as a general pattern. The Russian Revolution, fascism and Nazism were alternative proposals, which defied understandings of Europe as democracy which also in the Western part was late and partial if regarded in terms of institutionalized fact rather than imagery.[12] In the discussion of similarities and differences across Europe it is important to distinguish between discourses and arguments on the one side and the political implementation of the arguments through institution building on the other side. There was a gap between speeches and acts, and the outcome of the struggle between the forces for more or less radical change and the forces for restoration or accepting moderate change filled the gap.

The nineteenth century was the epoch of nationalism and nation building, with ethnic and religious demarcations within Europe. Nationalism emphasized the differences as to the meaning of Europe. From having been an instrument for change at the beginning of the nineteenth century it became ever more an instrument for restoration at the end of the century.

Before the Thirty Years War (1618–1648), Europe was rather subsumed under the superior category of Christianity but the atrocities of the religious war made religion problematic as a term with the aim to connote unity. However, Christianity as part of the identification in Europe remained nevertheless after 1648. Not only in religious but also in broader cultural terms the concept of Christian continued to unify and to divide. The Holy Alliance of Alexander I created in Vienna in 1815 tried to bridge the tension between the three main trends of Christianity – Russian orthodoxy, Catholicism and Protestantism. The Russian tsar, the Austrian emperor and the King of Prussia who signed the pact represented the 'three branches of the One family' under the 'Sovereign of Heaven'. They would protect 'Religion, Peace and Justice'. Other powers were welcome to join the pact if they respected these sacred principles. Most of them did so, but the pope and sultan felt unable to accede to a pact subscribed to by so many sectarians and infidels.[13] The Holy Alliance intertwined in its outline political conservatism and authoritarianism, Enlightenment ideals and Christian pietistic mysticism. As political practice it came to support the throne-altar compacts. It was contradictory, but its contradictions reflected a European

Zeitgeist looking for orientation between old and new, between the past and the future. The Holy Alliance was basically a legitimizing tool, which tried to unify Europe through a pattern of throne-altar compacts. As Chapter 7 will demonstrate, religious protest, which at the same time was political protest, continuously undermined these compacts emphasizing the divisive trends. On the other side, as a core dimension of the imagery of a European civilization mission in the world, Christianity in a more cultural meaning continued to unify.

Religion became, despite the Holy Alliance, a key tool for the cultural division of Europe when the three religions linked to linguistic-ethnic divisions between the Slavic, the Latin and the Germanic peoples. In this cultural construction of difference, the Slavic-Orthodox, the Latin-Catholic and the Germanic-Protestant cultures represented different stages of development on a religio-linguistic-ethnic scale which went from the East and the South to the West, from backward to modern.

After the Peace of Westphalia, 'Europe' became an alternative unification project replacing the failed Christian community. Imageries of European unification emerged as peace projects, for instance. Dreams of a more peaceful Europe emerged in a wide range of approaches from continental peace based on power balance to peace based on reason (Kant), on international law, or on peace movements and peace activism. A peaceful Europe was often seen as equal to a peaceful world. The perspective was Eurocentric.

Colonialism unified Europe and its colonies through the imagery of a civilizing task in the world, but it split Europe through power struggles over the colonies. Europe was imagined as a balance of power between its states with their colonial annexes. Europe was also centre and periphery within Europe, divided between the Western centre and the Southern, Eastern and partially Nordic peripheries. In a global version the polarity distinguished the imperial civilizing centre and the (still) uncivilized colonial periphery.

After the US revolt in 1776 against their colonial status and after the Latin American revolt against Spain in the early nineteenth century, an important question dealt with the distinction between Europe and the West and between Europe and its colonies.

After the Second World War the geopolitical demarcation developed the old Enlightenment trope of Europe as an East-West division where the trend in the latter part was to identify it with Europe as a whole. The Europe of progress and modernity outlined by the Enlightenment philosophers was by implication Western Europe. Promotors of this view looked with contempt and disdain on the Eastern part as backward and pre-modern.[14] The fact that this view on Eastern Europe dominated in the literary salons of the Enlightenment era in Western Europe did not, as we saw, mean that Western Europe in institutional terms was less authoritarian.

On the basis of the Enlightenment philosophers and the French Revolution, Napoleon created a unified Europe with the sword rather than the word. This was the most systematic, and, at the same time, the most violent modern definition of the borders of Europe so far.

Napoleon unified Europe twice. The second unification was an outcome of the resistance against him that he provoked. The aim of the unification created in Vienna in 1815 was restoration of pre-revolutionary Europe with big power coordination of the states of Europe as its fundament. From the 1820s the revolutionary ideology of nationalism confronted this architecture. One influential trend driven by Giuseppe Mazzini tried to combine nationalism with a cosmopolitan liberal dream of a European unification, but the long-term trend was that nationalism split Europe.

The liberal incapacity to cope with the social question, which emerged with the spread of industrial capitalism, and which during the economic depression in the 1870s became the class question (Chapter 5), triggered a more conservative social and ethnic nationalism which cut the connections to the idea of European unification. The fifty years before the First World War can be epitomized as a Europe of expanding and competing nation-states and empires. Expansion in a bounded space meant clash. Hitler exploited this situation.

Before the post-1945 (West) European integration the most spectacular unification proposal after Napoleon was Richard Coudenhove-Kalergi's plan in the 1920s for Pan-Europe, narrowing down the global vision of the League of Nations in 1919 with the aim to give Europe a more prominent place in the world again after the 1914–1918 disaster, including the European continent and its colonies but excluding the Soviet Union and the British Empire.[15] The plans for Pan-Europe petered out against the backdrop of economic crisis.

Hitler's Europe was the second unification through military violence after Napoleon's European order. In both cases the Russian winter choked the dream of a Europe united with weapons. Like after the defeat of Napoleon the defeat of Hitler led to an alternative European unification, or rather, two European unifications: the Western and Eastern appendixes of the hegemons of the Cold War.

In the bicentenary sequence of 'postwar-prewar-war-postwar-prewar-war-postwar' since 1815, 'postwar' meant the concerted attempts at European unification under the motto of 'never again', 'prewar' meant the erosion and 'war' the collapse of these attempts.[16] There were, in particular, three formulations heralding a lasting European peace, expressed in the motto of 'never again'. They emerged after the revolutionary and Napoleonic wars (1792–1815), in which the French Revolution widened into a European world war about global power, and the conflicts conventionally referred to as the First World War (1914–1918) and Second World War (1939–1945). Each of these three European world wars – and their predecessor the Seven Years War (1756–1763) – exceeded the previous in terms of violence and systematic mass killing. They represent a cycle over 250 years of violent European conflicts about global commercial and military power and the continual resetting of a new peace utopia based on a project for European unification and redefinition of Europe. The postwar designs were all attempts to transcend the nations as the locus of political community. They all aimed at creating a European order or community; in Versailles in 1919 the goal was even a global international community around the League of Nations. The repeated attempts and failures after major wars to transcend the nations as organizational principle reject teleological understandings of Europe.[17]

Europe in the colonial mirror

The idea of European unification necessarily involves a demarcation with respect to the non-European. This external framework for discourses of European integration has a long history of contestation, contradiction and ambiguity. It is important to see the rhetoric of European unification against the backdrop of self-images in mirrors of the Other. European community emerged through the construction of mutually reinforcing xeno- and auto-stereotypes.

In this construction the idea of Europe as a cultural value emerged closely linked to the idea and concept of 'civilization'. Europe became the home of civilization, and the lack of civilization became a means of demarcating the Other. The idea of civilization was connected to a philosophy of historical evolution. This intellectual framework was characterized by a system of oppositions: civilization – barbarism, virtue – corruption, development – backwardness, progress – stagnation, and so on.[18] A point of departure for the idea of civilization was the geographical exploration of the globe and the early phases of colonialism in the sixteenth century. The colonial order was, in turn, reconfirmed by the civilization language. The very concept of civilization was an eighteenth-century neologism expressing the idea of Europe as a cultural value.

The colonial order, however, was based not only on ideas of European cultural superiority but also on military, economic and political power. It meant conquest, control and exploitation of regions outside the primary territories of the colonizers. The colonial order, since the early modern era based on trade stations in other continents and, as we will come back to in Chapter 5, trade with slaves and raw materials, changed with the spread of industrial capitalism in the nineteenth century. However, the imagery of European superiority in economic, political and cultural terms remained throughout the century.

The goal of finding new sources of raw materials and new markets in an ever more global economy was of paramount importance for the industrializing nations. Britain, France, Germany, Italy, Belgium and the Netherlands were the main colonial powers. They shared among themselves large parts of Africa and Asia, either by reaching agreements at conferences like that in Berlin in 1884–1885, or through military confrontation. Like

America after its 'discovery' by Columbus, black Africa was considered a *terra nullius*, without government, and wide-open for the first civilized people who claimed it. They were integrated as inferior parts of the European self-understanding, belonging to but yet not belonging to Europe.

Thus, Europe was not only a project that unfolded through internal force, but was also in close interaction with other continents. A considerable part of Europe's relationships with the world dealt with exploitation of populations and natural resources (Chapter 5). The global environment was the basis on which Europe rose to world power. The triangular trade was an early lever for global economic and military power. Europeans bought slaves in Africa for weapons and other commodities and sold the slaves in America for sugar and other plantation crops for consumption and as raw materials for the emerging industry in Europe.

In retrospect, many of the conquered regions were of limited economic value, but in the race among colonizers, colonies were often established simply to prevent their being overtaken by others in this competition; the bid for prestige by political power played a considerable role during this expansion.

Colonialism was associated with the idea of white supremacy over other population groups, which in turn occurred under the assumption of the superiority of European civilization and the duty to spread it to other cultures – Kipling's 'white man's burden', Europe as imperial centre and colonial periphery. The idea of the superiority of European civilization functioned as a demarcation of the Other, but all the same, it did not prevent struggles or (civil) wars within this civilization, ideologically underpinned by vulgar readings of Darwin's and Spencer's evolution theories and biological classification of races.

At the end of the nineteenth century, the concept of imperialism was increasingly used to describe this process which, from its early basis of private interests, ever more involved governments, and the use of state power, in particular military but also legal and normative power, was mobilized in more efficient ways. In 1902, the English socialist J.A. Hobson published an influential book on the concept entitled *Imperialism. A Study*.[19] He was not the inventor of the concept – it had been in use for quite some time – but he was the first to develop something that resembled a theory of imperialism. He was quite clear about the meaning of the term: imperialism was the establishment of political control. He was also clear when he argued that its origin was in the financial milieu of the mother country. At the end of the nineteenth century a great and sudden extension of empire took place as a consequence of intensified industrialization and subsequent developments in European economy and society. Statesmen, soldiers and missionaries might have played some role, but the final determination rested with the financial powers. It was the consequence of a lack of domestic demand that made capitalist interests look for markets in other continents. In a pre-Keynesian way he suggested the domestic increase of the purchasing power of the lower classes as an instrument against imperialism (Chapter 5). Imperialism, Hobson suggested, was the font of a capitalist revival, a formulation which was, in a way, echoed by Lenin who, some fifteen years later during the First World War, described imperialism as the highest stage of capitalism.

The meaning of Europe was empire and imperialism as much as nation and nationalism. Europe as empires and Europe as nations clashed as well as overlapped and reinforced each other. Nationalist revivalism challenged imperial rule from within or reinforced imperial power against other empires within and without Europe. Europe as imperialism and nationalism was a complex pattern of cooperation and conflict between shifting coalitions.

The debate on colonialism and imperialism constituted a crucial dimension of the demarcation of Europe and its Other, as well as of the self-understandings in Europe and in the colonies and in what, after 1945, became the former colonies. The debate had been going on since the late nineteenth century. It continued around new key concepts like decolonization and postcolonialism after formal independence in the 1950s and 1960s. The issue at stake was whether formal independence also meant real independence.[20]

The initial relative consensus under the concept of decolonization about imperialism as a historical category broke down in the 1960s against the backdrop of the Cold War and competition between the super-powers in the former colonies. The old dependencies remained in new form. The hope that the end of empire after the era of the world wars had opened up a new stage in the development of the world overseas was not fulfilled. Independence brought neither an end to economic problems nor to economic dependencies. Indeed, some of the new states became ever more involved in and depended on the Western-dominated world system than they had been during colonial rule.

This was the framework in which the term *Tiers Monde* in the 1950s was launched. It was launched as an emancipative concept which lost meaning when it was translated into English, however. The term '*tiers monde*' ('Third World') was formulated as an analogy with '*le tiers état*' (the 'third estate') in the French Revolution. Demographer Alfred Sauvy wrote in a newspaper article: 'For in the end this *Tiers Monde*, ignored, exploited and despised, exactly as the Third Estate was before the Revolution, also wants to become something.'[21]

Sauvy attempted to draw the attention of the French public to the fact that (according to his own research) the population of Europe as a whole grew less rapidly than the population in the rest of the world. This would mean that within half a century or so, according to Sauvy's estimates, Europeans would lose their global cultural, economic, political and social hegemony. If such a shift did not occur peacefully, then it would come about as the result of a bloody world revolution. The point he made was that 'they, the Others' threaten the European ego. Practically everybody in Europe, he warned, was blind to this relatively slow and gradual, but also powerful change. By making a clear allusion to the French Revolution through the formulation of the metaphor *'tiers monde'*, Sauvy tried to provoke the public debate in early 1950s by arguing that the 'Others' of the *'tiers monde'* threatened to set in motion a revolution that would shake Europe.[22]

Sauvy played on the distinction between *tiers*, in the sense of one-third of the whole, alluding to the historical meaning that the term got in the French Revolution, and *troisième*, the third in the ordinal sense. When translated into English this connotation got lost. What remained was something 'third', which was linked to the polarity of the Cold War with its Western first and Eastern second world. In France the connotation of *tiers monde* adjusted in the 1960s to the scenario of the Cold War and to the Third World in English. The link to the revolution was lost. The immediate experiences of the Cold War superseded the retrospect imagery of the Revolution.

It is noticeable that, in the early 1950s, in his defence of Europe's interests, Sauvy held a rather positive opinion about colonialism and European intervention in Africa. He used the term 'under-developed' (*sous-développé*) as an argument for new relationships between Europe and Africa. Africa was scarcely populated and rich in raw materials. Europe and Africa should engage in a form of exchange for mutual profit: the Europeans would offer 'development' and the Africans could, in return, provide 'space'.

Sauvy defended colonialism building his argument on the concepts of 'developed' and 'under-developed'. Just as he argued that Europe should govern Africa, he also asserted that France should lead Europe. Also, if the connection between Europe and Africa was strong, the specific relationship between France and Algeria was even stronger: the Franco-Algerian bond was the most solid of all the ties that connected Europe to Africa.

This relation between France and Algeria was soon to be tested. In late 1954, the Algerian uprising against French colonial rule started. The Algerian War had a major impact on the conceptual history of the 'Third World'. Frantz Fanon, in his bestseller *Les damnés de la terre* gave Sauvy's *tiers monde* scenario a new twist. His conceptualization of the relationships between Africa and Europe did not connect to the French Revolution as a threat but as a promise, as an emancipating legacy for the exploited to turn against their masters. Fanon tried to maintain the original connotation to the French Revolution when the trend in France was to adjust the meaning of the *tiers monde* to the meaning in English with the connotation of being a third part of the bipolar Cold War, although not strong enough to make the world structure triangular.[23]

Parallel to these developments Swedish economist Gunnar Myrdal published a book called *Economic Theory and Under-developed Regions*.[24] In this book, Myrdal discussed the rapid increase in international inequalities. He also outlined some possible solution by, like Sauvy, arguing in terms of 'developed' and 'under-developed' countries and regions but from a modernization perspective with a development optimism where universal features develop according to a historical logic, even though some parts of the world had developed faster and further than others. The problem to be tackled, according to Myrdal, was how to achieve international equality and balanced, universal development on a global scale. In Myrdal's view, the system of colonialism had become obsolete and would soon dissolve:

> In the era of awakened nationalism in the under-developed world the colonial system is now doomed, and its liquidation is one of the most important political avalanches taking place before our eyes. [...] The ideas about this system as a vehicle for a national 'civilizing mission' in history, which under the epoch of colonialism had emerged and become a part of the ideological structures and phraseologies of the different metropolitan countries, will for a considerable time be earnestly upheld by writers, statesmen and the common citizens. Fundamentally, these ideas are, however, largely rationalisations of economic interests.[25]

Myrdal differentiated between 'under-developed' and 'developed', and he did not once refer to the term *tiers monde*. As opposed to Sauvy, he did not distinguish between 'us' and 'the Other'. In Myrdal's view, there was only universal humankind. Universal modernization was the instrument with which the Western world would overcome both communism and poverty.

The dynamics of the Cold War were stronger than Myrdal and Fanon. The semantics around the imagery of a tripartite world began to describe an existing order with ever less ambitions to change it. The two super-powers, one European and Asian, the other a European descendant, and their European annexes disseminated their competition about military and economic power rather than development to the Third World.

Europe in the American mirror

The American Revolution was experienced as something new in the history of humankind, or mankind as was the term at the time. Writing more than 150 years after the revolution, the German-American philosopher Hannah Arendt referred to it as 'the feeling of a new beginning' shared by both Americans and Europeans. Europe was ruled by tradition and habits, whereas the Americans discussed and chose their constitution.[26] Arendt's view was not, of course, new.

The rejection or affirmation of modernity in Europe has been channelled through observations of America in a variety of views. For Europeans, America was as distinct from Asia and Africa as it could be from the moment it emerged. The so-called discoverers did not expect anybody or anything there where America happened to be found. The inhabitants of Asia and Africa had always already been known about – so it seemed – but America was like a *tabula rasa*. The native Americans appeared as the unknown radical Other. John Locke suggested that something like the state of nature had prevailed in America, a kind of state of nature before human order had been formed by means of contact. Europe saw its original state of nature in America.[27]

To Hegel in 1822, half a century after the American declaration of independence, American society had not yet made its way into world-history. His lectures on the philosophy of history, which subdivided the world into the 'Oriental', the 'Greek', the 'Roman' and the 'Germanic' parts, dealt only briefly with the 'New World'. He wanted to anchor the experiences of the French Revolution in a flow of history with the Greek and the Christian as the sources. The radicality of what went on on the other side of the Atlantic escaped him. Like Locke he regarded America as a somewhat belated beginning of society and history, as a point of reflection about the origins of social and political life.

Only a little bit more than ten years later, a few years after Hegel had passed away, this view changed totally. When Alexis de Tocqueville travelled to America he was not looking for the origin of Europe in the contemporary world but for its future. He was convinced that democracy, the key concept that strong opinions in Europe feared since the excesses of the French Revolution, in its American application represented the future of Europe, the future as both promise and threat but unavoidable.[28]

In the mid-nineteenth century, Leopold von Ranke wrote that the American Revolution was more revolutionary than any of the revolutions that had preceded it, and that it had meant a total shift of perspective. Ranke was interested in the American Revolution because republicanism was no longer an abstract idea but had a firm foundation in a state. Europe might learn from America.[29] Ranke said this in a time that was still before the European invocation of the French Revolution as the beginning of modernity and modern Europe had begun to extinguish the American Revolution from the European consciousness, emphasizing the distinction between Europe and the USA rather than their shared history.[30] Before the American Revolution, the world was governed by kings with God's grace. With the American Revolution, the idea was born that the power lies with the people. Ranke discerned two views – two worlds – that stood against each other: one was the Old World, and the other the New. They were seen as the two poles in a moral world order. Earlier, the American Indian, as the elevated noble savage, had been contrasted to the depraved European. From the 1780s, the revolutionary creator of a new social order took the place of the Indian. However, it should be added that what was seen in the American mirror was also an element of the European Enlightenment rhetoric in which Rousseau and others who lauded the natural, primeval state and criticized civilization were advancing the ideas of modernity.

Reinhard Koselleck has described this shift of perspective in the American mirror as the emergence of a manichaean world-view, where the old world of despotism and the new world of freedom became polarized yet, simultaneously, became dependent on one another. In the nineteenth century, within Europe a parallel manicheism emerged in the contrast between liberal Britain and reactionary Russia. In the American mirror Europe and America were seen as two connected vessels: when the one was emptied the other was filled. This moral geography took on historical necessity, a necessity which was intrinsic in the metaphor itself. Being the Old World meant that the days of Europe were numbered. The future belonged to America as the New World.[31] However, the metaphor also contained other possibilities. Europe stood for experience and wisdom which, during the nineteenth century, emerged as an alternative view in the American mirror and could also be related to the white man's burden, which was seen reflected in the Asian and African mirrors. Europe had an educating mission: it stood for science-based classical culture and education and aesthetic values expressed in art, music and literature. This cultural Europe was contrasted to an America without culture, history and morality, an America with the immoral Wild West. 'Moral' and 'immoral' as labels for Europe and America shifted with respect to the image of an Old World, no longer predominantly 'depraved' and a New World, no longer predominantly 'revolutionary'.

Both these interpretative frameworks were underpinned by the frontier myth, which emerged in nineteenth-century America as a kind of foundation myth. This was the Puritan myth of New England as God's New Israel, in which 'exodus' was the term used for the migration of the Pilgrim Fathers to America. The idea of the North American continent as a new Garden of Eden was cultivated in both the Old and New Worlds. In this mythology, frontier was the *limes* between Euro-American colonization and the wildness, which was not a deterrent, but rather an invitation to cultivate the free land in the West, and civilize or exterminate its original inhabitants. The metaphor was used to describe both the process of migration and colonization and the form of social organization on this border of civilization. The myth legitimized collective expansion as a manifest destiny and promoted the emergence of fundamentalism – as opposed to pragmatism – as a key element in American political culture.[32] In the extension of this manifest destiny, the native Indians no longer appeared as the noble savage in contrast to the depraved European, and the violent confrontation with the aboriginal inhabitants was celebrated as a regenerating experience where the white pioneer emerged strengthened and purified as the New Man. The mythologization of the frontier as the place which gave rise to the unique emancipatory social and political order of America based on a democratic-egalitarian spirit and a confident pioneer individualism, released American democracy from its European connection. Freedom and equality were seen as essentialist American products. The 'frontier thesis' by historian Frederick Jackson Turner in 1893 was important for this image, however, this image must be related to the entire ideological embedding of the American dream based on Christianity and ideas of eternal renewal rendered possible by infinite space. The huge migration of over 50 million Europeans to North America during the century after the 1820s maintained and confirmed the frontier myth. They populated and cultivated, 'civilized' the land behind the moving frontier.

The American-European historical relationship can be described as two plots. The Enlightenment philosophers looked upon post-revolutionary America as a kind of better Europe, as a place of an applied Enlightenment. This was the view that Alexis de Tocqueville mediated when he went to the USA to investigate American democracy, which he admired and feared at the same time as he saw it as the for better or for worse unavoidable future also for Europe.

The Enlightenment discourse on constitutionalism, tolerance and citizenship was in relation to Africa seen as the dissemination of a European value canon through a civilizing mission. In the American comparison the discourse mirrored America as the future of Europe. Although America had not yet made any great steps in science, art or literature, these were all areas where something great could be expected from the young republic, the heir of the republican states of antiquity. The competing plot, entangled with this first one, concerned the wild, uncultivated and violent America of the Wild West as opposed to the civilized, dignified and mature Europe.

This kind of spirituality as spatiality and cultural naivety was to be repeated half a century later in the Soviet Union's enormous projects to divert the course of rivers in Siberia. Of course, the point of departure in the USSR was located in a different form of spirituality, and the ever-present American cultural 'openness' was absent. In the early 1920s the young Soviet experiment and the United States vied briefly with one another for European attention. The Soviet Union became the model for the European Left and President Wilson's USA became the guarantee for a liberal Europe of global democracy and peace. However, soon the liberal American model eclipsed the socialist Soviet model at the same time as liberal became less left. Following the First World War the United States became extremely attractive and emerged more than ever as a, if not *the*, production model to emulate. The interest in American production methods had already begun in the 1890s but in the 1920s it accelerated at an unprecedented rate. Rationalism, Taylorism and other key concepts mediated the belief in a science-based management of production to secure a prosperous economy and a better world. This view on America was reaffirmed and strengthened following the Second World War and persisted virtually unchallenged until the Vietnam War and the dollar collapse in the 1970s, when a more critical point of view was established.[33]

Europe in the Asian and African mirrors

In the Asian mirror, European self-esteem was also ambiguous. Like the American mirror the Asian mirror offered various possibilities of identification and demarcation. One of the discursive fields in the imagery of the Orient was defined by the opposition of enlightenment and despotism where Europe stood for enlightenment and the Orient for despotism. However, the translation of *A Thousand and One Nights* into French at the beginning of the eighteenth century painted the picture of a miraculous Orient which had already been glimpsed in Bartélemy d'Herbelot's Islamic encyclopaedia, *Bibliothèque orientale*, of 1697. Whereas some regarded Muhammed as a cheat, others saw him as an enlightened philosopher. Voltaire, for instance, admired Muslim tolerance which he contrasted to Christian intolerance. Of course, there was also the demarcation between an enlightened Christianity and a fanatic Islam, and there were mergers of the Enlightenment and despotism views like in the notion of enlightened absolutism.[34] Also, the recurring enthusiasm for China and India enriched and problematized the European self-image as a civilizing project.

Friedrich Nietzsche condemned Buddhism as nihilistic but he also in his own struggle with the issue of nihilism referred to himself as the Buddha of Europe. The question of nihilism steered his curiosity towards Buddhism. He was fascinated by Buddhism at the same time as he rejected it. He saw himself and Europe in the mirror of Buddha. The question of how to overcome aversion to an impermanent world in which nothing, including the ego, remained stable tied Nietzsche to Siddharta in sympathy and rejection.[35] In *Thus Spoke Zarathustra* Nietzsche viewed Zoroaster, the Persian prophet, as his arch antagonist, whom he admired but failed to overcome, an opponent of similar power and stature. Zarathustra was the alter ego of Nietzsche worthy of Zoroaster's greatness.

Karl Marx was less ambiguous when he saw the capitalist production mode in Europe in the mirror of what he called the Asian production mode. Despotic urban ruling cliques exploited surpluses from undifferentiated village communities and held Asiatic societies in thrall as opposed to the more developed production relationships of industrial capitalism demarcated from the agrarian world in Europe.

In the African mirror the view was somewhat different. There was less identification than contrast. Africa represented the colonial world which still was uncivilized. Europe 'invented' an Africa that was impenetrable and dangerous.[36] Africa was the main target of the fulfilment of the Enlightenment promise through a civilizing mission. Irrespective of identification or dissociation, or a mix, the imaginary of Europe emerged in comparison with the American, Asian or African Other.

Edward Saïd has documented these developments in *Orientalism* where he translated the historical experiences of the meeting between Europe and its Others in other countries, in particular the Orient, from the Enlightenment to the emerging imagery of postcolonialism in the 1970s.[37] He criticized the cultural representation of the Orient in Western studies and discourses. The imagery that the orientalists outlined reflected the imperialist societies which produced them and since the imagery was powerful the peoples in the Orient took over this external imposition. The xeno-stereotype became also an auto-stereotype.[38]

Orientalism became a milestone in the debate on postcolonialism, which in the 1970s began to draw a demarcation to the earlier optimistic concept of decolonialization. Other influential contributions that emphasized the power relationships in the cultural representations of the Other were those by Jacques Derrida, who questioned the assumptions of the Western philosophical tradition and the dominating discourses, and Dipesh Chakrabarty, who made a strong argument for the relativizing of Europe's role in the shaping of the world through colonialism and imperialism.[39] Chakrabarty moved the focus in postcolonial studies from unilateral imposition of power from the colonial centres towards views that emphasized entanglements, resistance and softer counter-strategies in the confrontation with the imperial powers. The persistence of Enlightenment thought and imageries of modernization and civilization was not only a one-way imposition of power but offered also possibilities for resistance and appropriation through adjustment. Of course, the spirit of Foucault and his imagery of epistemic power structures and knowledge regimes hovered over this debate.[40]

In Africa, there was the philosophy accompanying the politics of decolonization and struggle for independence that emerged in two versions. There were those like Léopold Senghor who argued for an ethno-philosophy based on ideas of *négritude*, a counter agenda to the Western/European civilizing mission project, and those like Frantz Fanon and Paulin Hountondji who argued for a more universalist transformation of Enlightenment thought, which had been developed by the West but could be appropriated and used for resistance also by the rest, emphasizing the universal dimension and potential of critique and human rights rather than as something specifically Western or exclusively an expression of colonial power.[41] This was the line of thought that Dipesh Chakrabarty so powerfully developed. Against the backdrop of the new perspective on the past that the reactions to Saïd had opened up, philosophers like Valentine Mudimbe, Achille Mbembe and Patrice Nganang began to reconsider the one-way view after the initial euphoria after independence, irrespective of whether the one-way represented confidence in *négritude*, i.e. the African opposite of the European one-way view, or in the capacity to appropriate and transform the Enlightenment discourse. They developed continuities as well as discontinuities across the old border line between the colonizers and the colonized and across the rupture of the present between the worse past and the better future.[42]

Europe, in its African, Asian and American mirrors, took shape as a relational concept in a global framework. The self-reflection in Europe dealt with the understanding of Europe as part of the world rather than as a closed totality developing and depending on itself. There is a potential for increased complexity in this European self-reflection: to critically connect to the growing self-esteem among the former colonized peoples when they consider themselves in their European mirrors in terms of resistance, opposition, subjugation, adjustment and cooperation.

The Cold War: the European division and unification

The Cold War thus divided Europe as the debate on the Third World reflected. The iron curtain located the significant Other within Europe. However, there was opposition in Eastern Europe against the Russian hegemon and in Western Europe against American leadership. In the West there was a continuous tension between those who wanted close relationships to the USA and those who argued for more independence from the USA. When in 1947–1948 the US administration in the framework of the Marshall Plan suggested the formation of the United States of Europe (USE), seeing the USA as a blueprint of the USE, resistance among the West European leaders was massive and the US administration had to drop the idea. However, in this agreement the disagreement began. There were continuously mixed feelings and various answers to the question of whether the USA was an Other or one of 'Us'. The European integration project beginning with the European Coal and Steel Community in 1951 and continuing with the European Communities in 1957 tried to mediate between the two positions, but there was never unanimity about Europe's position in this respect, although few denied that the integration project was a more autonomous alternative than NATO cooperation.

In Western Europe the trend was to explain away Eastern Europe as not being part of the Enlightenment project. The real Europe was equal to Western Europe. The Western part appropriated the term Europe. The European integration project was a West European integration project but it was not called so.

An important debate dealt with the character of the West European integration project. A crucial question was whether Western Europe was heading towards a supranational federation or an intergovernmental confederation. Was European cooperation about the dissolution of the nation-states or the reinforcement of them? The answers were contested and in a way the debate was reminiscent of that among the socialists on revolution or reform, where revolution at the end became a long-term goal with little present relevance and little contention, a goal to which one would arrive when time was mature. The goal did not require any particular political action in the present. The European federation would emerge slowly and gradually according to the interpretative framework that functionalist theories provided. Functionalism told that ever-tighter cooperation would occur through the spread of integration to ever more fields. This was the belief of those who dreamt of a federal Europe represented by its Western part but who were not prepared to take action in the immediate future. Few imagined any end to the East-West division.

The French president Charles de Gaulle transcended this duality with his argument about a Europe of the nations ('*l'Europe des patries*') and their unification under French leadership in his imagery of Europe from the Atlantic to the Ural. The goal of de Gaulle was to escape the American umbrella, which in his view also included Britain. De Gaulle wanted to transcend the borders of the Cold War through the imagery of a unified Europe covering the territory between the Atlantic coast of the continent and the Ural Mountains excluding Britain but including Russia in an imagined post-Soviet future scenario. The Soviet Union represented in the view of the French president historical continuity connecting the present of the Cold War to the Russian Empire.

After de Gaulle's resignation in 1969 the dreams of a federal (Western) Europe returned. Also on another point the European leaders broke with de Gaulle's European imagery. They welcomed Great Britain to become part of their (Western) Europe in the 1973 enlargement from the Six (France, Germany, Italy and the Benelux countries) to the Nine (UK, Ireland, Denmark). On the other side, the vision of a more independent Europe under demarcation from the US hegemon remained after de Gaulle against the backdrop of growing doubts on the American capacity to guarantee the (West) European peoples' military security through protection in a nuclear war and financial security through the dollar.

Willy Brandt developed de Gaulle's vision of Europe extended to the Ural in new directions through his politics of entente with the Soviet bloc. He was aware that this move potentially might provoke historical memories and concerns in France. Therefore, he worked for increased West European integration in a federal direction to prevent suspicions of a German solo performance. The negotiations in the 1970s on the Werner Plan for an economic and monetary union with a shared (West) European fiscal policy and the Davignon Plan for a (West) European security political union hinted at a federal step in the European unification under growing demarcation from the USA. The collapse of the international order based on the dollar and of key industries, leading to mass unemployment in Europe for the first time since the 1930s, became a stumbling-block to the federative efforts. The declaration on a European identity by the West European leaders in December 1973 was an attempt to maintain momentum in the negotiations. It called forth the imagery of a European people but without any institutional follow-up consequences it remained an empty phrase.

The economic and the social in European unification after 1990

The end of the Cold War provoked feelings of a new European unification, this time one that transcended the old East-West demarcation. The Maastricht Treaty in 1992 with the decision on the European Monetary Union consolidated a *West* European union but the contours of a truly

European unification transcending the East-West division of the Cold War emerged. The dream of European unity eroded rapidly at about the time of the fratricide in the Balkans in the mid-1990s but it recurred and was realized in 2004 with the enlargement from EU 15 to EU 25 and the inclusion of the former Soviet satellite states into the European Union.

Russia did not join the EU but the relations were harmonious at this time. There was since the early 1990s talk about long-term Eurasian market integration from Vladivostok in the East to Lisbon in the West. The Baltic became after the Cold War a European inland sea as opposed to its earlier function as a divide. In the general euphoria of the early 1990s work began on making the Mediterranean another European inland sea which connected Europe with Turkey and North Africa in a large market area. The imagery of a new Europe emerged with dissolution of the Cold War borders between its Eastern and Western parts and the prospects of the transcending and long-term dissolution of the borders to Asia and Africa, Europe in a global seamless entanglement. There was little thought on state power and social integration in this new brave world which rested on the power of economic integration.

The long Cold War dream of final European unification became real in 2004 through the enlargement to Eastern Europe, which glossed over the Yugoslavian implosion. But for Slovenia, however, the ex-Yugoslavian countries were not part of the enlargement or of the new Europe.

The neglect of paying attention to the social issue in the new architecture of Europe soon became an imminent threat. The social differences within the EU between its Eastern and Western parts grew with unification and even more so did the *feelings* of new dramatic threats where cheap labour from the East would flood the labour markets in the West and industries in the West would close down and move to the East where labour was cheaper. The idea of a new constitution for Europe to seal the unification ended in a horror scenario for the European leaders when in 2005 French and Dutch voters turned down the proposal in referendums. The social issue was a main trigger of resistance against the constitution.

In 2000 the EU decided on the motto of 'unity in diversity'. The decision was a creative response to the failure of the essentializing idea of a European identity with a European demos and it was also a response to the civil war in the former Yugoslavia. One might ask whether the European leaders were inspired by South Africa in their choice of the new motto. Emancipated from apartheid the new South African constitution in 1996 contained the formula 'united in our diversity'. The European leaders can hardly have been unaware of this fact. The old Europe after the civil war in the wake of the dissolution of Yugoslavia did not necessarily represent the global future and the promise of democracy and peace. South Africa at this time no doubt belonged to the future.

However, the Euro crisis triggered by the collapse of the global financial markets in 2008, and the state debt and austerity politics in response to it, destroyed this imagery of united in diversity, which shifted to a view where the South-North divide extends the old one between East and West of the Cold War (and before).

The ever-louder voices of ethnic and social nationalism and the recurrence to authoritarian government styles reinforce the external borders of Europe as well as the divides between Eastern and Western, and Southern and Northern Europe. A growing re-nationalization and de-Europeanization erodes the European integration project.

Europe as a value community

There is a tension built into the imagery of universal Enlightenment values as the core of Europe. The philosophical debate has pointed at this tension since the early twentieth century. The argument emerged in the debate that the imagery of Europe as the embodiment of the universal is hypocritical. The elevation of particular European ideals, values and principles to universal proportions occurred through exclusion and subjugation. Universalism is a European invention and has thus a particular rather than universal origin. References to this universal hegemony have underpinned Europe's imperialist past. European particularism as universalism has justified exclusion and domination as well as promoted interests of particular parties.[43]

The European promise of universality was and is only fulfilled as a strong but often empty discourse, and the values as such were and are neither absolute nor universal but contested. Political practices have repeatedly deviated from them. The articulation of Europe as universal was always contentious and its content was always preliminary under permanent reformulation.

During the Enlightenment discourse in the eighteenth century and the romanticist reaction to/transformation of Enlightenment in the early nineteenth century the nations were the carriers of universalism and universalism reflected the (European) nations. Hegel's philosophy on the dynamics of the spirit of the nations and the world spirit is a case in point. Hegel unified Enlightenment and romanticism, the universal and the nation.

Disappointments and frustration with the ways in which nineteenth-century politics implemented the Enlightenment values of national and global community, liberty and equality in the wake of the spread of industrial capitalism paved the way for the emergence of liberal and social democracy but also of fascism, Nazism and Stalinism. They were all new contentious propagators of European universalism.

Europe as value contention about giving meaning to key concepts like freedom and equality, security and community does not mean that Europe is value-nihilism and relativism but that the claims for universal values are disputed and clash in a permanent work on value construction. There is neither a zero- nor an end-point in this attempt to demarcate and define Europe. There is a permanent search for a meta-normative definition of Europe but there is no place and time where it can be finally defined. Until the mid-twentieth century the search for European universalism operated with the implicit or explicit understanding of Europe as a normative centre of the world. Half a century of decolonialization and postcolonialism has not necessarily led to a better world, in any case not to the promised land contained in these two concepts, but the development has promoted the insight that European universalism is not necessarily realizable only in Europe but that this can occur in any country and that it does not depend on Europe for its sustainability. The conclusion of this development is that the normative demarcations of Europe are eroding, making the concept of Europe more diffuse.

Is it possible to fall back on a set of common values in the sense of historically emerged shared values? How does the idea of universal human rights fit with the idea of value pluralism? How does the idea of a specific European Christian heritage (in demarcation to Judaism and Islam) fit with the Enlightenment idea of religion as an individual private issue? These questions all have a bearing on the larger question of what Europe is and whether it can be understood as a value community.

Often the idea of common and universal values is translated into liberalism by implication, not in a narrow political sense, but in a broader philosophical sense of Enlightenment, in connotation with freedom, where liberalism connotes universal values about emancipation from subjugation. However, what is freedom? Rather than underpinning the commitment of Europe to a single, unequivocal, and normatively superior concept of freedom, post-Enlightenment debate was marked by a continuous interpretive struggle, with lines reaching from G.W.F. Hegel to Axel Honneth in the attempt to elaborate and defend a comprehensive notion of freedom, and from Benjamin Constant to Isaiah Berlin in the attempt to define a liberal notion of freedom (we return to the debates over freedom in Chapter 6).

Values such as enlightenment, humanism and Christianity referring to notions of individual freedom, religious tolerance and a liberal capitalist economy were unproblematic during the Cold War when they could be propagated by West European actors in support of one side in a bi-polarized world where the Western welfare states levelled the tension between individual liberties and social solidarity. For a short while after the end of the Cold War these values supported the idea that history had come to an end in 1989/1991 and – in some optimistic version – that perpetual peace was feasible. After the fall of the Berlin Wall, liberalism ruled the roost without competition. It looked like after the end of the Cold War the only value order to survive as a point of reference for political action was the Western form of capitalist democracy. However, developments would demonstrate how problematic apparently universal concepts, such as freedom, were and are in their implementation in political and economic (commercial) practice. Freedom became more or less exclusively negative freedom in its emphasis on the (strong) individual. The meaning of society shifted to market society. The imagery of the welfare state declined.

In the war on terror proclaimed by the USA after 11 September 2001, Enlightenment values were mobilized on what was depictured as the struggle of Good against Evil. Throughout the debate on the war on Iraq the same set of European values served to condemn the war on the one side (the governments in France and Germany) and on the other to legitimize war (the governments in Britain, Italy, Spain and Poland). President George W. Bush referred to those who hesitated to embark on a military crusade against Sadam Hussein as Old Europe as opposed to his own coalition of the willing with the Young Europe recently liberated from the Soviet yoke and mainly supporting Bush. Of course, hypocrisy accompanied the propagation of Christian values. The declaration of war was based on a lie.

In one major line of its self-understanding, Europe is liberal enlightenment. The whole twentieth century, however, can be described as a *crisis* of liberal enlightenment in that sense (two world wars, Nazism with the Holocaust, fascism, Stalinism, and, at the end, a new genocide). Within Europe, totalitarian projects from the left and from the right have been at least as influential as liberalism. The twentieth century can be seen as a century of continuous European civil wars culminating in genocide twice. This historical experience must be integrated into any discussion of European values. Rationalization and instrumentalization of technological and industrial capacity resulted not only in the European welfare states but also in the railway transports to the Holocaust camps and the Gulag. The ambiguities and contradictions in what is proclaimed to be universal and univocal constitutes the European value canon.

Beyond Europe's geographical borders, the main European legacy is the colonial project of the nineteenth and first half of the twentieth century that was based on ideas of a supreme Western civilization with values like whiteness and Christianity, and ideals of a civilizing global mission under the motto of white man's burden. The gauge of this project was set in temporal terms of backwardness against progress. An important driving force of the civilizing mission was the geopolitical competition among European nation-states for military strongholds, extraction of raw materials and exploitation of labour. In our self-understanding we prefer to see the 1960s as the end of the colonial experience, and it might be true that the European motor was changed for the dynamics produced by the Cold War and competition between the USA and the Soviet Union, with the aim and to the effect that the European division of the world in interest spheres continued with other sources. It is not difficult to interpret also the post-1989 world unified by the globalization language in a long continuity where the world is unified through military and economic power.

The idea of a European and later Western progressive development towards mastery of the world, which, in turn, paved the way for the ideal of freedom, was subsumed under the term of modernity. The concept has often been seen in connection with the Enlightenment. A more or less evolutionary development towards an ever-better society has been the thrust of this view. 'Social engineering' is a concept that disseminates this view. Confidence in the capacity of social and economic sciences to contribute to the improvement of society has been an important proponent of the view, which exists both in a Marxist and a liberal functionalist version.

On the other hand, there was also the national-socialist view on the connection between the Enlightenment and modernity. In this view the civilizational critique of modern technique, capitalism and a pluralistic society, experienced as atomistic, paved the way for fascism/Nazism through its promotion of dreams about *Volksgemeinschaft*, holistic community and 'back to nature'. The distinction between modernity and anti-modernity was not chronological but razor thin and what appeared as anti-modernity was not necessarily the predecessor of modernity but could as well become its consequence. Lenin's utopia of a final socialist community after a transitional phase of iron fist dictatorship ended up in overstretched modernity. This development had historical models. The maxim of the French Revolution – freedom, equality, fraternity – ended in the Jacobin guillotines and in terror. Social criticism did not always end in emancipation.

Max Weber's modernization view on Europe was pessimistic. Progress as bureaucratization and rationalization means loss of enchantment and leads to the end of modernity when contentious politics become consensual administration and democracy becomes technocracy. Modernity is a permanent process of mystification and demystification, where demystification at the end leads to difficulties to maintain the belief in progress.[44]

This is a view that Koselleck seems to share in his critique-crisis motor of modernity with its pessimistic subtext. Critique did and does not only precipitate societies into crisis and social reforms in response to the crisis. The victors in history often preferred to respond to crisis with hypocrisy. Koselleck's case was the development of the maxim of the French Revolution: while it was held together in the revolutionary language in one cohesive imagery, it split up into two competing principles, hypocritically defended by the two mutually-exclusive ideological languages of liberalism and socialism, which in the 1950s, when Koselleck published his *Critique and Crisis*, had brought the world to the brink of nuclear extinction.[45]

Koselleck saw modernity as a continuous interpretation of past experiences and the translation of these experiences into future-oriented horizons of expectation. However, because of the overwhelming and exponentially growing experiences, not least due to the expansion of information and knowledge, and because of the fact that too often past expectations have become experiences of disappointment, it becomes ever more difficult to outline new expectations. Reinhart Koselleck talked about the overstretching of the gap between experiences and horizons of expectation. The capacity to outline new convincing future horizons of expectations declined through the accumulating experiences of disappointment and potentially at the end collapsed.

In his 'post-modern' approach from a somewhat different point of departure Zygmunt Bauman shares Weber's and Koselleck's pessimistic view in order to explain the Holocaust, which he sees as a consequence of modernity and its *Zweckrationalität*.[46]

This chapter has demonstrated that there is no final answer to the question at the beginning of the chapter: what is Europe? There are many answers posed but no unambiguous definition. The chapter has furthermore argued that Europe as a value project based on the Enlightenment heritage and a progressive movement from backwardness towards modernity, a predominating narrative historically and still in the present debate on Europe, is biased. The pretension that Europe is universal is provincial. Democracy went historically hand in hand with various forms of authoritarianism and totalitarian regimes and enlightenment was from early on connected to absolutism and imageries of absolute values as much as emancipative pluralist liberalism and tolerance. The argument of the chapter is also that the dark shadows of Europe's historical legacy must be integrated in any understanding of Europe. This integration does not necessarily mean the collapse either of Europe or of modernity as the rest of the book will show. On the contrary, the integration is a tool to reinforce both concepts.

PART TWO

European Interpretations of Modernity

4

Europe's Hesitations with Democracy

European democracy: evolution or discontinuity?

A change of perspective

For a long time, the democratic revolutions of the late eighteenth century were seen in the long tradition of the evolution of Western societies towards political modernity, indeed as the 'breakthroughs' after which only gradual further change was needed – change that, in most recent terminology, is described as 'democratization'. As Marcel Detienne mockingly puts it, 'Common sense likes to believe not only that *politics* or *the political* have fallen from the sky, on one beautiful day in "classical" Athens, in the miraculous and certified form of *the* democracy, but also that it is evident that a divinely linear history guides us by its hand from the American Revolution and then the "French Revolution" towards our Western societies, which are happily convinced that their mission is to convert all peoples to the true religion of democracy.'[1] Detienne may overestimate the number of current believers in such a straight and strong account, but he rightly observes that even leading specialists in classic history evoke continuity between ancient Athens and the present. Christian Meier, for instance, speaks of the battle of Salamis as the 'needle's eye of world-history'.[2] This metaphor rightly gives importance to events rather than structures or processes. However, to continue with it, Meier also thinks that the thread that passed through this needle's eye was never cut since. It may have been lost for some time, but found again in the Renaissance. Thus, in his view, 'world-history' took 'a new beginning' in ancient Greece in 480 BCE.[3] Similarly, though mostly devoid of Meier's sophistication, the frequent use of the term 'democratization' today suggests that it is far too easy to believe that democracy, once it exists, has such a compelling force that it will spread across both time and space with ease.

This is not the only view, though. From the 1960s onwards, the history of political thought experienced its own version of the broader linguistic turn in the social sciences and humanities, and this turn led to stronger emphasis on discontinuities in conceptual history. The move to understand political thought in its specific contexts, in particular, entailed the rejection of the view that there are 'perennial problems'[4] in human social life, towards the solution of which such key concepts as liberty or democracy are first elaborated and then only improved, which in essence gives them validity even across major historical transformations. Rather than providing a history of invention and later refinement, as it used to do, conceptual history began to look at variations in context that do not necessarily support any particular and steady evolution of political thought. More specifically, the period between 1770 and 1830 came to be seen as a major divide in the history of political thought – a divide across which concepts and problems changed so radically that it is hardly possible to recognize them as 'the same' from beginning to end. Despite all differences, the three main approaches developed since the 1960s – the Cambridge contextual history of political thought led by Quentin Skinner, the German *Begriffsgeschichte* initiated by Reinhart Koselleck, and the analysis of discourse formations inspired by Michel Foucault – all share the general assumption of rather radical discontinuity and tend to agree on the approximate timing of the latest profound conceptual transformation.

In this new perspective, thus, the period around 1800 remains highly significant. If we still consider it a breakthrough, we will have to ask: a breakthrough towards what? At a closer look, it becomes clear that the political transformations of the time were no breakthrough to democracy at all. The idea that this period marks the onset of political modernity requires considerable specification, to say the least. This chapter approaches the question of European democracy by relating the history of political concepts to politico-institutional change in Europe. It will do so by confronting the ancient Greek conception of, and experience with, democracy with the European approaches from the late eighteenth century onwards. This method does not entail any strong prior assumptions about Greek democracy, as will be discussed in a moment. Rather, it is adopted because European thinkers themselves reasoned politically by comparison and confrontation with Greek experience. After a preliminary reflection on the nature of politics and democracy in this light, the chapter will proceed in two large steps. First, the history of the European attitude to democracy is reconstructed across three periods: rejection after the revolutionary moment around 1800; reluctant coming to terms with the democratic political imaginary in the later nineteenth century; and adoption of the commitment to democracy after a major conceptual transformation. In the second step, the chapter discusses this transformation under three headings: the relation between political action and political representation; the relation between stability and change of political institutions; and the relation between inclusion and exclusion with regard to the resident members of a polity. The aim is to grasp the key challenges to the democratic self-understanding in the form in which it prevailed in (Western) Europe around 1960. This will serve as a basis for investigating in the later course of our analysis, in Chapter 9, how this self-understanding eroded rapidly during the past half century, a process that is as yet little understood.

The democratic political imaginary

Before embarking on this analysis, though, a few paragraphs are needed to identify the subject matter that concerns us here: what is the specific kind of politics that we refer to when we speak about democracy, and why are we using terms of Greek origin when doing so? There is no doubt that a major politico-cultural transformation occurred in the Greek city-states, in particular in Athens, during the sixth to fourth centuries BCE (that is, during the supposed Axial Age; see Chapter 2 above), but there is some dispute about what this precisely entailed. Some authors assert strongly that the Greeks invented politics (or the political) during this period, and it is significant that they include a leading historian of antiquity, Christian Meier, and one of the most thoughtful social and political philosophers of the second half of the twentieth century, Cornelius Castoriadis.[5] If one accepts this interpretation, then the Greeks created an unprecedented novelty that should be of lasting significance across all later world-history. Even though the innovation itself would apparently get lost again for numerous centuries, its past existence and the available record about it made it possible to reconnect to it and to reassess its suitability and desirability for later societies. This was to become true in the Renaissance and, maybe more significantly, with the revolutionary period in the late eighteenth century or, as some may hold, during the entire period that stretches from the Renaissance to 1800, to which historians of Europe refer as early modernity.

Without denying the significance of the Greek events, there are good reasons to be more cautious. There is, to start with, an ongoing debate about the distinction between 'politics' (*la politique*, *Politik*) and 'the political' (*le politique*, *das Politische*). We shall not reconstruct this debate here, not least because it is confusing by virtue of the fact that no consolidated definitions have emerged, so that one author may call 'politics' that which another author refers to as 'the political'.[6] That some distinction is needed, however, is plausible. All human collectivities need to determine their rules for living together, and the term 'politics' or some derivative of it can be used to describe the ways of determining such rules. Some human collectivities, though, created for that purpose specific and explicit institutions that are separate from other aspects of social life, even though not entirely disconnected from the latter. The Greeks can lay no claim to having invented the former, but they did create novelty with regard to the latter. The conscious creation of sub-collectivities for purposes of political participation, of organizational forms to arrive at the expression of a common will, and of subsidiary rules – such as ostracism or payment for civic service – to keep the new arrangement functioning was, to the best of our knowledge, at the time unique in the world.[7]

If we underline novelty too strongly, though, we may lose sight of the fact that Greek political practices were very specific to the context in which they developed and should not be mistaken for general features of politics. In other words, novelty does not rule out comparison; it rather demands comparison to understand what is truly new. In this spirit, Marcel Detienne has suggested that there may be general requirements that apply to all politics, in the sense of having a specific place for political action, such as the need to get together; the need for someone to start speaking; some idea of having something in common; some recognition of the other participants in the conversation as similar or equal; some notion of wanting to act together.[8] None of this is self-evident in human social life. All of this was present and explicit in ancient Greek politics. But much of this can also be found in other societies, who did not borrow from ancient Greece but whom we nevertheless do not credit with the invention of the political.

What stands out, in comparison, is thus the *explicitness* and the *reflexivity* with which the Greeks developed their politics. In addition to archaeological evidence, we know this thanks to the written sources we can consult (even though the absence of such sources elsewhere does not necessarily mean the absence of the phenomenon). From those sources we recognize changes in the Greek political self-understanding through the emergence of new concepts such as freedom, equality and democracy.[9] We may surmise that they arose in response to problems that the Greeks were facing, but these responses were also creating new problems in turn. Once you are committed to freedom of speech, the question arises naturally whether this freedom needs limits so as not to endanger the collectivity. Once you are committed to equality, you need justifications for any exclusion from political participation, as scholars such as Aristotle duly tried to provide for the exclusion of women, slaves and manual workers. Once you contemplate government by the many, you need sound expectations about why the collective will that emerges from broad involvement is adequate for handling common matters – or even superior to other ways, as Pericles suggested in the Funeral Oration. In other words, explicitness and reflexivity led to a *radicality* in formulating political matters that – again, to the best of our knowledge – did not exist elsewhere.

Based on these brief reflections, we propose the following conclusions. In the ancient Greek context, the so-called invention of politics meant the explication of rules of self-government that, in a very broad sense, also existed elsewhere, though not in such explicitness.[10] We will call this the creation of the democratic political imaginary. Explicitness led to radicalization in the ways in which questions could be posed, and this is what we inherit from ancient Greek political thought.[11] The answers the Greeks gave to the questions they themselves raised are much more context-specific than the questions. Beyond helping to understand the Greek *polis*, their current usefulness lies in recognizing ways of responding to issues rather than in the supra-historical significance of the solutions as such. Or, to return to the question of the perennial nature, or lack thereof, of political problems, we may restate the issue as follows: there are indeed no perennial problems in the strict sense because both the contexts of political action and the conceptual resources to address political issues are highly variable across situations. Once we refer to a context in which the democratic political imaginary is at work, however – that is, a context in which there is high explicitness about political matters as well as a commitment to searching autonomously for ways to address them – then we may hold that there is an identifiable set of basic *problématiques* that recur across situations. Even then, though, they may be formulated as different problems in a context-specific way, as specific interpretations of the more general *problématiques*.[12]

Having said this, we can now move to analyse how the reference to Greek democracy served to understand and conceptualize issues that political actors were facing during the revolutionary transformations around 1800. From those debates questions arise that we can recognize as general features of the political *problématique* of modernity, that is, of determining the rules for communal life on the basis of collective self-determination. These questions were addressed by the ancient Athenians; they were retrieved, discussed and newly addressed by the revolutionaries of 1789 as well as their opponents; and they need to be addressed in our present time. The answers to these questions, though, depended crucially on the socio-historical context. Returning to Greece therefore provides resources for widening the horizon of thought and action but no solution to contemporary problems.

From rejection to reluctant acceptance: democracy in Europe, 1789 to the 1960s

The political moment around 1800: a democratic revolution?

The significance of the ancient Greek experience in the history of political thought is immediately evident when one looks at the political debates of the decades around 1800 – a time for which the term 'democratic revolution' has been used.[13] This was the period in which the reference to both the ancient Greek *polis* and the Roman Republic became much more frequent than they had been for centuries.[14] Up to this moment, the term 'democracy' had remained present in scholarly use to broadly refer to popular self-government, but it had no longer been used in political documents. It is only between 1780 and 1800 that it becomes again a 'political concept';[15] and it did so with reference to its origins in Greek antiquity.

This occurred in a highly ambiguous way. On the one hand, the ancient political experiences served as a reference-point for the present. Both Greece and Rome had experienced politically tumultuous times, and had faced them without the certainties of revealed religion, and something similar seemed to occur from the late eighteenth century onwards. Greece seemed to provide support in understanding the nature of political action, in particular the action of founding a polity. Rome, in turn, served to understand the relations between aristocracy and peasantry and the elaboration of a constitution that gave space to the multitude without abolishing all privileges of the few. These were sufficient reasons for an interested look at the ancient political experience.

As the political and economic transformations in late eighteenth-century Europe went on, on the other hand, observers increasingly saw themselves forced to conclude that an entirely new kind of socio-political formation was being created that had little in common with the ancient world. Jean-Jacques Rousseau was a prescient interpreter when he addressed the citizens of Geneva already in 1764 as follows: 'The ancient peoples are no longer a model for the moderns: they are too strange for them in all respects. You Genevans, in particular, [. . .] you are neither Romans nor Spartans, you are not even Athenians. Leave aside the great names that do not lead you anywhere. You are merchants, craftsmen, bourgeois, always occupied with your private interests, people for whom freedom itself is nothing but a means to acquire without hindrance and to possess with certainty.'[16]

This is an early expression of a view that was to become common half a century later, and it is significant that Rousseau, critically, voices it with regard to a commercial city that, on the one hand, could be inclined to look for similarities in antiquity because it was a small republic but, on the other hand, was socio-economically very different from territorial states such as France and Prussia in which, almost as in ancient times, agriculture prevailed. When Rousseau wrote, the latter only began to face the market-industrial revolution that was to give much more weight than ever before to the commercial bonds between people (see Chapter 5 below). By 1819, in turn, this change was so much more visible that Benjamin Constant's distinction between ancient and modern liberty, reiterating and elaborating on Rousseau's point, could become a canonical statement for almost two centuries to come.[17] In contrast to Rousseau, Constant, and with him many later writers, welcomed or at least accepted the change. At this point, antiquity had been a main point of reference in political debate for a few decades, but this was much less the case during the later nineteenth and twentieth centuries because institutions of the ancient world were increasingly seen as superseded by the outcome of the ongoing social transformations.

This is particularly true for the reference to ancient Greece and to democracy. The outcome of conceptual struggle over several decades, to put it very briefly here, was to favour the term 'republic' over 'democracy' when characterizing the new political reality, or the one that was to be striven for, depending on speaker and circumstance. Recent debate seems to have taken this 'choice' as an indication of the prevalence of Rome over Greece in political debates, and some authors even speak of 'neo-Roman' political thought.[18] True, the term 'republic' entered into modern thinking through the emphasis the Renaissance placed on the Roman Republic over the Empire. It also emerged, however, as a new direct translation of *politeia* in Aristotle, without Roman mediation and in contrast to earlier renderings inspired by Christian thought on community.[19] More importantly for our purposes, and in line with Aristotle's usage of *politeia*, the term refers to the form of a political order, to a 'polity', as we can now felicitously say, not to the extent of popular participation in political decision-making, in contrast to *demokratia*. With regard to the latter issue, speakers at around 1800 were well aware that 'democracy' means wide participation, in distinction from monarchy and aristocracy (or oligarchy). Those who spoke against the use of this term saw considerable risks in such wide participation, but they may nevertheless have been in favour of a 'republic', as, for instance, Immanuel Kant was. Making this terminological choice, they were not neglecting the Greek in favour of the Roman experience. Rather, they were favouring a democracy-critical interpretation of the Greek experience over other interpretations, and by doing so they could well rely on Plato, to some extent Aristotle, and other voices of dissent in ancient Athens.[20]

In this usage, the term 'republic' as *politeia* leaves the extent of participation open. Looking at the temporary outcome of the struggle, it is clear, though, that most European societies rejected or strongly restricted participation. Most of them remained monarchies. To offset tyrannical tendencies of one-person rule, well known from ancient debates, the monarchs were increasingly flanked by parliaments elected by relatively small numbers of property-owning male citizens, and limited in their actions by the idea of rights of the individual, sometimes laid down in constitutions. But nothing that would have been recognizable as 'democracy' was created in Europe. R.R. Palmer was not wrong in talking about a 'democratic' revolution but it needs underlining that the revolution largely failed and that the 'aristocratic' side kept the upper hand in the struggle.[21] The polities that emerged from the 'democratic revolution' were not modelled on ancient Greek democracy. Rather, they were elaborated in conscious rejection of Greek democracy by the elites in European societies.

A central concern of the late-Enlightenment revolutions was freedom, in several respects: first, as personal freedom *from* arbitrary and unjustified rule and *for* self-expression and self-realization; secondly, as commercial freedom that was expected to both promote peace and wealth; and thirdly, as collective self-determination.[22] In reflection on the Greek experience, the latter concept of freedom came to be seen to be in tension with the former two. While freedom was requested, what was to be avoided was the uncertainty that the expression of collective self-determination created in Athens. The response that crystallized after 1800 was what we now know as a liberal concept of freedom, a freedom that was not emerging from the collectivity but needed to be protected against the collectivity. Such protection was to be achieved through the concepts of individual rights and of a constitution that would safeguard those rights. This double institutionalization has since been hailed as the major accomplishment of political modernity, the co-emergence of human rights and the rule of law. It has less often been observed that democracy does not figure explicitly in this account. Some liberal thinkers, such as Isaiah Berlin, have indeed acknowledged that a commitment to individual liberty is fully compatible with non-democratic government.[23] The idea of enlightened rule was widely accepted in nineteenth-century political liberalism, a rule that accepts limits to state interference with private lives, even protects private liberties, but is entirely devoid of any democratic self-understanding.

In contrast to what one is currently inclined to believe, therefore, the democratic imaginary did not break through during the period of the so-called democratic revolutions. Given that it was strongly present in the debates about transforming the polities of that time, we have to conclude that it was rather consciously rejected. The debates remained within the ancient frame of thinking by including only property-owning males into the citizenry. Against the background of Enlightenment thinking, however, slavery was no longer justifiable and the equality of women had at least been brought on to the political agenda, even though the theme kept being suppressed. This meant that, in contrast to the ancient Athenians who referred to a regime in which only 'free men' participated as 'the rule of the people', the term democracy came to refer to the idea that all adult residents in a territory (at least all men) would participate in political deliberation and decision-making. This was a conception, though, that almost all members of the political elites around 1800 rejected, even most revolutionaries – even if there are some exceptions as early as the 1647 Putney debates in England. As a result, as mentioned above, the modern polity came to be called 'republic' rather than, and often in deliberate contrast to, 'democracy.'

'Democracy' in Europe after the democratic revolution: the nineteenth century

Given this rejection of the Athenian model of democracy, the political view of ancient Greece changed considerably in the aftermath of the late eighteenth-century revolutions.[24] In a first instance, ancient Greece was seen as a world that had been lost. Contemporary society was devoid of something that had existed in the ancient world and was worthy of being recalled, even though in most views it was impossible to retrieve it. Significantly, the praise of Greece ceased to refer to political matters and emphasized 'cultural' ones instead, such as philosophy and the arts (see Chapter 3 above). By the middle of the nineteenth century, however, the view emerged that ancient Greece had prepared the ground for the modern form of liberal democracy, the contours of which were more clearly emerging at the time. The differences between ancient and modern politics were downplayed by seeing the former as a stage preceding the latter, for example by referring to Athens as the source of the idea of popular sovereignty and of universal suffrage while disregarding the exclusion of slaves and women from the right to political participation.[25] This is the view that informs the notion of Greece as a 'seedbed' for political modernity, still widespread today.

Significantly, this interpretation singles out Cleisthenes' reforms at the end of the sixth century BCE as the key-event of Athenian political history, thus giving primacy to an *institutional* reform with features comparable to modern constitutions over socio-political change that would need to be read as a new *form-giving of society* (Claude Lefort, with reference to Tocqueville; see Chapter 2 above for this notion in general). It tended to assimilate Greek society, in particular Athens, to contemporary society by emphasizing the elements of personal freedom and the development of commerce.[26] Referring to George Grote's *History of Greece* among other works, John Stuart Mill drew on the Athenian experience of democracy to argue that a democratic polity could entail the flourishing of personal liberties and provide for social dynamics in the arts and commerce as well.[27] Though not a model to emulate, ancient Athenian democracy here became a forerunner to 'modern' liberal democracy.

Introducing evolutionary thinking into the relation between antiquity and the present, this kind of interpretation also opened the way for emphasizing the differences between Athens and nineteenth-century Europe against the background of the alleged similarities. Thus, critics of emerging 'bourgeois' society could use the comparison to urge for further socio-political transformation. In the German context, proponents of democracy were seen as 'radicals' because they insisted on the link between individual and collective freedom. At mid-century, Arnold Ruge called for the 'overcoming of liberalism by democratism'.[28] Karl Marx famously made the distinction between 'political emancipation,' that is, full inclusion in terms of political participation, and 'human emancipation' as the overcoming of the situation of new enslavement related to the need to sell one's labour.

This interpretation perpetuated the reference to antiquity in political thought, but it did so now within an evolutionary frame of thinking. For the 'bourgeois' interpreters, ancient Greece took a significant step towards political modernity, one on which the democratic revolutions could build directly. For the radical or socialist interpreters, too, a look at Greece helped to grasp the evolutionary logic of history, but in their view this history was marked by a series of radical transformations of which one more would be needed to achieve a satisfactory state of socio-political organization. The adoption of such an evolutionary frame went along with changes in the understanding of democracy, of which only the most significant shall be singled out here. First, the term 'democracy' moved closer to that of 'republic', after their separation in the aftermath of the revolution. Second, the specificity of the ancient experience was downplayed by, among other elements, allowing for a larger size of democratic polities and representation in place of direct participation. Thirdly, partly in the light of the European reception of Tocqueville's analysis of American democracy, the state of democracy was associated more with equality of condition than with broad political participation.[29] In sum, these moves made 'democracy' in its new guise more compatible with the prevailing socio-political situation. As Reinhart Koselleck pointed out, 'democracy' became a 'universal expectational concept', a term that went far beyond the political experiences of the time but expressed the expectation of future political development.[30]

Democratic thought at the time of 'democratization': the twentieth century

If there is any historical date at which 'democratization' found its first full expression it is 1918/19, the moment at the end of the First World War in which universal suffrage was introduced in many European countries, as a combined result of the mobilization of the masses for the war and the rising strength of the workers' movement more than of the insight in the desirability of democracy. Now it became clear even to reluctant observers, such as Max Weber, that the institution of democracy would mark political forms of the future.

European societies witnessed the advent of inclusive democracy – also discussed as a 'transformation of democracy'[31] – at a moment of extreme political uncertainty, marked by the Russian Revolution and the increasing strength of the socialist movement in general, by the geopolitical changes caused by the First World War together with the wider acceptance of the notion of collective self-determination, and brought to a climax by the world economic crisis of 1929 and after. In this context, politico-theoretical debate was dominated, once again, by critics of democracy rather than supporters of it. Few were those who, like maybe most significantly Karl Mannheim, recognized the major challenge of 'fundamental democratization' and simultaneously remained committed to democracy. Much more forceful was the voice of those, on both the political right and left, who considered universal suffrage and competitive-party democracy as unstable, undesirable or both.[32]

After the Second World War, the experience of the totalitarian breakdown of democracy overshadowed political thinking as well as political practice. Since this breakdown was associated with the mobilization of politically immature masses, one could have expected a revival of the critique of democracy. However, one consequence of the oppression and mass murder under totalitarian regimes was the renewal of the commitment to universal human rights, first voiced during the later eighteenth-century period of the 'democratic revolution' and now reiterated in the United Nations Universal Declaration of Human Rights of 1948. Thus, no justification for exclusion from formal political participation could be provided any longer.³³ Given the risks of democracy, as explored in earlier debates, political thought concentrated on developing a new model of politics, often now referred to as the Schumpeterian model, in which democracy means the selection of a minority of political decision-makers by an inclusively defined citizenry that remains apathetic outside of the brief moments of election campaigns and elections.³⁴

From the 1960s onwards, critical responses to such thinking were forthcoming, pointing to forms of domination implied in such an understanding of democracy and calling for broader participation and more widely extended deliberation. Among a wide array of critical authors only two stand out for whom the ancient Greek political experience was important in retrieving a broader conception of politics and democracy: Hannah Arendt and Cornelius Castoriadis, who both emphasized the connection between a fundamental concept of autonomy and freedom on the one hand, and a view of politics as the conscious exercise of collective autonomy on the other, and identified the origins of this connection in ancient Greece.³⁵ Both also acknowledged that a radical concept of autonomy goes along with an emphasis on uncertainty and contingency; in other words, they recognized the risks that one incurs by a commitment to democracy. But despite periods of intense reception, in particular of Arendt's work, both authors have remained marginal to post-Second World War analyses of democracy.

Stepping out of a strongly contextual reading of the history of political thought, as briefly pursued in the above sketch, one can identify a number of arguments that suggest that the framework for political action was altered so profoundly in the course of European history that conceptual rethinking was necessary. Such observations include: (1) the growing size of polities requiring representation rather than direct participation; (2) the need to stabilize political orders and thus institutionalization rather than permanent openness to consider what we now call constitutional issues in everyday politics; and, maybe most importantly, (3) the novel inclusiveness of modern polities making every adult member a full citizen on equal terms with all others rather than excluding those who take care of the household (women) and most people who do manual work (slaves and craftsmen). We will briefly discuss all three issues in turn, focusing though on the third as, in our view, the most crucial one.

Transformations of democracy up to the 1960s: three key tensions

Action and representation: size and self-understanding of ancient and modern democracy

The observation that the mode of operation of ancient democracies was simply 'technically' no longer feasible under 'modern' conditions already emerged during the Enlightenment debates and persisted ever since. It has been discussed in terms of numbers, arguing that political communication oriented towards democratic decision-making was possible only among relatively small political collectivities – Aristotle already was concerned about the best size of the *polis* in this sense. And it has as well been addressed in terms of the physical requirements for democratic debate. Inclusive direct democracy needs both a space large enough for all citizens to meet and distances short enough, with given means of transport, for citizens to regularly reach this space for meetings. Thus it could convincingly be argued for, and applied, in small settings, such as the city of Geneva or Swiss cantons more generally.[36] The polities in which the idea of universal-suffrage democracy emerged, such as prototypically revolutionary France, were normally too large both in numbers of adult residents and in spatial extension. Significantly, some revolutionary advocates of self-government made virtue out of necessity and resorted to the idea of representation as a way of overcoming the limitations of ancient democracy and achieving stable forms of self-government adequate to the conditions of the time.

In as far as they were based on self-government, often contained within constitutional monarchies, European polities adopted systems of representation requiring neither full assembly nor movement of large numbers of citizens, with the exception of Switzerland. At the same time, they most often retained restrictions to suffrage during all of the nineteenth century and sometimes longer, that were due to domination or justified by other reasons (see below the discussion of exclusion). But such 'restricted liberal modernity'[37] withered away in the transformation towards inclusive democracies in the early twentieth century. Those democracies overcame the size/space issue by fully resorting to representation instead of direct action. During the interwar period of the twentieth century, though, representation by political parties in formal institutions was underpinned by high factional organization and strong mobilization of the electorate. There was, one could say, some form of direct involvement of the citizenry, reminiscent of, even though very different from, ancient democracy. Thus, the 'technical' issue of size and space that demanded the building of democracy on representation moved out of the centre of concern and was replaced by debates about the 'political' consequences of democracy under conditions of mass mobilization.

Subsequently, the instability of these high-mobilization polities gave rise to the idea of citizen apathy being necessary for the stability of inclusive democracy, theorized and practised after the Second World War. At the same time, such polities were open to the criticism that they had abandoned the idea of democracy and become 'liberal oligarchies', by and large guaranteeing human and civil rights but limiting the exercise of rule to the very few.[38] When these practices were challenged from the late 1960s onwards, critical debate often emphasized that the prevalent institutional form of democracy concealed a mode of domination. Many observers, furthermore, also took pains to show that the functional argument against stronger and more direct participation of the citizenry was less compelling than had been assumed. Thus, current debates about, and experiments with, deliberative and participatory democracy demonstrate, not that the issue of size and space is irrelevant for democratic practice, but that it can be addressed without renouncing the commitment to citizen involvement and action and resorting exclusively to representation in politics.

The instituting and the instituted: stability and change in democracy

The second major difference between the self-understanding of ancient democracy and the modern one is the limitation of the substantive reach of democratic decision-making. The ancients did not recognize any such limitation. Collective self-determination was not determined by any external force or reason. It could set its limits only from within, by the very process of deliberation. The risk of such a self-understanding was recognized in contemporary debate, as for instance the concern for hubris shows.[39] But this risk, too, could not be averted by other means than the reasonable action of the democratic citizens themselves. 'Modern' political reasoning, in contrast, has always used institutional design with a view to stabilizing a political form that, like the ancient one, had no evident outer limit, in contrast to the religiously justified rule that preceded it in early modern Europe. The key means towards that end came to be the distinction between normal laws to be determined in deliberation and higher laws to be set out in a constitution that could not, or only with more difficulty, be altered by agreement between contemporary actors.[40]

Two concerns enter into the justification for such a limitation of democratic action. On the one hand, the modern political self-understanding can be seen as not entirely without foundations, 'without banisters',[41] but built on the unanimous and unalterable commitment to some 'universal' principles and 'inalienable' rights, such as those set out in the UN Declaration. In this view, one needs to underline, political modernity is not about radical autonomy, in some contrast to ancient Greek democracy,[42] but about autonomy within the limits of a kind of modern reason that emphasizes the need to master potentially dangerous situations. On the other hand, constitutional limitations also addressed a different concern, namely the possibility of a 'tyranny of the majority' (Tocqueville) that used its democratically acquired power to further its own interest rather than the common good. This concern was already present in Aristotle who sometimes distinguished 'democracy' as the rule of the many in their own interest from 'polity' as the rule of the many with a view to the common good. It re-emerged after the 'democratic revolution' and then expressed the fear of the old elites that the long excluded groups in society might use the suffrage, once it had to be granted to them, to dominate over the former rulers.[43]

To conceptually characterize the difference between ancient and modern self-understandings in this respect, we can resort to Castoriadis's distinction between 'instituting' and 'instituted' moments in society. The latter term refers to a situation in which there is consolidated agreement about the basic rules of living together, and this agreement is expressed in institutional rules. The former term, in contrast, refers to a situation in which a collectivity acts together to establish the rules for living together. For Castoriadis, every society needs to be instituted, but an autonomous society remains capable of questioning its own institutions and transforming them in response to such questioning, re-instituting itself. Ancient Greek democracy had such capacity; but 'modern' constitutional republics can be seen as having renounced radical questioning of their own rules by exempting key components of them from alteration through autonomous action.

We need to add, though, that with regard to both the above arguments for self-limitation recent debate has somewhat re-opened the issue. On the one hand, global debates have widened the understanding of that which should be considered 'universal' and 'inalienable'. It is now recognized that universal claims have not only historical roots but a history of struggle that is marked by contingencies.[44] Furthermore, every single formulation of basic normative commitments may be seen as marked by 'incompleteness', making a 'diatopical hermeneutics' across different conceptions necessary.[45] On the other hand, and possibly related to greater confidence about the broad adoption of some version of shared normative commitments, current thinkers suggest widening the scope of collective self-determination with a view to making constitutions more open for reconsideration in the light of new situations. The attempt at creating a constitutional treatise of the European Union, for instance, was interpreted as a re-instituting; and the fact that it failed does not decrease the significance of the attempt and its interpretation as an instituting moment.[46]

There is a broad similarity between the two issues of distinction between ancient and modern democracy discussed up to this point, and thus an interim summary is useful. As regards these two issues, the relation between action and representation and the relation between instituting and instituted moments, the consensus of the decades after the Second World War meant fully abandoning the ancient Greek understanding of democracy. Democracy indeed had been transformed into the expression of popular will by aggregating individual views at large intervals and confined to selecting the governing group, on the one side, and, on the other side, democratic political action had simultaneously been limited to that which remained within the bounds of the constitutions that had often not been the expression of the collective self-determination of the living citizens but of their forebears. Both of these conceptions are very alien to the ancient Greeks. The term 'democratization' as applied to political developments of the past half century is a misnomer in this light, since it suggests a historical reference that at a closer look is absent (or would need to be located in a much more recent past than the term appears to imply).

But if we look at the past few decades only, roughly the period from the 1970s to the present, the reasons for the limitation of democracy have been found much less convincing than they were seen in the mainstream early post-Second World War view. Democracy is more often seen as extendable, in terms of both the intensity and the scope of political action, and to many observers and practitioners such extensions are seen as desirable. (What such re-opening of political debate in a new context entails for the practices of collective self-determination will be discussed below in Chapter 9.)

Exclusion and inclusion: the relation between political citizenship and economic involvement

The question of the inclusiveness of democracy, the third issue under our comparative consideration, poses itself differently. We witness here a conscious turn away from the ancient Greek self-understanding by moving to full inclusion of all members of a collectivity, even of those who deal with the necessities of life, into the concept of the *demos*. This turn was not taken during the 'democratic revolution', as argued above, but it was imposed on European (and North and South American) elites in the course of the nineteenth century through the struggles of the excluded in the name of the democratic imaginary. But this inclusion, ironically, came to be referred to as democracy in the new usage of the term; and from Grote onwards, though with decreasing frequency, ancient Athens was associated with such inclusive practice, identifying the Athenian free men with the *demoi* of modern Europe, reading the Greek reforms as a widening of the suffrage similar to late nineteenth-century European developments, and downplaying the significance of exclusion in ancient democracies.[47]

Arguably, however, this is the socio-political fact that most divides us from the ancients: slavery and the denial of citizenship to women and slaves (importantly, we keep denying citizenship to resident aliens). The novel inclusiveness is not a mere matter of size nor of intensity of political participation, but marks a fundamental difference in the social relations underlying a polity (as for instance developed in Aldo Schiavone's view).[48] As such, it prohibits us to simply return to ancient concepts when analysing contemporary polities. This difference, though, should be considered as a challenge to make comparison possible across the divide. Even if we allow for radical reinterpretations, we need to acknowledge the fact that Western socio-political language derives many of its key concepts from ancient Greek (and Latin). Grote and his successors captured something significant of the Greek political experience when they focused on the extension and institutionalization of participation; and they were even right in suggesting that there is a significance *for us*. But what exactly is it? To answer the question more fully, we need to first try to understand the Greek political distinction between categories of persons.

As explored in the two preceding sections, the ancient Greeks pursued a radical, one may want to say, highly modern approach to political matters. They subjected the rules for the life in common to nothing but the collective self-determination, to the autonomy of the citizens, with very few higher inviolable rules and with little significant intermediation between the views of citizens and collective decision-making. Their democracy remains a radical example; even though one may have reasons to shy away from some of its aspects, its exemplary character remains. But the ancient Greeks also excluded categories of persons from this commitment to autonomy; the collective autonomy of the citizens meant domination over others. If everything was open to questioning, why was this feature not questioned? In contrast to nineteenth- and twentieth-century reasoning in nationalist and racist terms, the exclusion was not based on characteristics of the persons themselves. Rather, it was based on a conceptual distinction between political matters, which were amenable to freedom in speech and action, and economic matters, which were governed and determined by the necessities of life. The separation of these two activities was hierarchical: political action was free because it was not conditioned by needs. Thus, dealing with needs was to be done in a separate realm so that political action could indeed be free. Those who dealt with needs, in other words, provided the condition for autonomy in political matters, but they were at the same time deprived of exercising this autonomy. Women, workers and craftsmen were dealing with needs; this was why they could not be free, and could not participate in the handling of political matters.[49]

Modern democratic thinkers today reject the conclusion, for good reasons. But how do we instead deal with the issues that led the ancient Greeks to that conclusion? At this point we have to briefly return to the reasons why 'democracy' was rejected after the 'democratic revolution'. Through all of the debate leading from Machiavelli to the French Revolution, revived by authors such as J.G.A. Pocock and Quentin Skinner under the label republicanism, there was consensus about the requirements made of those who could be citizens of a republic. Labelled in different terms, the common view was that citizens had to be (able to be) responsible, and one precondition for responsibility was not to be dependent on others. For this reason, property ownership loomed large in pre-revolutionary republican thinking; and the argument served to restrict participation in post-revolutionary polities throughout the nineteenth century. The basic connection between personal freedom, conceived as independence from others, and citizenship was already made by Aristotle and did not change significantly until the late eighteenth century.

What about the democratic political imaginary then, with the commitment to equal liberty? As we have shown, it was defeated in the revolution, but it did exist and remained powerful. Rather than arguing that the majority of the population was not independent and thus not qualified for citizenship, some authors reasoned the other way round: if it is valid to connect citizenship to the capacity to act responsibly and thus to independence, then the new post-revolutionary society should make sure that all of its members become independent. As David Casassas demonstrated, the plea for market society in Adam Smith's political economy was based on his political philosophy of an inclusive republicanism, which could be inclusive precisely because the widening of commerce could turn everyone into an independent producer and thus responsible citizen.[50] This reasoning stands within the tradition of Aristotelianism and civic republicanism, but in contrast to the main line of those traditions Smith believed to have found in commerce a different, inclusion-oriented answer to the question that for all his predecessors had led into the necessary political exclusion of many members of a society.

As we know, such market society of independent producers, a conceptual possibility of which Marx was still aware, did not emerge in the course of the nineteenth century, but a capitalist society instead in which most members remained dependent on others because of the need to sell their labour-power in the absence of other property. For this reason, full inclusion was forced by social movements on the elites of the persisting Old Regime in the course of the nineteenth and early twentieth centuries rather than having been found convincing in its own right. And when inclusive, equal-suffrage democracy arrived, the critics had an easy target because the tension between the idea of independence as a condition for citizenship and the fact that the majority of voters depended on others for their livelihood was not resolved.

Has this tension been resolved since? There is a line of reasoning in the history of socio-economic thought that suggests that it has. 'Modern' societies are both commercial and democratic societies. A division of social labour exists in them that enhances productivity and wealth, on the one hand, and, on the other hand, makes all members of these societies interdependent with all others, thus creating strong social bonds between them: 'organic solidarity', as Émile Durkheim called this link. This interdependence, well understood, is the new basis for responsible political behaviour, no longer the individual property earned through the right to the product of one's own labour. And it is common to all members, not limited to a class of property-owners. In political thought, in contrast, the mainstream view of democracy after the Second World War, as described above, can be taken to consider the tension irresolvable. Very active citizens tend to make irresponsibly excessive demands on the polity, that is why citizen apathy is necessary. In the absence of such apathy, liberal democracies enter into a 'governability crisis' and 'legitimacy problems' arise because the democratic state does not respond to the demands of its citizens.[51]

Confronting these two views, the question arises whether the interdependence diagnosed by social theory should not rather be seen as an asymmetric dependence of some citizens on others. More precisely, it is a situation in which a majority depends for their material well-being on the (economic) decisions of a minority, all the while this majority among equal citizens in a democracy holds the (political) power of calling on the resources owned by the minority. This issue was not unknown to the ancient Athenians. Our current vocabulary permits us to see it as a tension between a social situation and a political form; more broadly, it raises the issue of the social preconditions for democracy to be viable.

And this issue has not disappeared in contemporary politics. At a closer look, we find fully inclusive and rather stable democracies only for a short period in a rather small part of the world, mostly in the north of Europe between the 1950s and the 1980s. Elsewhere and at other times, democratic polities were either rather restricted in terms of participation or highly unstable. If neither of the two, then they often relied for their material needs on highly asymmetric terms of trade, in colonial or neo-colonial fashion, and exported and thus externalized the problem of dealing with needs (reminiscent of the notion that empire was a condition for Athenian democracy) or on the immigration of workers who only after very extended periods of residence become citizens. The latter is true for (Western) Europe (and North America) today, that is, for polities that otherwise appear as inclusive and rather stable democracies. Thus, even though modern democracy has strengthened the argument that exclusion is not justifiable on grounds of an alleged different 'nature' of certain human beings, it has not resolved the tension between the need for citizens not to be dependent on others to be free and responsible and the fact that many residents of democratic polities live in some form of dependence under current societal conditions. This issue, difficult as it may be, does not distinguish post-1800 societies fundamentally from preceding ones, as we will explore in more detail in the following chapter. It is one that stays with democratic polities and remains in need of a convincing answer.

5

The Market-industrial Revolution in Global Perspective:

Colonial Heritage and the Social Question

The Eurocentric legacy

In the conventional view, modernity based on capitalism and the economic imagery of progress, growth and expansion did not only *emerge* in Europe, from where it spread across the world, but it *had to* emerge there because of specific prepositions inherent in Europe itself. Economic and political modernity was, in this view, drawing on both Adam Smith and Karl Marx, inherent in the European culture and history. Europe became the heartland of modernity.

David Landes is one of the most outspoken twentieth-century representatives of this view with respect to the Industrial Revolution and the diffusion of capitalism. His economic history published in 1969 had the expressive title *The Unbound Prometheus*. The titan symbolized the emancipating industry.[1] The imagination of welfare and economic progress, of political and economic emancipation went hand in hand in this view of liberalism with a social face. Capitalism reinforced democracy and vice versa in a development that distinguished Europe from the rest of the world. This post-Second World War imagery of the nineteenth century as capitalist economic growth and emerging democratic welfare in mutually reinforcing dynamics ignored fully the fact that it is difficult to connect the nineteenth century to democracy, as we saw in the previous chapter.

Landes's perspective at the end of the 1960s was not only Eurocentric but also pronouncedly progressive. The Industrial Revolution began in England in the eighteenth century and spread from there to continental Europe and a few overseas areas transforming in the span of scarce two generations the life of the Western world and the relationships to the other peoples. The heart of the Industrial Revolution was an interrelated succession of technological changes. Steam power replaced human and animal force. New means of transport driven by steam made large-scale movements of rapidly growing amounts of iron, textiles, chemicals and other goods, people and information on land and sea possible. They conveyed the raw materials from the sources into the factories and out again to near and distant markets: 'And so on, in ever-widening circles.' New kinds of information opened up widening horizons for human agency. Landes described a virtuous expanding circle with self-generating dynamics.[2]

Opportunity was not necessarily achievement and economic progress not always even but marked by spurts as well as recessions. However, there was little doubt about the prospects of an indefinite climb. Technological advance was certainly not necessarily a smooth balanced process. Each innovation had a life span of its own comprising periods of youth, maturity and old age. Its marginal yield diminished giving way to newer, more advantageous techniques. However, the declining momentum of the early-modernizing branches was more than compensated for by the rise of new industries based on spectacular advances in chemical and electrical science and on the mobile source of power, the internal combustion engine.

Landes put the question why all this happened in (Western) Europe and not elsewhere and found the answer in the simple fact that Europe 'was ready to take off', which, in turn, depended on a complex causality where a long list of factors had been established by the historians without unanimity about their internal relationships or weight. He understood the Industrial Revolution writ large through a comparison of Europe and non-Europe, and within Europe. Landes himself emphasized in particular two decisive factors: (1) the emergence of private economic enterprises in Western Europe based on labour relations of contract rather than force; and (2) a rationalist culture based on a long historical tradition of distinction between Caesar and God, a pragmatic creativity of European science, nation-states promoting science and competition but also providing protection (mercantilism) when necessary and, finally, a Faustian spirit of mastery, a restless and reckless thirst for knowledge.

There is a strong Weberian blend in the outline of Landes. Max Weber argued that the West was unique in its capacity of rationalization based on and reinforcing science, technology and a methodical way of living, which resulted in the emergence of capitalist market economies, bureaucratic states and a disenchanted culture. The Marxist narrative shared some basic features with that of Weber, although there were obvious differences. Both approaches saw capitalism as the motor of modern economic development and as a European invention. Europe was different and more dynamic. The world outside Europe never developed the dynamics that led to the emergence of capitalism. Marx referred with condescension to the inferior Asian mode of production.

The legacy of African labour and American soil

This chapter is going to confront the Eurocentric legend and argue that the rise of Europe in the nineteenth century through industrial capitalism was a regional part of a major global transformation rather than a development inherent in a project of European modernity. The point in making Landes and his embedding in the West-focused modernization narrative of the 1960s our point of departure is not to kill him once more. To take issue with his tale is not very controversial any more. We depart from him because he in such a distinct way stands for an older understanding of the Industrial Revolution and its origin where Europe becomes the gauge of everything. He serves as a kind of Weberian ideal type from which we can separate ourselves. We will do this by drawing attention to the triangular African-American-European commerce with labour and commodities across the Atlantic which had slowly emerged since the beginning of 'modernity' around 1500 and which provided the foundation of the European take-off. The unique combination of African labour, American soil and European military power overcame constraints to economic growth that other regions of the world faced. There was nothing inherent in the European culture but human agency exploiting global preconditions and opportunities. The European expansion took shape in close interaction with and exploitation of other peoples and civilizations. It was this global meeting, in the double sense of towards and against one another, rather than an intrinsic European development motor that shaped economic modernity.

Smith's concept of trade-led growth missed the point that global trade was not just a matter of the unfolding of forces inherent in European history and culture, but also, and in particular, a matter of exploitation of opportunities that were created in the meeting with other peoples on other continents and that this creation and exploitation of opportunities was often supported by weapons and violence. Two hundred and fifty years of debate on the origin of the Industrial Revolution and the European economic take-off has conspicuously often circumvented these *inter*-dynamics between the European and the global. There is certainly a long debate on colonialism and imperialism but in historically oriented academic disciplines rather than in economics. However, also in the historical analyses of imperialism the emphasis is on a development from a European centre imposing its power on a passive periphery. Dependency theory and world systems analysis with a neo-Marxist flair building on classical Marxism emphasize exploitation from a Western centre. Their point of departure is less the Smithian market economy with fair and free competition, however, but capitalism as monopoly and coercion in close cooperation with the state. Immanuel Wallerstein's analysis of the development of the capitalist world system defined 'real' capitalism as anti-market and state-driven.[3] Capitalism was a dynamic force that from its very beginning was a transnational force which spread from its Western centre and created the modern world system incorporating a passive and peripheral non-developing 'Rest'.[4]

Our emphasis is on the mutually reinforcing dynamics between external and internal driving forces. The dynamics between 'from within' and 'from without', 'external' and 'internal' were intertwined and in practice difficult to separate. It does not make sense to emphasize the one or the other. Together they triggered industrial capitalism. The old imagery where industrial capitalism spread like ripples in water from its British origin is misleading. There was not one development motor but interrelationships between exports and imports, incorporation of foreign ideas about a new production mode, translating them to domestic habits and practices, and adjusting them to and exploiting market prospects.

Islands of capitalist industrial production emerged all over Europe, although the permeation was much greater in Britain and Western Europe. The pattern within Europe was more complex than a modernizing Western part and an agricultural Eastern and Southern part lagging behind. There were islands of industrial capitalism in parts of Eastern and Southern Europe and considerable parts of Western Europe remained agricultural. Agricultural production was not a stagnant point of reference representing the world of yesterday but became ever more market and capital dependent entangled with industrial capitalism. In an analogous way, Europe was entangled with other continents through production, commerce and labour migration. Modern production methods within and without Europe were entangled with more traditional modes where traditional did not mean 'standstill'.

Kenneth Pomeranz was one of the most prominent and earliest critics of Landes's view. He argued that several other regions of the world during the decades before 1800 shared the status of dense population and commercial sophistication as well as ecological constraints. China, for instance, had as much coal as Britain, the source of the new industrial technology. Standards of living in Western Europe did not differ very much from the maritime provinces of China and Southern India. He and other historians who made the same observation began to ask new questions about the origin of the fact that the economies in Western Europe began to grow faster after 1800. They confronted earlier views from Landes onwards in which Europe's cultures and political and legal frameworks with private property rights, institutions for knowledge production and technological innovation, a scientific and legal culture with arrangements for the diffusion of knowledge, and commercial and financial organizations, trading networks and markets for commodities, labour and capital were simply seen as more efficient. These factors, Landes and his adherents argued, had for centuries provided better framework conditions for the emergence of mechanized industry, and capitalist production and sales methods.

The target of the critique was the Eurocentric idea that Europe took off through internal dynamics. Pomeranz and others observed and documented a range of advanced and less developed regions across Europe and Asia where it is difficult to discern a particular European pattern as distinguished from an Asian one. It cannot after their documentation be taken for given that during the centuries before the Industrial Revolution Europe became predetermined for an exceptional transition to capitalism through more efficient cultural, legal and political institutional frameworks.[5]

The debate dealt with what was called the 'Great Divergence' which emerged around 1800 as a huge gap between rich and poor, industrializing and agricultural countries. The California School, as it was called, based around Pomeranz, Roy Bin Wong, Jack Goldstone, Andre Gunder Frank and several others, reversed the story of the West as a long process of gradual advances in Europe leaving the rest of the world behind. They argue that societies in Asia and the Middle East were the world leaders in economic terms, in science and technology, in shipping, trade and exploration until around 1500.[6] Some of them emphasized Europe's backwardness before 1500. Andre Gunder Frank argued that Europe was a marginal player in the world economy until the second half of the eighteenth century with a permanent trade deficit with Asia. When Europe began to climb, it did so on Asian shoulders with money that 'they had somehow found, stolen, extorted or earned'.[7] Pomeranz and others were less extreme and emphasized instead similarity, arguing that the Rest was not necessarily backward and the West not that different.[8]

The Industrial Revolution did not begin at Hour Zero. Modern economic growth accelerated with factory-based industrial production but it had a longer history than Richard Arkwright's invention of the water frame for the mechanical spinning of cotton thread and James Watt's improved steam engine, which for a while made Britain the workshop of the world and the future of the others. Recent views contend that Britain's – and Europe's – modern economic growth depended more on a long history of capitalism than on the Industrial Revolution *per se*. Capitalism emerged, to a large extent, in enterprises of modest scale which created markets for efficient allocation of resources and incentives for accumulation of capital and wealth. Goods and factor markets in the late medieval period and the following centuries rested on growing agricultural productivity and efficient service industries. They paved the way for the take-off in the nineteenth century through extension of commodity markets from local or regional subsistence arrangements to global exploitation of opportunities.[9] However, the point is that this long-term market development was not uniquely European but occurred also in China and other parts of Asia, for instance.

The same goes for another long-term influence. State building accompanied the creation of markets. They developed legal and institutional frameworks for the market relations. They developed a regulating as well as financial capacity. The financial capacity had not least a military side that supported the opening of markets. Only towards the end of the nineteenth century did states get, against the backdrop of the breakthrough of industrial capitalism, a particular European profile with a capacity for social politics, which we will come back to. Before that there was little European uniqueness as to the regulating and supporting role of emerging state institutions.[10]

There was less European exclusiveness than in the canonical Smithian narrative on growth of Europe's economies emerging gradually but inexorably on distinctive market-led trajectories. In the view of Pomeranz, China and Britain were on similar trajectories of diminishing returns and rising costs for the production of food, fuel and fibres. Britain's uniqueness was that it circumvented these problems through a source of cheap energy in the form of coal, as well as the invention of the steam engine *and* free access to exogenous American overseas resources.

One must to the argument about the colonial connection add that it was Europeans, not Chinese, Arabs and Indians who 'discovered', conquered, infected, plundered, colonized and finally established beneficial commercial relationships with the Americas and Africa.[11] The establishment of colonies along mercantilist lines based on trade with slaves for the plantations in the New World turned the terms of trade in favour of Europe rather than commerce with Asia.

America and Africa in particular, and colonialism and world trade more generally, gave Europe a different accumulation regime which ever more drew Europe into a global economy, an expansion which was ever more supported by state capacity, in particular military. It was a different commercial regime than the old one based on the oriental trade companies and their trade with spices and what were considered luxury consumption goods. The new exchange regime translated to the first steps towards mass consumption. These developments accelerated in the nineteenth century.

These developments were European but there was no necessity that they had to be. Zheng He's expeditionary voyages at the beginning of the fifteenth century, for instance, went as far as East Africa on ships more than four times as long as Columbus's *Santa Maria* with hundreds of sailors on four tiers of decks.[12] What would have happened if he had continued around what at the end of that century was to be called the Cape of Good Hope and found the seaway to Europe and the Americas half a century before the Europeans explored the seaways in the other direction?

The question is contra-factual but nevertheless worth reflecting on. It hints at the role of contingency and chance in the creation and exploitation of opportunities in the history of economic modernity. It emphasizes an openness towards the future in historical processes. References to 'contingency', 'fortune', 'luck', 'accidental', 'windfall' and the like abound in the texts on the great divide produced by the California School. Pomeranz refers to the 'fortuitous' availability for Britain of extra resources in the form of coal and colonies which goes a long way to explaining its industrialization.[13]

However, on the other side, one might with Peer Vries ask whether the capacity to create and exploit resources is just a matter of luck. Britain was already on a much more energy-intensive route than China *before* industrialization and was by 1700 by far the biggest coal user in the world. Long before industrialization there was an inclination to look for mechanical solutions and large-scale centrally coordinated production was on the increase. Technology, increasingly science-based, as well as steam power and factories played a substantial role in Britain's industrialization, and this made a fundamental difference for Britain in the Great Divergence, as not only Vries but also the California School explicitly underline. Vries refers also to the role of trade. In the end, British traders and the British state earned much more through trade than their Chinese counterparts. China might have been a leading producer of consumables but this did not necessarily mean that the Chinese economy was superior. This would be to misinterpret the logic of mercantile capitalism. For the British economy, income from services by British ship-owners, insurers, financiers and investors was very important.

The question is to what extent these differences were accidental and to what extent they built on specific capacity to create and exploit resources, in the British case, for instance, as solutions to an experienced Malthusian problem. The successes in the exploration of the world oceans in the sixteenth century might to a certain extent have been accidental as the comparison with Zheng He suggests, but the establishment of colonies and the exploitation of them was not necessarily random. The point is maybe not to settle the issue of exactly how European the industrial take-off really was, but to demonstrate that it did not happen as the logical evolution of some intrinsic force in the European economies but in their global framework of production, consumption and trade through a combination of factors where initial success to create and develop global markets provided the preconditions for increased military and economic strength, which, in turn, reinforced the successes in a virtuous cycle. The point is the early global dimension of European economic modernity and how this global dimension through exploitation of resources (humans, commodities and raw materials) early on led to superior economic power.

The triangle of trade between Europe, Africa and the Americas was an important source of economic dynamics. Slave labour was bought at trading forts in Western Africa, in particular Guinea, for commodities produced in Europe like manufactured goods, cloth and muskets, and on European keels brought to the Caribbean for work on the plantations in the production of sugar, cotton, palm oil and tobacco. These products were then brought to Europe where there was growing demand for them.

A movement for the abolition of the slave trade, not slavery as such, emerged at a time when trade was becoming less profitable and the prospects of yields were growing in the emerging British manufacturing industries through the direct exploitation of labour in plantations in Africa rather than through trade with it. Trade in commodities from Africa like palm oil as grease for the machinery in the emerging manufacturing and mechanical industry, cotton for the expanding textiles industry, and sugar for the alimentary industry began to become more profitable than trade with slave labour. Also, improvements in ship design, in particular the clipper ships, speeded up the seaborne transports of raw materials and manufactured products and also facilitated trade with more fragile commodities.

The declining interest in the slave trade went hand in hand with the emergence of a new global production and trade regime in the wake of the Industrial Revolution after its take-off.

The future yields were in the new dynamics of mutual bilateral exchange of raw materials and manufactured products on expanding markets for both categories. The triangular trade based on capture and sales of slaves began to lag behind in terms of productivity and future prospects during the decades after 1800. The direct import of raw materials and alimentary commodities from Africa to Europe grew and the structure of the trade shifted from a triangular pattern to a bilateral European-African. The European processing of the raw materials and sale of the manufactured products on the African markets provided better returns than the slaves. The mechanization in new industries in Britain reduced labour costs and in relative terms slave labour transported from Africa to America became more expensive. Slaves did not have incomes but the new industrial capitalism based on contract-based wage work led to growing purchasing power and a growing demand for industrial goods. The result was that for the emerging British and later European manufacturing and mechanized industry it was more profitable to keep the slaves as cheap plantation labour in Africa contributing to the growing productions of agricultural raw materials for the industries in Britain and Europe.

Whatever gap existed in 1780 between incomes per head in Western Europe and North America on the one hand, and the economic centres of Asia and the rest of the world on the other – the issue is disputed – it is clear that the economic expansion sustained by naval and military use of industrial technology turned it into a gulf during the first half of the nineteenth century. The Chinese emperor could no longer dismiss a British request to open diplomatic relations as happened in the 1790s. The opportunities of the European powers to impose their interests by force increased and the costs for doing so decreased. The Industrial Revolution generated a historic transformation of commercial relations between Europe and Asia. Instead of European countries running a permanent trade deficit with India, South East Asia and China, having to pay for Asian goods with bullion because the Asians did not want European goods, the introduction of the power loom in Manchester led to a European take-over of Asian consumer markets. British ships brought British factory-made cotton cloth into Africa and Asia instead of reselling the products of Indian handlooms. The weavers in India lost their jobs. Increasing competition from imported manufactures in India and other parts of Asia and in Africa destroyed local traditional production modes there.[14]

The economic success for the new pattern of exchange triggered new success in a virtuous circle. The manufacturing processes improved and increased the demand for raw materials and the search for new markets for the products. In America, there was better economy in promoting the birth rates of the slaves there than in importing them from Africa. This shift of perspective explains why the United States accepted the abolition of slave imports one year after the British abolition act. The issue at stake was less about the morals of slavery but the economy of the slave trade. Soon after the break with Britain the independent colonies in the Northeast developed mechanical manufacturing and textile factories like in Britain and a corresponding bilateral economy based on export of plantation products from the South to the industry in the North emerged.[15]

Sven Beckert has, in an impressive study of the global cotton capitalism, developed and sharpened the argument of Pomeranz.[16] He does not understand capitalism as a European phenomenon but in its global frame. He investigates the movements of capital, people, goods and raw materials around the globe and demonstrates how the connections between distant areas of the world were at the core of the grand transformation of capitalism in the wake of the Industrial Revolution. Industrial capitalism around cotton re-created the world introducing new ways of organizing production, trade and consumption. Slavery (even after the abolition of the slave trade), the expropriation and exploitation of indigenous peoples, imperial expansion, armed trade, and the assertion of sovereignty over people and land by entrepreneurs were at its core. Beckert calls this emerging order war capitalism, which flourished not in the factory but in the field, land- and labour-intensive rather than mechanized, resting on the violent expropriation of land and labour in Africa and the Americas. These expropriations produced wealth and new knowledge, which in turn strengthened European institutions and states and created the preconditions for Europe's economic development in the nineteenth century. This pre-phase of capitalism was based on slavery rather than free labour, on violence and bodily coercion rather than contracts, and on massive expropriations rather than property rights and secure ownership. Global colonialism based on naval power over the oceans since the sixteenth century, which in the nineteenth century ever more involved state power in military and administrative fiscal and legal terms became the key to the European *Sonderweg* when it began to take form after 1800.

War capitalism and imperialism was the foundation from which emerged the more familiar industrial capitalism characterized by powerful states with huge administrative, military, legal and infrastructural capacities. At first, industrial capitalism remained tightly linked to slavery and expropriated lands, but as wage labour and property rights gained strength and became mobile on a global scale, they enabled a new and different form of integration of the labour, raw materials and capital markets in huge swaths of the world driving the revolutions of capitalism into ever more corners of the world.

The production of agricultural commodities in the colonies increased the rate of the commodity exchange with industrializing Europe. During the second half of the nineteenth century, particularly after the 1870s, the economic interest in the exploitation of raw materials in Africa and Asia as input for the industry in Europe increased and required ever more state support in military and administrative terms. Imperialism became the name of the new pattern of state-protected exploitation by private enterprises looking for raw materials and markets for sales of industrial products.

A legal framework guaranteeing the Europeans extraterritorial rights emerged. Jurisprudence provided the legal basis for the colonial project.[17] Private European interests in land were protected by the natural law arguments, which linked arguments about territorial rights to the cultivation of land, and implied the distinction between nomadic and sedentary populations, thus opening much the largest part of non-European territory for European settlement.[18] The colonial and imperial arrangements were built on the ambiguities in concepts like sovereignty.[19]

However, imperialism was much more complex than being a unilateral European penetration and exploitation of the colonial world. Different power strategies were used from military violence to peaceful cooperation and the oppressed developed a multitude of resistance and compliance strategies. The European expansion was very much a matter of local negotiation. A network of legal and political arrangements regulated the colonial relationships and enmeshed the expanding industrial capitalism in a global framework for the exploitation of the opportunities that the Industrial Revolution offered.[20]

By 1878 the Western states claimed control of 67 per cent of the earth's land surface, and by 1919 85 per cent. The implication was that most of the world came to be ruled by European laws. This did not occur under any well-planned or cohesive strategy but through converging formal and informal practices. The rule of law expanded within and beyond Europe as the principle that property was to be respected, contracts were to be kept and public authorities were not to overstep the limits of their legally determined jurisdiction, in particular not disrespect laws of private property.[21]

There were myriad variations of European formal and informal rule, of entanglements between indigenous populations and their chieftains, kings or emperors and the European powers, between military, commercial, cultural and political relationships, between native resistance strategies and complying with the situation, between doing as much as possible via cooperation or as little as possible through conflict. The development of the European interests in Asia and Africa resulted in a variety of colonial arrangements. These ranged from commercial treaties to gunboat diplomacy to military occupation. Japan and Siam are examples of traditional regimes remaining 'independent' through Western modernization and reforms.

The European exploitation of opportunities based on military power enmeshed the world by means of mobilizing key words like development, progress, growth, wealth and civilizing mission. This was much more than a matter of economic power radiation. The political and military dimension of the permeation was obvious and the military conflicts were not only between the Europeans and the native population but also between the European powers in hard competition about markets and raw materials.

In the conclusion of his history of the global cotton industry Beckert rejects the conceptualization of the nineteenth century as an age of 'bourgeois civilisation' in nice contrast with the twentieth century, 'the age of catastrophe' (as termed by Eric Hobsbawm). The label of bourgeois civilization derives from a vision of the world that focuses its moral judgements on Europe. Looked at from the perspective of much of Asia, Africa and the Americas, one can argue just the opposite, that the nineteenth century was an age of barbarity and catastrophe, as slavery and imperialism devastated first one pocket of the globe and then another. The twentieth century was in this view, rather than catastrophe, emancipating decolonization even if emancipation was a long and tough struggle.[22]

The nineteenth century brought, in the view of Hobsbawm, the unfettered capitalism where new practices, institutions and legal arrangements about property and labour at the end subjugated the labour of the world.[23] Like Karl Marx he did not hesitate to see the Industrial Revolution as a European invention. In an early book he discussed why it happened in Britain and from there spread to Europe and at the end to other continents. He emphasized both the role of the market as an institution where supply and demand met, and of the state as a supporting instrument of political and military power when the markets were opened up. By the sixteenth century it was fairly obvious, he argued, that if industrial revolution would occur anywhere in the world it would be somewhere in the European economy. Then he began to investigate why it happened in Britain. The answer he found in the relationship between making profit and technological innovation.[24]

Although the origin was in Britain, Hobsbawm *did* see the global framework. The expansion of trade, in particular the trade connected with the colonial system, was crucial. The vaster, faster and growing circulation of goods did not only bring to Europe new needs, and the stimulus to manufacture foreign imports at home, but it also provided a limitless horizon of sales and profit for merchant and manufacturer. It was the British who by their policy and force as much as by their enterprise and inventive skill captured these markets. The industrial economy grew out of the commerce, in particular the commerce with the under-developed world.[25]

The subtitle of this section, 'The legacy of African labour and American soil', seems to fit like hand in glove with Hobsbawm's scenario. However, we want to say something different, closer to Christopher Bayly. We want to go beyond Hobsbawm's globalized Eurocentrism. The take-off period of the world economy in the nineteenth century does not know any point of departure or initial process but is a confluence of multi-centric economic spaces with a multiplicity of political, economic, scientific, technological and, not least, military factors leading to accelerating and condensing global developments. Before the Industrial Revolution there was the 'industrious revolution' – the terminology draws on Jan de Vries – operating with more settled patterns of daily life, rigorous time keeping, and exploitation of low-level advances in artisan industry in a Euro-American version with non-European analogues. The development was global not only – but also – in terms of European exploitation of markets, raw materials and labour. It is in the view of Bayly too reductionist to look for a single or even a predominating cause of global change, like capitalism, industrialization, or a rationalist science-organizing Western state. Instead the key is the concatenation of changes produced by the interactions of political, economic and ideological change at many different levels. It explains both the 'Great Divergence' between Europe and the rest of the world at the beginning of the nineteenth century and the great acceleration of social conflict and social change at its end.[26] Bayly describes the world in the nineteenth century as a complex of overlapping networks of global reach, while at the same time acknowledging the vast differential of power which belonged to them. He emphasizes the capacity of European companies, administrators and intellectuals to co-opt and bend to their will existing global networks of commerce, faith and power, a capacity which explains their dominance in terms of subordination rather than collaboration.[27]

The global movement of labour

One of the experienced threats in Europe that accompanied the early industrial capitalist mode of production was overpopulation. Death rates decreased in the wake of the Industrial Revolution. Thomas Malthus (1766–1834), a clergyman, political economist and demographer with a broad research agenda, and the most prominent sceptic of permanent growth, developed a demographic theory which argued that population grows faster than food with long-term starvation and population stagnation as consequences. It was a theory with a clearly moral and colonial dimension resting on a distinction between societies which controlled sexual behaviour, fertility patterns and population growth and those savage tribes which did not. Malthus misinterpreted his figures but created a scenario of the future which was remarkably long lasting, concluding that poverty could not be defeated by growing productivity because natural resources were limited. Malthus distinguished between government-supported welfare and public charity. Government poor relief should be gradually abolished, because it worked against the long-term interests of the poor by decreasing their incitements. A man, whose labour society did not want, 'has no claim of right to the smallest portion of food, and, in fact, has no business to be where he is. At nature's mighty feast there is no vacant cover for him.'[28]

The experienced threat of overpopulation in Europe became one of the driving forces of colonialism hand in hand with the search for markets and raw materials under mutually reinforcing dynamics. Colonial settlements in other continents supplemented the early trading stations along the African and Asian coasts.

However, migration to other continents was not only a reaction to the threat of overpopulation and the everyday realities of poverty and destitution experienced by many people in the dynamic nineteenth century, despite the fact that the rates of economic growth increased. Migration was also a reaction to the promise of a better future in some other part of the world. Push as well as pull factors triggered migration and maintained it.

The Industrial Revolution was thus not only about overseas capital and commodity movements. Also, labour moved between the continents. Migration between countries within and between continents is an old phenomenon over many centuries. However, from the 1820s global migrations changed dramatically. The number of migrants and the distance they moved increased to levels far beyond what had earlier been the case. The most intense migration movement was across the Atlantic. The 'discovery' of America over 300 years earlier had triggered a transatlantic movement of people. By 1820 some 11.3 million had travelled to the 'New World', a term which like 'discovery' reflected deep Euro-centrism. Eighty per cent of them were slaves from Africa for the American plantations. Among the rest were many convicts and indentured servants from Europe. In the 1780s the British government began to send convicts to Australia. During the ninety years the traffic lasted, 160,000 convicts were deported. The 'New World' recruited labour through coercion and contracts. The contracts as a rule meant prepaid travel to jobs with paltry pay and miserable working conditions. Furthermore, the contracts as a rule were signed for years of work under such conditions. As opposed to slaves they were signed by 'free' individuals. The difference between slaves and 'free' labour was often subtle, although in legal terms there was a distinction.[29]

Between the 1820s and the 1920s almost 60 million people crossed the Atlantic, two-thirds of them to the USA. The change from trade with humans to their free movement seems to be big. However, as we saw, 'free' did not necessarily mean free in the conventional understanding of the term. The term was often a euphemism. For millions, the emigration was a coerced escape from wretched living conditions, hunger and starvation, or political oppression and persecution. Many of them emigrated to other forms of exploitation and subjugation, although most of the migrants probably experienced that they improved their living conditions. Moreover, although the slave trade declined it was not until the 1880s that the cumulative sum of European migrants matched that of slave labour from Africa in the Americas.

There were two gigantic global migration movements during the century after 1820, the European exodus and the Asian exodus, each involving 50–60 million people on the move, the European somewhat bigger. Escape from poverty and persecution welded together the world. This was one important part of economic modernity although less noticed in its global dimension than the commodity expansion and the economic growth. In 1860, the USA was, after Great Britain, the strongest industrializing economic power of the world, which besides the industrial production also benefitted from a strong agricultural export sector. A globally ramified communication network facilitated the input of new labour when the demand so required. The vast majority of the migrants to the USA came from Europe before the First World War. The annual average after 1820 was 50,000. In the 1840s the annual average grew to 250,000 and in the early 1850s to 340,000. During the world economic depression after the Crimean War in the 1850s and the American Civil War of 1861–1865 the European immigration decreased considerably, but thereafter the increase of the annual average continued, although the world economic stagnation in the 1870s again led to decreasing annual averages. From the 1880s until 1914 the culmination of the European immigration occurred. At the end of the 1880s, 800,000 Europeans migrated annually to North America and after 1900 the figure rose to 1.3 million. In comparison to this European exodus few immigrants came from other continents. Between 1849, when the gold rush to California began, and 1882, 300,000 Chinese arrived, mainly attracted by the gold fever and the job opportunities as navvies in the railway industry.[30]

The Neo-European settlements in the Americas and in the Pacific meant the repulsion of the native populations into peripheral spaces or genocide. The invasion led to marginalization of traditional economic and social systems, power relationships and cultural patterns. 'Modernity' in the wake of industrial capitalism had a predatory dimension.

The early nineteenth century migrant streams were often led by farmers and artisans from rural districts, travelling in family groups with the intention to acquire land and settle permanently. Although many in the later emigration waves continued to have rural roots they were, towards the end of the century, increasingly coming from urban areas and industrial occupations. Although they were not necessarily among the most poor, they were typically unskilled and poorer than the earlier emigrant groups. Their formal schooling and training was limited. They migrated individually rather than in families. This shift during the nineteenth century from skilled towards unskilled, from better paid towards lower paid, from older towards younger, and from families towards individuals was not least conditioned by cheaper travel cost through the shift from horses to railways and from sailing ships to steamships.[31] Around 1900 the crossing of the Atlantic took one week as opposed to six weeks at the time of the sailing ships before the mid-nineteenth century. The travel in the steamships was also more secure. The decision to emigrate was not to the same extent a choice for life. It became much easier to return, which made more people dare the step.

The overseas traffic with steamships, was, after 1880, ever more organized in an ever-tighter network of liner services. Transport markets were opened up by globally competing and operating shipping companies. A tight network of agents with modern canvassing and advertisement methods, browsed through and discovered ever new emigration regions in order to fill the ships. Migration was business. The agents coordinated the railway and sea transports. The steamships and the expanding continental railway network in Europe and North America led to a spectacular rise of person and goods kilometres at ever shorter transport times. The expansion of the physical infrastructure for transport of commodities and people was through the telegraph accompanied by a not less dynamic expansion of intellectual communication. New newspapers mushroomed with ever larger circulation sizes. The possibilities to get information about settlement or employment increased rapidly and decreased the migration barriers that followed from lack of information.[32]

Like the capital movements, migrating labour entangled Europe in a global network where the transatlantic movements were particularly intense. The labour dimension of industrial capitalism and European modernity must be seen in its global relations.

The economic and the social in the Industrial Revolution

The spread of industrial capitalism meant the emergence of new forms of property as opposed to the old feudal order around landed property. New movable capital property was based on private contract rather than birth. Shareholdings with limited ownership responsibilities and trading of shares on stock markets decreased the personal risks and increased the propensity of risk-taking. The speculative dimension of the economy increased. New organization of credits through new forms of commercial banks emerged underlining the speculative trend. The opportunities of social climbing increased but also the risks of social fall. Industrial capitalism was more dynamic and more turbulent than traditional economic regimes. The vision of progress triggered dynamics in various directions.

Adam Smith, and the school of political thought linked to his name, developed, in particular, the liberal idea of the market as the motor of social life. They imagined market expansion through increased distribution of labour leading to economic growth. The market became a growth machine that propelled by itself. There was an insight in the emerging view that social problems might occur, but the view was also that the growth would mitigate them. The key concepts in Smith's approach were market and labour, in particular, division of labour.

John Locke, the empiricist and social contract theorist – remaining within the framework of natural law, but breaking with the idea of an unchangeable natural order – had paved the way for the new approach by arguing that labour justified property rights and conferred value upon things in a new and better world.[33] In making a distinction between usefully productive labouring individuals and uselessly privileged pleasure-searching individuals, a new economically and morally justified principle of achievement became the gauge. Work became a productive activity measured according to its economic impact and yield. It became an instrument of demarcation between a bourgeois value order, based on diligence and industriousness, and what was considered to be an obsolete value order based on birthright. The meaning of 'idleness' and 'inactivity' changed when charges of moral worthlessness on account of sloth turned the focus from the lowest to the highest strata of society. The meaning of the concept of liberty changed from connoting a privilege for a social group with birthrights towards a universal right of all people. It is precisely on this re-evaluation of work, from an instrument for the maintenance of to an instrument for the change of the social order that Smith based *The Wealth of Nations* (1776). The entrepreneurial work of the commercial class challenged the privileges of the landowning class as Locke had argued. In the new theoretical construction of a growing economy in moral philosophy, as political economy was called, labour became a means, not only to maintain existence, but also to create expanding capital.

In the 1830s, the observation of growing social problems in the wake of the spread of the capitalist market economy provoked a debate about how self-regulating the market really was and whether growth automatically mitigated social problems. The question was put whether the social problems were not built into the market expansion system. These observations connected the new forms of private property with new forms of poverty and proletarianization. The ruling classes began to fear social unrest and new revolutions. The debate on the social question dealt with the protection against social unrest from the perspective of the ruling classes.

The amalgamation of workers on individual wage contracts rather than paternalist employment relationships of the crafts meant that the workers had to confront new kinds of social problems on their own. Workers were hired and fired according to the demands and supplies on the markets for commodities and labour. A core of employees was tied to the company by means of better working conditions and job security whereas many were hired on temporary contracts with occasional employment. The commodification of labour was as the slave trade demonstrated not new, but the labour relationships changed with the invention of 'free' contract-based individuals on a market who got more responsibility for their situation.

The amalgamation of wage workers with bad working and living conditions and uncertain future prospects provoked fears of social unrest and new revolutions among the ruling economic and political elites and the growing middle classes. Poverty went hand in hand with property and there was obviously a connection between the two but more precisely what kind of connection was disputed. However, it was clear that the problem was more complex than just being a matter of blaming the poor and unemployed individuals themselves for their precarious situations as had been the case in the pauperism of the agricultural societies.

The identification of social problems in the wake of the spread of industrial capitalism and wage work changed the political debate and the economic theories. Classical economic theory became after Adam Smith more fragmented, more contested, more technical and more abstract. The imagery of Smith and other moral philosophers depicted a seamless global economy of general growth through international distribution of labour and market expansion. There was an awareness of social problems in the wake of industrial capitalism, but, as we saw, the conviction was that economic growth would mitigate them. The world of Smith was still that of the small artisan workshops and the ingenious distribution of labour. This world-view eroded when the spread of contract-based wage labour, factory work and industrial capital accumulation led to new kinds of social problems. In particular, the issue of poverty fundamentally changed the character of the debate. The focus shifted from international distribution of labour towards national distribution of income and systematic imbalances intrinsic in a theory that predicted equilibrium.

Work and ownership of the means of production were increasingly separated. Thus the breakthrough of an industrial economy was accompanied by social inequality between owners of capital (and land), and those who did not own capital or land which highlighted the problem of social equilibrium. The producers produced for the market, which is an abstract entity, without knowing what the existing needs and desires really were. The knowledge of the producer in the old order, where s/he could follow the result of her/his work until the fruits of it were consumed, was forever lost. The producer could not know the needs which s/he should satisfy. S/he worked incessantly to fill the common barns without knowing how the fruits of the work are distributed. The producer in the new order of wage work was no longer the worker who manufactured the commodities but the capital owner who provided capital for their production.[34]

Swiss economist Sismonde de Sismondi developed a humanitarian protest against the dominant economic orthodoxy of his time. His central argument in the 1820s was that consumption depended on the income levels of consumers rather than on the aggregate production. He refuted the Smithian argument that efficient production delivered superior outcomes in distributive terms. This was the terrain of the big glut controversy of the 1820s, where Sismondi criticized the inequalities provoked by capital-intensive manufacturing and expressed concerns about private property regimes where available capital dictated production rather than demand.

The key question dealt with how to link the social and the economic and whether supply created its own demand. Key terms included 'overproduction', 'glut' and 'underconsumption'. Sismondi urged governments not to fall back on the resources of the state through subsidies to manufacturing enterprises. The situation required a careful regulation of the competition, not state subsidies, Sismondi argued.[35]

One of the protagonists in the debate was French economist Jean-Baptiste Say, who had argued in his *Traité d'économie politique* (1803) that production finds its markets, supply its demand, and that there is no glut or overproduction and no underconsumption ('Say's law'). He expounded the theories of Adam Smith as a proclamation of faith that the new industrialism was a harmonious, virtually automatic economic mechanism, which did not require any customs.[36]

In Britain James Mill (1773–1836) and David Ricardo (1772–1823) maintained a similar Smithian position as Say. Ricardo was a British political economist, stock trader, financier and speculator, MP and businessman, who accumulated a considerable personal fortune, and was among the most influential explorers of economic theory after Smith, in continuous controversial debate with Sismondi and Say. Sismondi, in his *Nouveaux principes d'économie politique*, argued that the infinitive advance of productivity promised by Say would be checked by society's real capacity for consumption meaning that the limitation of growth was less the productivity than the distribution of income.

Refuting thinkers such as Smith, Say and Ricardo, Sismondi rejected the idea that economic equilibrium leading to full employment would be immediately and spontaneously achieved. A certain kind of equilibrium might be established in the long run, but only after a frightful level of suffering.[37] Sismondi argued that the interests of the social groups participating in the production of riches were far from converging. Those social classes engaged in production are not unified in a harmonious relation, rather they are antagonists.

In modern societies, need had ceased to be the regulator of production, Sismondi argued. Need had been replaced by profit and by wealth. Not the production value but the exchange value had become the coordinator of the emerging new order which provoked a problem of distribution. Work and ownership of the means of production were increasingly separated. Social inequality accompanied the breakthrough of an industrial economy which highlighted the problem of social equilibrium. Sismondi anticipated a debate that Marx would continue.

In the 1870s, after debate lasting almost half a century on the social question from the perspective of liberal market economy, Karl Marx broke through with an alternative view to that of Smith and his adherents arguing that class struggle was the motor of social life. The Manifesto was forgotten soon after the knock-down of the 1848 revolution, but Marx continued to build up his view in the public debate in the 1850s and after he had published

Capital in 1867 he attracted ever more attention. However, it was the Paris Commune in 1871 which made him a famous, as well as feared, man and the working class in singular to stand up as a promise for many and a threat for others. Marx's *The Civil War in France*, written in London in 1871, was a necrology of the Commune and its destiny, which conferred a mythic status on its author. It was reprinted in three editions in two months and was translated into most European languages. The headline 'Grand Chef de l'Internationale' in the *Paris Journal* was repeated everywhere in the radical European press. It was a common belief that the Paris Commune had been the work of the International. The conservative press throughout Europe denounced Marx as the leader of a secret communist international workers' conspiracy. The International was depicted as one of Europe's great powers. Marx transformed the social question into the class question and shifted the top-down perspective of a social threat to ward off to the bottom-up perspective of a social opportunity of emancipation.

A variety of views and theories emerged during the bicentenary debate on the connection between the economic and the social. The liberal market-oriented view and the Marxist view focusing on labour and work co-existed and merged in complex and contradictory ways, overlapped and competed during the nineteenth and twentieth centuries. They shared basically the optimism as to the inherent potential of a better future, whatever that meant, through the capitalist mode of production.[38]

What, then, was the significance of the two views?

Their most important novelty was probably the idea that work and labour can be liberated from their human-divine paradigm. The market view saw them as carried by free individuals with a capacity to negotiate their wages and working conditions with the capital owners and agree on new forms of private contracts. The liberal view emphasized the work that the capitalists invested in their enterprises and *their* rights to benefit by the yields of their work rather than the remuneration to the workers for *their* work. The Marxist view emphasized the workers as exploited individuals who had to sell their labour. They had a collectively shared interest against the exploitation of the capitalists who bought their labour. Marx referred to the sale and purchase of labour on a market under demarcation from paternalist employment relationships in the old pre-industrial society. Labour and work were no longer simply something one *did*, but also something one *had* (owned), *was* (as a commodity), and *offered* (on the market).[39]

In the wake of the imagery of market expansion, a more expansive view on work and labour emerged in both the Smithian and the Marxian narratives. Both emphasized economic growth. The issue at stake was the distribution of the yields of that growth.

By the mid-nineteenth century Friedrich Engels and Karl Marx did not only outline the emerging industrial capitalist order driven by class conflict but also took issue with Malthus's population theory from new points of departure. They turned Malthus upside down. What Malthus saw as the problem of a population pressure on the means of production they saw as the problem of a means of production pressure on the population. They coined the term 'reserve army' to describe labour without employment arguing that the excess of labour emerged as a product of a dynamic capitalist economy. The excess situation they discerned was temporary rather than definite and existential as with Malthus and it was connected to a new kind of crisis inherent in the capitalist mode of production.

Karl Marx captured and conceptualized a series of ideological and intellectual trends during a turbulent period of European modernity and translated them into theoretical reasoning. In his development of a new interpretative framework for how to understand the affluence and the poverty in the wake of industrial capitalism he was ambiguous between arguments for history and historical experiences as the only basis of knowledge about how societies function and arguments for knowledge through the discovery of general laws guiding humans and societies. Marx was contradictory and contextual, not least depending on the time. In the preface of *Kritik der politischen Ökonomie* (1859) he developed turns of phrase which must be interpreted as arguments for the existence of development laws inherent in the structures of capitalism. This view was later invested with a doctrinaire character in orthodox Marxism. On other occasions, he emphasized historicity in a non-universal sense.[40] He linked current politics to utopian theoretical predictions. As such he was a restless observer who repeatedly strove to correct his predictions and the conclusions.

Using an empirical-historical basis, Marx elaborated on the structural economic, social and political inequality of individuals that issued from their class position as wage labour or capital owners. This served to separate the capitalist mode of production from an imagined society of small commodity producers that was common to classical economics. Through his emphasis on the production relationships Marx demonstrated, largely on the basis of classical economic theory, in particular its labour value thesis, that rather than wealth of nations the organization of the economy led to the exploitation of one class by another, resulting in long-term economic instability. Marx represented a modified Ricardian approach to political economy. A key concept in David Ricardo's view was the iron law of wages which fit with Marx's thought.[41]

Marx was above all concerned with the issue of private property. He confronted the Hegelian view that civil society mediated between the individuals, the family and the state. For Marx, instead the state was a political construct reflecting the power relationships in civil society, power relationships based on private property in the hands of the capitalist bourgeoisie. Democracy was in his view a bourgeois abstraction legitimizing unjust power relationships.

Marx's observation of and comment on the workers' class formation was in many respects correct, although much less so his prediction from the observations. His outline of a corresponding bourgeois class successfully confronting the feudal society and then becoming the losers to the working class did not come true. Often the emerging bourgeois economic elite merged with the aristocratic landed elites forming a new conservative and moderately liberal economic elite that ruled in Europe more or less successfully through what they understood as necessary concessions to labour.

Marx's prophecy notwithstanding, the emergence of mass labour movements in nineteenth-century Europe – including trade unions and political parties or movements such as Chartism in England, the socialists in France or the social democrats in Germany and Northern Europe – was in fact a reaction to conservative and liberal attempts to exclude the working classes from the political process. The aim of these attempts was democracy. Slowly, the representatives of the unrepresented obtained a foothold within political structures that were moving toward parliamentary forms as we saw in Chapter 4. However, we saw also that this development was far from a general breakthrough of democracy. The working classes, which increasingly identified themselves as the working class or labour movement in the singular, sought majority power in the parliaments, alone or in coalitions with other parties. Their aim was to obtain power over the state apparatus in order to effect social reforms. They sought to influence, rather than to destroy the 'bourgeois' state. Marxist and social democratic aims appeared to be close, both sought to empower the working class, but their means were ultimately quite distinct.[42]

Gustav Schmoller, the German sociologist and a protagonist in the European academic-political debate on the social and the class questions at the end of the nineteenth century, noted the magnitude of the new order. The new was not in some doctrine of trade or money, tariff barriers or navigation rules, but in something 'far greater': the total transformation of society and its organization as well as of the state and its institution, a transformation which replaced the local economy by the political economy of the national state.[43]

Free trade and protectionism

An early liberal argument dealt with free trade as the tool for a harmonious world order. Richard Cobden (1804–1865), a manufacturer and radical liberal statesman, and a successful entrepreneur in the Manchester printing industry, brought forward, in his vehement campaign for free trade in the 1840s and 1850s, the argument that free trade promoted peace and general wealth. He legitimized his argument with references to Smith. Cobden was associated with John Bright (1811–1889) in the formation of the Anti-Corn Law League, the political platform of Cobden, also called the Manchester School. The adherents were a group of middle-class radicals who identified their enemy in protectionist aristocrats and the landowning upper classes.[44]

Although their claims regarding Smith and other British Enlightenment philosophers as their intellectual antecedents were dubious, Cobden and his colleagues constructed a powerful rhetoric around the rubric of peace and free trade, the legacy of which continues to this day. Free trade theory also found adherents in France. One of them was Michel Chevalier (1806 –1879), a French engineer, statesman, economist and free market liberal. Together with Richard Cobden and John Bright, Chevalier prepared the free trade agreement of 1860 between the United Kingdom and France, referred to as the Cobden-Chevalier Treaty, which became a model for the spread of bilateral free-trade agreements. The model character of the treaty depended not least on its most-favoured-nation clause. If France subsequently signed a treaty which gave some other country lower tariff rates than England enjoyed, these rates were automatically to apply to British goods as well. France made similar treaties with other states between 1860 and 1866. Each treaty meant lower duties and some of these were passed on to British goods. Other countries made treaties with one another, and thus a network of low-tariff agreements over European trade was established, although this emerging order should not be mistaken for a general European free trade.[45]

Cobden's continental opponent was Friedrich List, who developed an idea of what could be called free-trade protectionism. He contrasted the 'British system' of *laissez-faire* capitalism to the 'American system' of developmental capitalism through tariff protection and government intervention, and argued that the devotion of the classical economists to international free trade was based on their interest, as British subjects, in keeping the rest of the world occupied in subordinate pursuits for an industrial England.

List was among the sharpest critics of the peace-through-trade argument. He connected Smith's argument about economic strength for the wealth of nations through international distribution of labour to global political and military strength rather than welfare.[46] According to List, nations could not be treated as a universal category but had to be seen in relation to their development stage: agricultural, industrial (developing manufacturing) and commercial (established manufacturing). For List, free trade was a desirable final goal, but for the two earlier stages some form of protection was crucial. Protective customs were necessary in order to prevent British domination over continental nations. List confronted Smith's cosmopolitan economy.

List highlighted the disparities in wealth and power between the states created by contemporary trade patterns under the British hegemon. He critically connected issues of welfare and warfare, economic performance and political management, arguing that trade might simply reshape, rather than negate, international rivalries. In the scenarios laid out by Smith and Say, growing competition between the nations would lead to the transformation of the product diversification into standardization. Sismondi warned that this would either lead to a race-to-the-bottom exploitation of labour or to the aggressive attempts to conquer markets by force. He suggested that nations specialize in particular products. List rejected this view, too, to argue that national specialization would only underpin the British economic hegemony.[47]

The myth of the nineteenth century as free trade is an ex post construction which was particularly activated as an instrument to give historical legitimization to the neoliberal globalization language in the 1990s. The myth made Cobden's ideological campaign for free trade in the 1840s, based on a biased reading of Smith, an implemented regime and a standard for a large part of the nineteenth century. Ideals of free trade and practices of protectionism have, as opposed to this myth, framed and driven Europe's economic modernity after 1800.

The economic modernity of Europe

To sum up this chapter: European economic modernity through the spread of the Industrial Revolution and industrial capitalism was a global issue and much more than an issue of market capitalism. The European economies, developed through expansion on global markets for commodities, labour and capital, were a special part of a development that involved the whole world, certainly not all as winners, and with a considerable degree of exploitation of people and nature. Europe was only one part of a specific global multi-centric conjuncture and confluence without a specific starting-point in time and space. The European particularity was one of several particularities in a general global pattern at the beginning of the nineteenth century which connected state power and market efficiency, technology and management of resources and labour in new ways with new institutions. The European particularity connected technology and science, ideologies and arguments about reason and rationality, about mobilization and ownership of capital and labour, to institutions for state administration and market efficiency. New forms of capital ownership and labour relationships supported by military power and naval control of the oceans paved the way for economic expansion, and the question of distribution of the yields of the economic expansion paved the way for social protests and social politics.

The second argument of this chapter is that economic modernity was far from a smooth process. The spread of industrial capitalism triggered and maintained from the 1830s onwards a long and heated debate on the social question and on how to come to terms with the growing observations that economic market integration went in tandem with social disintegration. The liberal narrative on global distribution of labour and market expansion for economic growth, which would mitigate the social problems, competed with an alternative view, which Karl Marx and Friedrich Engels had formulated in 1848, and which Marx developed theoretically in the 1850s and 1860s arguing that the growth would not mitigate the social problems which, so his argument ran, were inherent in the capitalist order. Growth would end up in capital concentration and the reserve armies of the workers of the world before a new world would emerge.

Another part of the liberal narrative was that free trade would not only promote growth but also peace. This contribution to Smith's liberal narrative was added on in the 1840s (Cobden). Strong counter-arguments emerged asserting that free trade was just an expression of British self-interests aiming at consolidating its commercial hegemony (List). The competing arguments about free trade or protectionism supplemented the two competing interpretations of the economy, the liberal and the Marxist, contributing to a much more complex framework of interpretation than in the standard view on the nineteenth century as economic liberalism. The label of liberal for the economies during the century after the publication of *Wealth of Nations* in 1776 requires considerable reservations and qualifications.

In the 1870s, the economic liberal order faced growing difficulties implying that the liberal narrative lost credibility and the Marxist interpretation gained convincing power. We will come back in Chapter 8 to the erosion and collapse of the liberal order as it had been shaped in the wake of Smith, with all oppositions and contradictions (*pace* Sismondi, List and Marx), and see how a new kind of organized modernity was created.

6

The Modern European and the Quest for Individual Autonomy

Institutions and self-understandings: a conceptual clarification

After having, in the two preceding chapters, discussed the two key institutional features that are often supposed to mark European modernity – liberal democracy and market capitalism – we now turn to a reconsideration of supposed key elements of the modern European self-understanding, namely individual autonomy and the separation of religion and politics. In the common view, modern Europeans are committed to individual autonomy, that is, the freedom of the individual is a basic principle and any interference with this freedom requires special justification. Similarly, the common view holds that modern Europeans clearly separate private from public matters. In particular, religion is considered to be a private matter, and therefore the public affairs of the state should be separated from religious concerns – this is one version of the reasoning about modernity being marked by secularization.

Following the approach taken in the two preceding chapters on 'modern' institutions, this and the following chapter will confront this common view about European modernity with the analysis of European thoughts and practices in the course of the supposed modernity. As before, the point is not to build a strawman only to set fire to it. We are well aware of the fact that what we call the 'common view' has widely been criticized in the past and in the present. Because this common view remains a point of reference in both scholarly and public debate despite its misconceptions and inaccuracies, however, more than criticism is needed. A confrontation of this perception with the actual thoughts and practices in Europe will permit us to understand the European self-understanding as one particular interpretation of modernity rather than a model of modernity.

Before we proceed with considerations on individual autonomy in this chapter and on the separation of religion and politics in the subsequent chapter, a broader conceptual remark is in order at this point. As mentioned earlier (in Chapter 1), we work with a distinction between institutional arrangements and ways of interpreting the world to arrive at a more appropriate understanding of modernity. Importantly, placing the focus on interpretations permits us to see existing institutions as one of several possible sedimentations of a modern way of interpreting the world. Thus, in our analysis of democracy (Chapter 4) we could see how a discrepancy arose between the political imaginary of modernity, oriented at democracy as expression of collective autonomy, and the political institutions of European societies during the nineteenth century. Similarly, our analysis of the organization of the economy in nineteenth-century Europe (Chapter 5) showed how ideas of the autonomy of the individual actor and of the increasing mastery of nature informed the moves towards freedom of commerce, free trade and industrialization, on the one hand, but also how, on the other hand, the colonial and the social question became the results of the prevailing organization of economic modernity. In both cases, the modern commitment to autonomy, both individual and collective, and to mastery clearly informed the institutional transformations. But it did so in a particular way in the context of the given European socio-political constellation. Thus, the institutional transformations should not be misunderstood as the gradual but universally inclined realization of the project of modernity.

In the following two chapters, we move from such institutional analysis to the underlying world-interpretations. And again we need to proceed by enlarging the horizon. The 'project' of European modernity is often seen as closely associated with the commitment to individual freedom and personal self-realization. But world-interpretations also need to address the relations between human beings. Therefore, a focus on the individual begs the question of the relation of such an individual to other human beings. In the history of sociological thought, this question has often been framed in dualistic ways, seeing individuals as members of societies, communities or collectivities. But this is already a specific way of formulating the issue. More generally stated, human beings are separate from others and indivisible in their corporeal reality soon after birth, but they are closely connected to other human beings from before birth and continue to do so in their lives. We might say, with Aristotle, that they are political animals. Sometimes – probably incorrectly – the term 'religion' is assumed to stem from 're-ligare', 're-connect', and to refer to that which binds human beings again to each other and to something superior that they see as having in common after the initial experience of individuation. Whatever social ontology one may opt for in detail, this brief observation suggests that politics and religion are terms that can be explored for understanding the ways in which Europeans have conceptualized their relations to one another, and to others, their similarity with others and their difference from others. For these reasons (and for reasons peculiar to European history to be detailed further on) the exploration of the European ways of world-interpretation takes here the forms of, first, an exploration of the notion of individual autonomy (this chapter) and, second, a parallel one on religion and politics in the history of Europe (Chapter 7).

Our reasoning on individual autonomy proceeds in five steps. We first reconstruct and discuss the widespread view that Europe is the historical home to 'a culture of individual autonomy'.[1] Concluding on the difficulty of asserting European origins of such culture, we subsequently trace more tangible events in European history that show a commitment to individual autonomy, namely, secondly, the advent of the notion of individual human rights and, thirdly, the emergence of an individualist ontology, this latter differentiated into its epistemic, political and economic claims. In each case, we explore the nature of the claims made as well as the countervailing claims that were made in response to the individualist claims. These reflections allow us to reconsider the European relation to individual autonomy in two ways. In socio-philosophical terms, fourthly, we discuss whether individual autonomy can be seen as the sole core value of European modernity. In socio-historical terms, fifthly, we consider whether individualization is a lasting and steady tendency in the history of European modernity.

The European discovery of the individual?

Conceptually, it is not precisely clear what 'individual autonomy' refers to. The term is sometimes used synonymously with individual freedom, but through the notion of 'autonomy', that is, setting one's own laws, it signifies more than the absence of constraints and includes an idea of actual capacity of self-determination – knowing what one wants and being able to do so. Furthermore, the meaning of the adjective 'individual' is unclear in the combination with 'autonomy': can one think of laws that pertain only to oneself and not to others? We will re-encounter these issues in a moment. But despite these reflections, the use to which the term 'individual autonomy' is normally put provides a sufficient basis for going on with our exploration. Charles Taylor, whose impressive *Sources of the Self* has become a key reference, offers the following specification for the 'culture of individual autonomy': this 'is a culture which is individualist [...]: it prizes autonomy; it gives an important place to self-exploration; and its visions of the good life involve personal commitment.'[2] As such, the term marks a distinction from supposed other cultures that accept heteronomy, that is, determination of behaviour through laws given by others; that value following a rule more than creativity; and in which the visions of the good life are given by habits and traditions. Across the past two centuries European thought also identified those other cultures. They were the so-called primitive societies, the traditional subject of anthropology, as well as Eastern societies, both of which were held to be marked by a pronouncedly greater degree of collectivism, integrating the singular human beings and their orientations rather firmly into the value frameworks of society. The relation to Europe's own past was more ambiguous. On the one hand, it was only the modernity of Europe that fully embraced the individual, thus earlier Europeans were guided by tradition not unlike Europe's others. On the other hand, however, the commitment to individual autonomy was to be traced to European origins some of which dated back long in time. We will first reconstruct and discuss this kind of reasoning.

The points of reference are numerous and manifold. The will to find European origins has been widespread, but it has encountered very different results. Sometimes the modern view of the individual is seen as having several ancient sources: one in the Greek injunction to 'know thyself' as a call for self-reflexivity as a precondition for action, another one in the idea of individual salvation in Christianity, and a third one in the Roman formalized concept of right. There are early documents that give evidence of rather deep self-inspection and conscious agency, such as Augustine's *Confessions* of 397 CE. In more socio-historical terms, it has been proposed for the same broad period that the combined effect of the decomposition of the institutions of the Roman Empire and the migration experience of the Northern invaders proved so unsettling for established practices that the ensuing uncertainty could not but lead to greater space for individual action.[3] There is also knowledge about experiences of liberty in rather self-governed cities from the early second millennium onwards; and these observations can be combined with those on cultural change associated with literature and teaching in the new universities.[4] Nevertheless the most common reference is to the Renaissance in which supposedly a whole culture of individual autonomy gradually emerged, indeed pointing back to what was seen as achievements of antiquity that had temporarily been lost and should be regained. The evidence is clearly sufficient to suggest that a commitment to individual autonomy did not suddenly emerge at the supposed onset of modernity but that practices and ideas that can be read in such light date to much earlier history.

Much of the evidence cited up to this point, in turn, sits uneasily with the thesis that there is a close connection between individual autonomy and modernity in Europe. One would need to employ some notion of very gradual, long-term evolution from early 'seed-beds' (see our earlier discussion in Chapters 2 and 4). But such an approach cannot easily be sustained since it is notoriously difficult to trace practices of selfhood and autonomy across large time-spans and with limited sources of information. Furthermore, such a view also contradicts the opinions held by many of the propagators of 'modernity' at around 1800. Thus, for instance, the 'liberty of the moderns' was seen as highly distinct from any view of liberty the ancients may have held, as in Benjamin Constant's famous formulation from 1819, and antiquity then resembles more what came to be called 'traditional society'. We will come to more recent events shaping the supposed 'culture of individual autonomy' in a moment.

The reasoning sketched up to this point about the origins or early expressions of individual autonomy suffers from two shortcomings. First, it tends to claim European particularity but is devoid of comparative observations or even reflections. Second, it tends to imply society-wide diffusion of the commitment to autonomy but draws on only a few, mostly very particular persons and their expressions as sources.

We have dealt with the former argument when discussing the Greek 'origins' of democracy (in Chapter 4). Thus, there is not much need to underline that many of the references point to occurrences outside any recognizable Europe, both in space and in time: Jesus was born in the Middle East, Augustine in North Africa, and the ancient Greeks looked northwestwards towards Europe. It is more important to emphasize that the existence of historical traces that can be interpreted as experiences of individual autonomy and self-exploration in some sites does not entail that that they are absent from others. It is a peculiar leap of the European imagination to stylize the above-mentioned occurrences and connect them to form a specifically European trajectory towards individual autonomy. Would it not have been more suggestive to consider them as evidence for a general human capacity, of which we just happen to find more traces in those world-regions from which numerous early documents have been preserved in writing?

Let us just give one example of an alternative representation. In her novel, *The Story of an African Farm* of 1883, the South African writer Olive Schreiner describes how children living on a farm in South Africa look at rock-paintings by the San people who lived in this area in earlier periods and were subjected by European settlers, who referred to them as 'Bushmen'. The author lets Waldo, a fourteen-year-old boy, say:

> 'It seems that the stones are really speaking – speaking of the old things, of the time when the strange fishes and animals lived that are turned into stone now, and the lakes were here; and then of the time when the little Bushmen lived here, so small and so ugly, and used to sleep in the wild dog holes, and in the sloots, and eat snakes, and shot the bucks with their poisoned arrows. It was one of them, one of these old wild Bushmen, that painted those,' said the boy, nodding toward the pictures – 'one who was different from the rest. He did not know why, but he wanted to make something beautiful – he wanted to make something, so he made these. He worked hard, very hard, to find the juice to make the paint; and then he found this place where the rocks hang over, and he painted them. To us they are only strange things, that make us laugh; but to him they were very beautiful.'[5]

Waldo mobilizes in his statement the prevalent imagination of colonial thought and its scholarly branch, anthropology, of the time. But he also recognizes a similarity between the painting 'Bushman' and himself: the desire to create and to express something of his view of the world, to make a difference. Obviously, Waldo is one of the voices of the author, Olive Schreiner, a white-skinned South African woman with an English cultural background. Schreiner's imagination avoids the leap of seeing the other as a radically different human being, the appearances that Waldo mentions notwithstanding. Rather, she recognizes something of her own – something that we can label individual autonomy and self-exploration, but can also characterize in other terms.

Waldo's words can also serve us to discuss the second weakness of the reasoning about the European culture of individual autonomy. Waldo makes a clear distinction between the painter and the other San: 'one who was different from the rest'. Without this being explicit for a long time, an underlying assumption in the history of individual autonomy similarly is that few human beings at a given moment are capable of, or are inclined to, individual autonomy and self-exploration. Waldo's usage emphasizes the 'difference' as decisive for the capacity to create, for artistic creativity. In the tradition of individualist political philosophy, as we shall see in a moment in more detail, autonomy, independence and responsibility are connected in such a way that by far not everyone in society has the preconditions to be free. Faced with claims made in the light of the democratic political imaginary, late nineteenth-century sociology operated with a distinction between elites and masses or crowds, where again only the elites are capable of reasoned and intentional agency. These examples may suffice to say that the 'culture of individual autonomy' has certainly not been 'European' in the sense of orientations and values being diffused across European societies. It was present in certain places and from certain times onwards, but it did not become widely diffused until late in the twentieth century.

We return to the current place of the commitment to individual autonomy in Europe in conclusion of this chapter. For the time being, our explorations in the history of such 'culture' have remained inconclusive. Even though there are clearly significant instances of the experience of, and commitment to, individual autonomy in Europe and in adjacent 'pre-European' world-regions, their existence neither suggests that such an individualistic culture was specific to Europe nor that it spread from early beginnings gradually through the entire European societies. To explain why such a view is nevertheless held, we now change approach and look at identifiable historical moments when thoughts and practices change in the direction of greater emphasis on individuals.

The individual as rights-holder

In a first step, we look at the notion of the individual human being as a rights-holder as a European invention that shows the commitment to individual autonomy. This case also lends itself to the change in approach. The notion, namely, that every human being has equal rights is sometimes traced back towards its alleged origins in European history. Then, a combination of elements is invoked which contains: components of ancient Greek philosophy, in particular the *stoa*; references to 'all human beings' in the New Testament and the notion that human beings were created in the image of God; and the concept of rights in Roman law. Any attempt to derive European origins of human rights from such observations, however, encounters the objections that we mentioned above. On this politically delicate matter, furthermore, counter-claims have not failed to arise. Alternative justifications for human rights in Confucianism were apparently already invoked at the drafting of the United Nations Declaration of Human Rights after the Second World War. The Cyrus cylinder, found in Persia and dating to the sixth century BCE, is sometimes considered the earliest known written statement of human rights. It is plausible to assume that the general idea that human beings should be considered as equal and that there is an obligation to treat them as equal is not the creation of any particular civilization, but has been proposed in many places and at many times.

In turn, the question is transformed when we look at instances in which human rights were invoked as such, namely explicitly as the equal rights of all individual human beings, and in which such invocation was meant to be put into practice to resolve significant topical issues. This, we argue, is the case from the early sixteenth century onwards. It happened in Europe, but it is not a 'European' affair.

Faced with the enslavement, subjection and killing of the native inhabitants whom the Spanish invaders encountered in America in the years after the first landing of their ships, Bartolomé de las Casas developed a doctrine of human rights and defended it against his opponent Ginés de Sepùlveda in what became known as the Valladolid-Salamanca debates of 1550–1551, officially organized by the Spanish king Charles V to receive scholarly advice on how to treat the native Americans. Organized human groups had always been aware of 'others', and had conceptualized their relations to them, such as between Hellenes and Barbarians, in terms of 'asymmetrical counter-concepts'.[6] These had, however, also always been somewhat specific others, about whom something was known or, at least, imagined. The native Americans, in contrast, had not been expected. They appeared, as Las Casas should underline, in their full 'innocence'. Thus, the encounter with them raised the question of the understanding of human beings as a species, and the limits of this species. The question was no longer how the 'other' was different from 'us', but whether those others were human beings. If this question was to be answered affirmatively, as Las Casas maintained, then ethical limits needed to be imposed on how one could deal with them and the lands they inhabited. This was the moment when the notion of human rights as the equal rights of all human beings emerged. It was a radical conceptual innovation, the importance of which is not diminished by the fact that the institutional conclusion derived from it, expressed in a decree by Charles V, was soon withdrawn under pressure from the Spanish merchants and the settlers who benefitted from exploiting America and the Americans. It was continued with the elaboration of the notion of natural rights and found a political culmination in the 1789

Declaration of the Rights of Man and Citizen in France. In 1948, the United Nations Declaration of Human Rights is the attempt at reaching global consensus about such notion of rights, including a detailed outline of their main contents. Across this trajectory, individual human beings were increasingly seen as rights-holder, arguably an important condition for developing individual autonomy. In the first instance, however, such view did not have ontological implications. The ways in which human beings entertained bonds with other human beings were not yet being reconsidered.

Individualist ontology (1): the knowledge-seeking subject

The encounter with the native Americans raised a question that had not been posed as such before. Similarly, politico-religious developments in Europe (to which we return in detail in Chapter 7) challenged what was hitherto considered as certain, namely the common moral basis of the communities of Christians organized within the Roman Church. Taking the encounter with the Americans and the split of the Christian churches in the aftermath of the Reformation together, Europe had entered into a period of marked uncertainty about the sources of knowledge and the justification of power. The resort to the individual human being turned out to be a possibility of restoring certainty and putting power on new foundations of legitimacy. In this sense, Las Casas's notion of human rights was meant to provide orientation for the attitudes and relations to the native Americans. It prepared the ground for a much more comprehensive rethinking of human nature.

The doubts about the humanness of the native Americans, the hitherto unknown ones, was a prelude to larger doubts. The wars among Christians in Europe further shook basic certainties in ways in which wars against known 'infidels', such as in the crusades or the '*reconquista*', had not done, because they undermined assumptions about the very possibility of common ethical bases. At such a moment of existential doubt, the need was perceived to reconstitute certainties on new foundations. Las Casas's move towards the individual human being served as a source of inspiration.[7] Arguably provoked by the troubles of the religious wars in France,[8] René Descartes provided with his *Discourse on Method* (1637) the outstanding example for going one step further, beyond the view of the individual as a rights-holder, and resort to the individual human being as the sole source of certainty: *cogito ergo sum*. His method, to be emulated by many followers and creating a major intellectual 'tradition of modernity' (Jacques Derrida), performs a double intellectual move. It first withdraws from the treacherous wealth of sensations that come from the socio-historical world to establish what they hold to be those very few indubitable assumptions from which theorizing can safely proceed. And subsequently, it reconstructs an entire world from those very few assumptions. Within the intellectual history of European modernity, the notion of autonomous individual subjects and their rationality has been the recurrent key assumption. In other words, this thinking takes the double modern signification of autonomy and mastery as an unquestionable starting-point of all reasoning. Thus, it sees human beings as giving themselves their own laws and as being capable of mastering the world. For both features to be fully attained, this human being needs to distance himself from the world, to step out of it and reach a superior position, to be able to consider the world as an object that can be both known and controlled. The proponents of the method tend to think that the first move *decontaminates understanding*, any arbitrary and contingent aspects being removed. And that the second move creates a *pure image* of the world, of scientific and/or philosophical validity, from which then further conclusions, including practical ones, can be drawn.

Without opening here a discussion of the possible merits of the first move,[9] it has often been objected that such move does not – and cannot – accomplish its objectives. The concepts of the individual and their rationality – or whatever other concepts are chosen as starting assumptions – are never pure, or merely procedural and formal, never devoid of substance. As a consequence, they cannot mark any unquestionable beginning, from which thinking can safely start out, and doubts can be raised about any world that is erected on their foundations, that is, about the subsequent second move. However, it was exactly doubt about the multifarious perceptions of uncertain epistemic status that emanate from the world that made this thinking arise in the first place.

John Dewey called this approach, critically, the 'spectator theory of knowing',[10] namely the view that the world is exposed to the human gaze and that it is exactly this distance between the knowing subject and the object to be known that allows for certain knowledge. This idea is sometimes – and arguably wrongly – traced to Plato's distinction between a realm of essence and a realm of appearance. However, it acquires its particular modern guise when it is developed in response to radical doubt about the certainty of the world. The spectator theory of knowing thus starts out from a radical scepticism, from the attitude that nothing can be taken for granted. And it is in response to the doubts about the world around us as we experience it that the quest for certainty needs to proceed through a distancing from the world to gain an 'outside' look at it. The distancing from the sensations of the world was considered a precondition for the identification of those very few indubitable assumptions on which claims for valid knowledge can be erected.

The critique of this attitude, in contrast, held that such modernist distancing was neither warranted nor achievable. It was not warranted since 'one doubts on specific grounds';[11] there are always – even for Descartes – claims 'beyond reasonable doubt' and knowledge would proceed from such claims. It was not achievable because unlimited doubt would even affect the proposition about such doubt itself. As Wittgenstein put it: 'If, therefore, I doubt or am uncertain about this being my hand (in whatever sense), why not in that case about the meaning of these words as well?'[12] He himself observes the distinction between these two arguments, but also the difficulty to keep them always distinct. 'There are cases where doubt is unreasonable, but others where it seems logically impossible. And there seems to be no clear boundary between them.'[13]

Individualist ontology (2): the individual as source of legitimation

Such criticism accompanied the modernist 'method' from its beginning. Nevertheless, the modernist approach spread to other areas, not least because of the urgency of the problems that needed to be addressed and the scarcity of other resources to address them. While Descartes defined the urgency in epistemic terms – as lack of certainty – his contemporary Thomas Hobbes, equally witness to religious strife, defined it in political terms – as lack of legitimacy and justification.

As is well known, Hobbes, and after him John Locke and Jean-Jacques Rousseau, developed the theory of a social contract as the foundation of a political order on the agreement between individuals. It is less often observed that they required an imaginary distancing in space to make their intellectual distancing device operable.[14] The social contract is that which moves human beings out of the state of nature into the state of political society. The hypothesis of the state of nature, in turn, became possible because of the encounter with the native Americans. 'In the beginning, all the world was America', as Locke said.[15]

Social-contract theorists imagined the native Americans as human beings before a state in which bonds between them had been created and higher forms of cooperation had emerged. That is why the theorists could transform them into individuals who have natural rights and on whose will political forms could only legitimately be based. They knew well that no such individuals existed in Europe or Asia, in the Old World, in which the state of nature had long been left behind. But supposedly witnessing such individuals elsewhere allowed them to endow contemporary Europe with a hypothetical history during which the leap from the state of nature to the state of civil society was taken. The recourse to this leap still provided legitimacy and justification for power in Hobbes's and Locke's time, but also an angle for critique for the latter and for Rousseau when observations suggested that this contract had been breached by the powers-that-be.

As a critique of illegitimate and unjustified power, social-contract theory inspired the US Declaration of Independence and the French Revolution, but during the nineteenth century it soon became considered too 'thin' a theory, to paraphrase Michael Walzer,[16] to base a polity upon. 'Thick' theories of the social bond emerged forcefully, in two main versions: the theory of the cultural-linguistic bond that inspired European nationalism, and the theory of the socio-economic bond that inspired socialist and communist thinking. After two world wars and the rise of political regimes that were based on extreme versions of such political theories, the individualist assumption returned into fashion. It was normatively championed by Isaiah Berlin in his 'Two Concepts of Liberty',[17] but it was fully returned to the politico-conceptual agenda by John Rawls in his *Theory of Justice* of 1971. This treatise rests its claim to superior insight on the construction of a decontextualized 'original position' from where individual human beings enter into contract with one another under a 'veil of ignorance'. Rawls's approach formalizes the 'method' that we have seen at work in Descartes. To isolate ourselves from all sensations coming from the world, we place ourselves under the veil, and this then provides the original position from which otherwise unsolvable problems can be successfully addressed. In contrast to Descartes, Rawls does not aim at enhancing knowledge. Rather, he is aware of an abundance of existing knowledge that needs to be forgotten, with the help of the veil of ignorance, to arrive at a viable polity. The emphasis on the individual no longer aims at enhancing the certainty of knowledge, it aims at providing justification, and this at the expense of knowledge.[18] Social-contract theory moves the modernist method from epistemology to politics.

Beyond ignoring the multitude of social bonds between human beings, modernist political thought also offers a very particular interpretation of the problem of constituting a polity. Focusing on the individual, it suggests that under conditions of equality free and reason-endowed human beings will arrive at an agreement between themselves about the most appropriate rules for the life in common – no other considerations are necessary. The underlying assumption is that political order will emerge as the aggregate of the preferences of free and equal individuals. This thinking underestimates the degree to which the exercise of collective autonomy may require more than just summing up individual wills – an issue of which Jean-Jacques Rousseau was aware, but which the individualist-liberal tradition of thinking prefers to ignore.[19]

Individualist ontology (3): the passions and the interests

One reason for this neglect was the urgency of the situation during the seventeenth century, during which faith in the individual was meant to overcome the social and political uncertainty. During the eighteenth century, however, another reason emerged, replacing the rather blind faith of the preceding century. Rather than postulating that freedom and reason of individuals were sufficient to gain certain knowledge and to ground a political order, mechanisms were now considered that would create and sustain new kinds of orders.

Like the notion of the social contract, the idea of expanding commerce also emerged in response to persistent strife, warfare and misery. Human beings were seen as driven by passions and by interests, none of which are *a priori* good or bad, but the latter ones were considered stable and predictable, whereas the former ones fluctuating and uncontrollable. While human nature could not be changed, society could possibly be transformed in such a way that social interactions are more driven by interests than by passions. When human beings increasingly trade goods with each other because of specialization and a division of labour, so the argument goes, then they depend on each other and will no longer fight wars against each other. In such an arrangement, furthermore, the pursuit of one's own interest in producing more and selling more of one's product will tend to maximize the general level of satisfaction of needs. The former reasoning is known as the 'sweet commerce' (*doux commerce*) argument, originating in Montesquieu, the latter one as the 'wealth of nations' argument, made famous by Adam Smith. Taken together, these were strong 'arguments for capitalism before its triumph', in Albert Hirschman's apt formula (even though they might better be called 'arguments for commercial society').[20] Rather than making a leap from individuals to social and political order, they now introduced arguments why the interaction between free and interest-driven individuals would lead to a form of self-regulation that optimizes collective outcomes. That this was not as straightforwardly true as initially suggested should already have become evident in the early nineteenth century.[21]

Up to this point, our reflections should have served to underline two observations. First, we find instances of experiences of, and commitments to, individual autonomy in the history of Europe and adjacent world-regions. However, these instances do not warrant the notion that the commitment to individual autonomy originated in Europe, and they are too selective to confirm that a 'culture of individual autonomy' spread across European societies from a certain time onwards. Secondly, we observe how a focus on the individual human being becomes a conceptual resource to deal with urgent and dramatic social and political problems. It is a resource of last resort, when other means fail, no triumphant discovery of a superior interpretation of the world. As such, though, it becomes increasingly persuasive as problems persist, and its use spreads from epistemic to political to economic matters.

Two further questions need to be asked to conclude these reflections on individual autonomy in Europe. First, we have to ask whether today individual autonomy has become the core value in European societies, and maybe for modernity in general. This question namely persists, whatever the reasons for the rise of individual autonomy may have been across history. Secondly, we need to ask whether the rise of such commitment and, importantly, its sedimentation in institutions has generated a social trend towards individualization, as has often been argued in sociological theory and tends to be today overwhelmingly confirmed in empirical social research. Both of these claims have been and are being made for European modernity, and we need to investigate them in the light of our preceding reflections.

Individual autonomy as the sole core value?

Historians of Europe characterize the nineteenth century often as the age of competing political ideologies, and sociologists complement this view by announcing from the 1960s onwards the end of ideologies. By the 1980s, that is, by the time of the fall of existing socialism and after the end of the varieties of authoritarianism in the south of Europe, the verdict seems clear: the commitment to individual autonomy was the telos of European modernity, and it had by and large been reached. To give just one significant example: the critical European philosopher Axel Honneth introduces his major study *Freedom's Right* by stating that 'of all the ethical values prevailing and competing for dominance in modern society, only one has been capable of leaving a truly lasting impression on our institutional order: freedom, i.e. the autonomy of the individual'.[22] And a few years later he gives his sequel volume on the idea of socialism an epigraph taken from Walt Whitman's poem 'To a foil'd European revolutionaire' from 1856, which includes the phrase: 'Liberty is to be subserv'd whatever the case'.[23] At first sight, this may seem to be an indication that the criticism of the commitment to individual liberty as an ontological starting-point, mentioned at several points above, had subsided. How should we understand this development, and what is indeed the adequate conclusion in our time?

Above, we had suggested that an individualist ontology had indeed been proposed and elaborated from the middle of the seventeenth to the beginning of the nineteenth century, but also that strong critiques had arisen during the nineteenth and early twentieth centuries, not least in the light of the experiences with the principle of individual liberty. In the course of those years, the case for individual liberty was repeatedly restated: from Benjamin Constant's early statement on the 'freedom of the moderns' in 1819 to James Stuart Mill's elaboration of the principle of liberty in 1858 to Isaiah Berlin's distinction, of 1958, between negative and positive liberty and his cautious but adamant defence of the former over the latter. These are the key contributors to the tradition of European political liberalism. Their thought constitutes a tradition as they restate the same basic principle in the light of different historical experiences. For Berlin, indeed, it is a cumulation of historical experiences, with totalitarianism as the latest one, that leads him to his defence of negative liberty.

Nevertheless, the history of European political thought cannot be written as one of the rise of such liberalism, which for the sake of clarity we will refer to as individualist liberalism.[24] This is so for a number of reasons. First, the individualist liberals have been unable to develop a coherent case for the primacy of individual liberty. Mostly, they have been aware of this: Constant acknowledged that ancient freedom had merits that modern freedom does not have; Mill recognized other forms of political thought in Europe that took aspects into account that he could not integrate; and Berlin had to state explicitly that he did not succeed in separating individual liberty from other significant political values. Secondly, there has been a European tradition of non-individualist liberalism that can be seen as reaching from Alexis de Tocqueville to Claude Lefort. These thinkers underline the form-giving of political society that constitutes the individual, not the other way round. Thus, democracy as a form of society can both provide freedom to singular human beings and constitute bonds of solidarity between them. Thirdly, even though it has been weakened by intellectual and political events, this other tradition has not subsided at all. To return to the example above: Axel Honneth, who gives primacy to individual autonomy does so by redefining liberty as 'social freedom'. His concerns are 'the social foundations of democratic life', and the rights of the individual are one of several components of the recognition of other human beings in social interaction.[25] Fourthly, current European institutions are clearly committed to the autonomy of the individual, but never exclusively so. To use a key example, not least because it is European and because it had recently generated intense debate: the Charter of Fundamental Rights of the European Union, agreed upon at the Nice summit in 2000 and made legally binding as part of the Lisbon treatise of 2009, commits the EU to 'solidarity' as well as 'the principle of democracy' on an equal level with the freedom of the individual. First appearances notwithstanding, thus, European modernity has never been committed to individual autonomy as the sole or most basic value. It is committed to individual autonomy, true, but it keeps leading an open and contested debate about the relation of this commitment to other ones such as, most importantly, solidarity and democracy.

Individualization as the direction of European history?

From the early nineteenth century onwards, juridical change such as the formalization of individual rights following the Declaration of the Rights of Man and of the Citizen and the granting of commercial freedom gave a push to the orientation towards individual autonomy. Thus, despite the qualifications mentioned above, it remains a possibility that the increasing institutional commitment to individual autonomy may have set in motion a process of individualization, understood as human beings seeing themselves more and more as individuals and less and less as members of collectivities such as societies, nations or classes. This has been a core theorem of sociological thought. A main and very striking statement remains the one by Karl Marx and Friedrich Engels in *The Communist Manifesto*:

> The bourgeoisie, wherever it has got the upper hand, has put an end to all feudal, patriarchal, idyllic relations. It has pitilessly torn asunder the motley feudal ties that bound man to his 'natural superiors', and has left remaining no other nexus between man and man than naked self-interest, than callous 'cash payment'. It has drowned the most heavenly ecstasies of religious fervour, of chivalrous enthusiasm, of philistine sentimentalism, in the icy water of egotistical calculation. It has resolved personal worth into exchange value, and in place of the numberless indefeasible chartered freedoms, has set up that single, unconscionable freedom – Free Trade.

Related arguments about individualization and rationalization, in different varieties, can be found in many early sociologists, such as Max Weber, Émile Durkheim and Georg Simmel. The assumption that such trends marked the history of modernity is very widespread, up to the present day.

Already in the course of the nineteenth century, however, negative consequences of such individualization came to be perceived. Rather than increasing the spaces for individual autonomy, it was seen as disembedding human beings from their social contexts. Thus, Tocqueville diagnosed the rise of conformism as a consequence of equal freedom in US democracy. Marx would identify a particular form of alienation as the result of commodification, namely human relations turning into relations between things when human beings encounter each other on markets. Somewhat later, Weber expressed his concern about the limited range of forms of conducting one's life when exposed to the rationalizing demands of modern capitalism. According to these analyses, the conditions for individual autonomy had not at all improved during nineteenth-century European modernity. True, one may have doubts about the adequacy of these diagnoses: possibly these observers mistakenly applied an aristocratic-bourgeois view of self-realization to the peasant and worker majority population to whom gaining equal freedom meant something different, at least as a first historical experience. Nevertheless, these analyses rightly question the immediacy of the connection between individual rights and individualization.

Subsequently, throughout the first two-thirds of the twentieth century, one can indeed observe a process of collectivization with the building of mass organizations such as parties and trade unions, often emerging from social movements of protest, and the standardizing of life-expectations and forms of behaviour, enhanced through schools, mass media and mass consumption. These collective conventions and institutions of 'organized modernity' (on which more in Chapter 8) include their members as individuals, true, but they do so by means of standardizing roles and homogenizing outlooks on the world. Thus, the term individualization is hardly useful to characterize the period between the 1890s and the 1950s in many societies. In turn, the social transformation that started during the 1960s is often seen as having led to highly increased individualization and new forms of individualism. How this new individualization should be understood and, in particular, whether it can be regarded as enhancing individual autonomy is currently under debate, with which we will engage in Chapter 9.

7

Religion and Modernity in Europe:

The Christians and the Others – the Religious-political Entanglement

Religion and politics

Both religion and politics deal with the symbolization and ritualization of order, and the normative legitimization of action. In this sense they are connected. They are mutually reinforcing one another at the same time as there is a tension between them. Religion and politics are nevertheless often seen as separated. In the paradigm of modernity as continuous differentiation, specialization and division of labour, religion came, like the political, the economic and the culture to be seen as a particular sector of social life, connected but separate. Not least the thesis of modernity as continuous secularization, within Weber's overall interpretation of modernity as a process of permanent disenchantment, underpinned the idea of religion as a separate sphere doomed to disappear in the long run.

The secularization thesis peaked in the 1960s as we will discuss in a later section of this chapter. The thesis became problematic against the backdrop of extensive empirical evidence of what some observers called a return of religion to the political arena and others referred to as the politicization of religion.[1]

On the basis of this development the idea of a principle separation between religion and politics, i.e. religion and modernity, is no longer tenable. Religion and politics are entangled. Johann Arnason talks about a religio-political nexus and argues that this nexus is old, emerging in the Axial Age civilizations (Chapter 2), but still relevant.[2] In the Christian Roman Empire, as well as in the Islamic caliphate, religion and imperial structures merged under the principle of one God, one emperor, one world empire, one belief, although the unity of *imperium* and *ecclesia* soon split up in the Holy Roman Empire of the German nation founded by Charlemagne and the Catholic Church under the pope.[3] However, even if they split up, they both consisted of a religio-political nexus with a meta-institutional status, where the political dimension, in the sense of an overall execution of power, intertwined with the religious power which in particular played a legitimizing role.

The legitimization of religious as well as political power in the nexus was contentiously opening up new possibilities of protest and critique. Rival cognitive doctrines emerged, in particular in monotheistic traditions. Religious criticism merged with social criticism linked to visions of a more just political order. The contrast between legitimizing and subversive trends linked up with a polarization between orthodoxy and heterodoxy.

Western Christendom experienced, in comparison with other religions, probably the most varied versions and the most momentous transformations of the religio-political nexus, but Islam had a similar profile. The early modern formation under the retrospect contested label of absolutism was a late product of this long history. Sacral foundations were crucial to the claims and practices of absolutism, 'the king by the Grace of God', and legitimized its influence. Modern nationalism and modern democracy as well as the revolutionary claims for democracy and the totalitarian transformation of the mass societies of the twentieth century were all significantly shaped by the absolutist religio-political background.[4]

Another link between religion and politics deals with monotheism and violence. Jan Assmann triggered a vivid debate with his argument that violence accompanied the emergence of monotheist religions, more precisely violence in the name of God, not as a logical consequence or as necessity but as a potential. He refers to the distinction between true and false that drives the orthodoxy-heterodoxy dynamics and the introduction of an emphatic concept of truth that implied the principle of incompatibility. The outcome was orthodoxy, the exegetics of the right doctrine which determined what was false and exterminated it. Assmann had violent truth claims *within* monotheist religions in mind and violent persecution of what was defined as disbelievers with Judaism as his case.[5]

Others have emphasized the violence *between* monotheistic religions.[6] The historical violence that emerged from monotheist religions did not only deal with internal conflicts between true and false, right and wrong, and with competing monotheisms with violent clashes with other religions, such as Christians against Jews and Muslims, but also with civilization campaigns against native polytheist religions driven by the truth claim and the demonstration of economic, political and cultural power.

There are different kinds of religion and different kinds of politics. There is the difference between 'absolute' politics and routine politics, where absolute politics does not see any boundaries to political will, and everything social is seen as transformable by politics. The refusal to accept the established order and to recognize any of its boundaries gives absolute politics ultimacy, and hence a religious character.[7] In the same sense there is the difference between softer forms of religion as cultural practices and rites and more fundamentalist approaches with theological arguments. Cross-cutting this general distinction, there are culturally specific differences among the historical religions and political cultures as to the symbolization of order.[8]

The question of what is religious and what is political is difficult to settle in an unequivocal way. The outbreak of the Crimean War (1853–1856) is a case in point. The Crimean War was a consequence of a Russian attempt to expand in the Balkans at the cost of the disintegrating Ottoman Empire, and in particular the British and French ambition to prevent this expansion. The direct trigger was the removal of the silver star from the Church of the Nativity in Bethlehem. Sultan Abdülmecid I removed the star in 1852 which provoked the Russian claim for a protectorate over Palestine. The French emperor Napoleon III refused to allow the Russian protection of the Orthodox Christians in the Balkans to stand for the protection of all Christians and raised claims to Palestine in the name of Roman Catholicism. The British government lurked in the background suspicious about the intentions of the Russian and the French emperors. Nobody would call the Crimean War a religious war even if there was a religious argument at the beginning. However, if we with the same question move back in history another couple of centuries and ask it about the Thirty Years War, some would probably see an immediate parallel to the Crimean War but more would argue that there was a religious dimension.

The examples demonstrate that the empirical distinction between religion and politics in the past to a large extent is a matter of historiographic conventions, and these conventions are often not neutral but expressions of particular perspectives which are more or less contested. One might even say that the conventions have a mythical dimension.[9] Walter Benjamin, in his famous little text 'Capitalism and Religion' in 1921, only four pages in print, reflected on the mythical and religious dimension of modern capitalism which dilutes the boundary between *Geld* and *Geist*, money and spirit, and thus dismantles a major cultural distinction.[10]

What is politics? What is religion? Iran after the revolution in 1979 can be described as a hierocracy or a theocracy with absolutist pretensions. Is it a religious state? Were the centralized and absolute European states supported by Lutheran or Catholic Orthodox churches in the seventeenth century religious states? Was the Thirty Years War a religious war? Were the European throne-altar compacts in the nineteenth century political or religious?

The answer to these and similar questions are hardly a clear yes or no. Religion was an instrument in military power struggles as well as in domestic social conflicts. The treaty in Augsburg in 1555 ('whose realm, his religion') implied the political instrumentalization of religion, since many princes did not primarily choose the confession of their states on the mere basis of personal belief but on the basis of political interest. Religion became an instrument in the European power game between the emperor and the princes of the empire, a power game that involved the close although rival relationship between the emperor and the pope. The instrument failed to stabilize Europe, however, as the Thirty Years War (1618–1648) demonstrates. Augsburg was just an armistice in a religious conflict that substantially dealt with much more than religion.

Although entanglement is the main relationship between religion and politics this does not mean that everything is entanglement. Today's Islamic State (IS) is not a theocracy or a hierocracy, it is neither Islamic nor a state in any conventional understanding of the terms, but brutal power which despite the *jihad* tradition has little to do with religion. It is rather reminiscent of terror movements like Pol Pot. The systematic destruction of irreparable cultural heritage treasures by the IS is not religious iconoclasm but just a raw demonstration of power.

The tradition of Holy War for political purposes is old. The crusades were one early expression. The nationalist movements in Europe in the early nineteenth century had a strong subtext of Holy War. In the German wars for unification, Napoleon was depicted as the Devil. Mazzini saw himself and Italy as the World Redeemer in his cosmopolitan national project for the Third Rome after the First Rome of the emperors and the Second Rome of the Catholic Church. Numerous wars and punishment expeditions in the colonies had a Christian underpinning of civilizing mission justifying cruelty and violence which triggered counter actions. Many anti-imperial revolts and wars in the nineteenth century had a religious motivation. The classical example is the Indian Sepoy rebellion of 1857. The Persian philosopher and ideologist Al-Afghani argued that the dictates of industrial and financial capitalism would destroy the culture of the Islamic countries. Although Al-Afghani himself was not a very pious Muslim, he became an uncompromising defender of Islam against Western outrages, urging for a global *jihad* under the direction of the Ottoman Empire. The charismatic Muhammad Ahmad in the 1870s commanded a violent chiliastic movement driven by religious salvation expectations against the Khedive of Egypt and his British ally proclaiming himself the Mahdi, the messianic redeemer of the Islamic faith. The Boxer Rebellion in China around 1900 is a third case of anti-Christian, anti-colonial and anti-West violent conflicts against white foreigners representing and disseminating Christendom, and native Christian converts.

The extremes along the religion–politics axis are easier to discern than the mixed forms. The same is true if we shift from the top-down perspective of the ruling elites to the bottom-up perspective of the socio-religious protest movements. The religious protest had historically, and continues to have, a social dimension. Religious fundamentalism and radicalism spilled over into political fundamentalism and radicalism and vice versa.

The philosophical and civilizational enlightenment project had not only a dimension of liberal tolerance but also one of intolerant educating fundamentalism. The Enlightenment had a dimension of civil religion around the master narrative of progress. Alexander Herzen, the Russian philosopher and writer on socialism, fellow of Marx and Bakunin in the organization of the International Workingmen's Association in London, referred to the eighteenth century as one of the most religious periods in history, blessed by 'Pope Voltaire' and the 'secular clericals' of the French Revolution. Liberalism was the last religion although not from another but from this world, he argued. He viewed the French Revolution as the end of history, the final stage in social development of a society based on humanism and harmony.[11]

The Enlightenment programme with science-based belief in progress which put reason against religious superstition took on itself religious proportions where the main difference was that the dream of perfection was located in this world. In the Marxist version there was even an apocalyptic dimension. The exegetics about the right way to perfection was not that different from the religious exegetics about the right way to redemption. Economic theory became dogmatic belief and the international law belief in the legal capacity to regulate the future became a utopian dream not that far from religious belief.[12]

Religion as authority and as protest

The dynamics and entanglements of religion and politics are particularly visible in the confrontation of authority by religious and political protest movements. In the meeting point between top-down rule and bottom-up challenge religion and politics reinforce one another mutually and produce movement. They are often entangled in ways that make it difficult to separate them. Max Weber drew attention to these clashes in his philosophy around the concepts of disenchantment and secularization. There is certainly a dystopian subtext of implacability in his reading of history. However, he also discerned a different kind of dynamics based on repeated eruptions of protest and establishment of religious sects ever since the institutionalization of churches. The religious protest operated between the poles of orthodoxy and heterodoxy, between the authority to proclaim the true doctrine of faith and challenges of that authority. In the wake of Weber, Shmuel Eisenstadt elaborated a historical panorama assessing the importance of heterodoxies and sects as forces of social transformation. The heterodoxies and sectarian movements emerged from within the world-religions offering alternative normative orders on the basis of reinterpretation of fundamental values of their respective traditions. Conflicts between religious orthodoxy and heterodoxies resulted in cultural-political reconstruction. These conflicts often had a fundamentalist dimension.[13]

Eisenstadt's investigation dealt with the Axial Age civilizations (c. 800–c. 200 BCE; see Chapter 2), but his matrix is applicable also for later periods. In the early tenth century, Western monasticism based on the principle of *ora et labora*, pray and work, had become ever more dependent on the local nobles who provided them with land but controlled all that belonged to the territories under their jurisdiction. The ascetic ideals were ever less practised in the monasteries. A reform movement began in the monastery in Cluny, France in the tenth century with the aim to restore the old practices and ideals of asceticism and poverty, and to break the secular interference and the Church's tight integration with the feudal order.[14]

This reform movement was the first in a long row of Christian religious protest with a political implication. By the beginning of the twelfth century new waves of organized dissident protests permeated urbanizing areas. The Waldensians were one of these movements, also referred to as the Poor Men of Lyons, a band organized by Peter Waldo, a wealthy merchant who gave away his property preaching poverty as the way to perfection. Waldensian teachings challenged the doxa and the power of the Catholic Church, which in 1215 declared the Waldensians heretical and made them subject to intense persecution. A reform movement within the Bogomil churches in Dalmatia and Bulgaria, calling for a return to the Christian message of perfection, poverty and preaching, spread as a popular mass movement to the urbanizing areas in Southwestern France: the Cathars, named from the Greek *katharsis*, meaning 'purification' or 'cleansing'. The movement had a centre in Albi in Languedoc. Therefore, they were also known as the Albigensians. In their dualistic theology heaven was the realm of God and earth the realm of Satan. On this ground they argued that civil authority had no claim since it represented the world of Satan. The movement rejected Catholic ceremonies and rites. Pope Innocent III launched the Albigensian or Cathar Crusade in 1209 which became a twenty-year military campaign supported by the inquisition against the movement.[15] The Dominican monastery order was established as papal instrument of the inquisition. The pope realized the need for internal church reform as an instrument to ward off the bottom-up attack in the struggle about theological and political power.

John Wycliffe was a fourteenth-century scholastic philosopher and reformer, and an influential dissident within the Catholic Church. He attacked the privileged status of the clergy and criticized the luxury and pomp of local parishes and church ceremonies, and emphasized the right to private interpretation of the Bible. He opposed the doctrines about good works and the sacraments as the key to salvation. The Lollards, the followers of Wycliffe, advocated iconoclasm and defended the caesaropapism of the East Roman Church where the emperor exercised a strong control over the ecclesiastical hierarchy. The Lollard movement was the precursor to the sixteenth-century church reformation movement in England.[16]

Jan Hus was a Czech philosopher and priest, Master at the Charles University in Prague, who followed up Wycliffe's English campaign on the continent. He was a key predecessor to protestantism. He had a strong influence on contemporary opinions in Central and Western Europe and a century later on Luther. He was burned at the stake for heresy at the concile in Konstanz in 1415. After his execution, the followers of his teaching against core church doctrines rebelled and defeated five consecutive papal crusades in the Hussite Wars (1420–1431).[17]

Girolamo Savonarola was another voice who a couple of generations after Hus, at the end of the fourteenth century, in renaissance Florence called for Christian renewal. He denounced clerical corruption, despotic rule and the exploitation of the poor. He prophesied the coming of a biblical flood and a new Cyrus from the north, who would reform the church. He became a punchball in the political and military power struggle between the French monarchy, the Florentine Medici republic and the pope and was, at the end, in 1498 hanged and burned in the main square in Florence.[18]

So far the continuous waves of religious protest against church abuse of power and discrepancy between preaching and practice had been treated as internal conflicts within the Catholic Church. This changed in the sixteenth century. The advance of Luther, and, in the wake of him, Calvin, Zwingli, and many others under the key concept of reformation certainly, as the term suggests, aimed at a radical change of core dimensions of doctrinaire, political and economic church structures and practices. However, 're-form' did not mean the creation of something new but the term suggested rather back to the roots, back to the situation before the false development had begun. The formal point of criticism was the sales of indulgencies where sales of grace had become an ever more important financial market for the church. However, this both concrete and symbolic point of the criticism was filled with political implications and embedded in a whole theological programme with among others claim for the translation of the Bible to vernacular languages. The programme was presented for the first time in October 1517 when Luther posted his ninety-five theses on the door of the Schloßkirche in Wittenberg – at least he did so according to the tradition; the event has never been historically documented. It is clear, however, that Luther did publish his theses, wherever he did it, and that they provoked great concern in the Vatican when the insight about their explosive power gradually emerged. In many respects the theses repeated claims that Wycliffe and Hus had already conveyed. However, then, a century and more earlier, they had not developed the same revolutionary dynamics. The time had become more condensed and the ideas more explosive in 1517.

Religion and the emergence of modernity

The Reformation movement unfolded as a rebellion of reason and enlightenment against what it argued to be obstinate and backward medieval obscurity and at the same time a campaign for a return to a pure origin. It was an event internal to Europe that had its counterpart in the change of outlook triggered by the crossing of the Atlantic Ocean, as mentioned earlier (Chapter 6). Columbus had found America believing that it was India in 1492 and Ferdinand Magellan was, when Luther began his campaign, about to prepare his circumnavigation of the earth, which would deliver the final evidence that the earth was round. The intellectual terrain was being prepared for the next revolutionary attack on the church authority as to the interpretation of the world: Copernicus's thesis in 1543 that the earth rotated around its own axis and around the sun, not the other way round as the church maintained. Global trade and financing developed rapidly and new avenues of communication at sea and land within Europe and between Europe and other continents emerged providing new perspectives on the imagery of Christianity as universal and Christendom as absolute. Gutenberg's invention of book printing provided totally new preconditions for the spread of intellectual messages. Leaflets and newspapers reported currently and fast. The preconditions of the public debate changed and it widened to involve new strata of the populations. The artists painted humans and nature close to reality with a focus on central deep perspectives and anatomy, and the humanists brought the Renaissance ideas to Europe north of the Alps. They wanted to translate the ancient sources and disseminate new education around the motto of *homo mensura*: the human being, i.e. not God, is the measure of everything.

The changes at the beginning of the sixteenth century did not only promote enlightenment and expectations for the better but also angst for the worst. The Osman sultanate had conquered Constantinople in 1453 and advanced towards the Reich. Apocalyptic visions about the approaching end of the world were recurring medieval topics, but around the turn of the sixteenth century they boomed. Hieronymus Bosch conveyed human guilt, divine punishment and sense of doom in his paintings of monsters and hellish inferno. Luther, too, was convinced that the end of time was approaching. The epoch was ambivalent as to the possibility of improvement and threat of destruction. It was a time of tension between feelings of religious and political possibilities with expectations in a better future and fears of a violent end.

In political terms the move from the divine towards the human triggered around 1500 a debate within the Roman Empire about the distribution of power between the emperor and the princes. The empire was in the worldview of the time seen as the worldly arm of the papal church in an order where they in distribution of labour between heavenly and worldly power mutually supported each other. Today one would rather see them as two global competitors which both had a political-military capacity and a legitimizing divine underpinning. The emperor was, like the pope, weakened by the rapid change of the world at the beginning of the sixteenth century, having to face new forms of critical debate. The princes were about to transform their feudal dependencies to sovereign monarchies which based their power on new kinds of centralized states with a capacity for warfare of a new kind. The princes in the German lands looked with envy on the consolidation of centralized state power in France and England in relative independence from pope and emperor. They defended themselves against the ambition of the emperor to regain and consolidate lost power in the name of protector of the church. The emperor defended the papal-imperial order. Luther became in this situation a powerful argument in the hands of the princes. This was obvious when the martial period that followed on Luther's thesis ended after almost forty years of violent conflicts with the Augsberg treaty of 1555 with the agreement of *cuius regio, eius religio*, 'whose realm, his religion', meaning that the religion of the ruler dictated the religion of his subjects. (The formula got its name only a generation later, in 1582, from the Greifswald legist Joachim Stephani.) Luther provided arguments for state confiscation of church property which fit hand in glove with the expansion of the state apparatuses and many princes therefore declared themselves supporters of the Protestant movement. The Catholic Church headed by the pope and supported by the emperor had to give up its authority over the protestant princes.

The Protestant movement triggered by Luther generated such dynamics that it went beyond being an internal church issue. It established itself as an external force and the pope treated it as such. The movement put pressure not only on the pope but also on the emperor and the princes. The pope and the emperor reacted with the Counter-Reformation. Among the princes many saw an opportunity to use the protest in their struggle against the emperor for more autonomy. The Protestant movement established itself as an independent force in opposition to the Catholic Church and the regime of the pope. However, the protection of the Protestants by the princes had a price. Luther's argument for the transfer of matters of belief from the clerical authority of the Catholic Church to the priesthood of all believers stopped half-way. The new Protestant priest reading and exposing the texts in vernacular language certainly slowly replaced the Latin-speaking Catholic priest. However, the shift from the authority of the Catholic Church to the state churches of the princes meant that Luther's priesthood of all believers became the believers obeying the priesthood of the new state churches. New orthodoxies emerged which in terms of obedience and discipline had many links to the old order. Hierarchy did not disappear.

The transformation of Lutheranism to new state church orthodoxies and hierarchies triggered new heterodoxies and new protest movements. Luther was far from the end of history. The old dynamics continued in new forms. John Calvin and Huldrych Zwingli required reform of the Lutheran Reformation. The reformist movement confronted the Lutheran Reformation orthodoxy claiming more puritan and iconoclastic approaches to religion. The imagery of the priesthood of all believers persisted despite church-hierarchical orthodox authority and triggered, in turn, new movements against Lutheran or reformist state church authority with claims for lay preachers and more religious fervour and devotedness: pietism, methodism, baptism, evangelicalism, the pentecostal movements and other kinds of free churches continuously confronted state church authority claiming more puritan and less hierarchical forms of religious practices. Many of them were fundamentalist and sectarian. The religious protest had a dimension of political protest in its challenge of hierarchy and orthodoxy. However, it also had a religious dimension. The social and material existence went hand in hand with the existence around religious symbols like sin and indulgence, justice and last judgement.

The breaking up of the reformation movement had a much broader political-religious basis than the catalyst that Luther and his Protestant fellow-combatants constituted. There was also a Catholic Reformation with Ignatius Loyola as a protagonist. The Protestant and Catholic reform movements marked a break-up on the threshold between the Middle Ages and modernity at a time when humans entered centre stage in the worldview, and Christ, half-human, half-God became the centre of the worship of the divine under the motto of *devotio moderna*. This early modern reform movement must moreover be seen in its broader framework connecting to Italian humanism, French critique of religion, and Spanish spiritualism.[19]

The 1555 treaty on religion in Augsburg did not create religious peace as the emperor and the princes had hoped for. The near future was to demonstrate that the religious peace treaty did not necessarily lead to peaceful relationships between the emperor and the princes. The Thirty Years War and the civil war in England in the mid-seventeenth century are cases in point which provoked new views. Philosophers on social contract like Hobbes and Locke reflected in the wake of these wars on the question of how to achieve domestic peace. Thomas Hobbes found the solution in an order where the subjects rendered over the authority of public political decisions to the prince who, in turn, guaranteed the subjects freedom of thought and religion in the private sphere. This was in the view of Reinhart Koselleck the 'unpolitical moment'. The contract minimized political action by people other than the sovereign. Politics became understood as administration under the ruler's discretion justified through philosophical, moral, legal and other doctrines. The grace of God no longer legitimized the ruler but the contract with the subjects, and the ruler no longer determined religious belief but the individual conscience in the private sphere. Thomas Hobbes in *Leviathan* gave a masterful account of this separation of the political and the moral, and of the public and the private: the apolitical moment.[20]

However, the individuals did not stay isolated in the private sphere as the contract with the ruler prescribed. They talked with others about things they found wrong, as well as about political matters, firstly in secret societies, but ever more in public. The new communication possibilities in the emerging embryo of mass societies were powerful in the spread of arguments which questioned the contract with the ruler that gave him exclusive priority to political decision-making. Lutheran or Catholic orthodoxy and church authority undermined the idea of religion as a private issue. Bottom-up approaches to politics and religion challenged the top-down ruler and church view. Public critique resulted in political crises and political attempts to respond to the critique. The successful responses silenced the critique but not for ever. New critique emerged from new points of departure. The dynamics between critique and crisis was a core dimension of modernity. The Enlightenment philosophers guided this movement. Politics recurred and merged with the moral issues again. In the name of morality, the civic Enlightenment intellectuals condemned the state. Their expectations of history, based on their definition of morality, triggered, in the view of Reinhart Koselleck, the crisis, which never ended, and to the most terrible outrages.[21] Religion became political as it always had been, as secret privacy or as open and public. The merger occurred under the motto of progress, the catchword of the time. The religious protest movements from pietism onwards had a prominent place in this scenario. They could draw on a long legacy of socio-religious protest since the Middle Ages.

What was religion and what was politics when top-down and bottom-up clashed about religious and social values? The protesting socio-religious people's movements (*folkrörelser/folkbevegelser*) in Northern Europe during the half-century before 1914 had an outspoken or implicit religious value subtext based on Lutheran and puritan ideals emphasizing individual responsibility, and at the same time pronounced social and political goals drove them. The conservative throne-altar complex around the state church and the court, which the people's movements confronted in the Oscarian Sweden, tried to ward off the attack with religious moralism (cf. Wilhelminian Germany and Victorian Britain), which some would call bigoted and hypocritical rather than Christian, although they were founded on arguments with provenance in Lutheran state church orthodoxy. These were obviously not the same Lutheran values as those articulated by the people's movements, or, better, the same Lutheran values were used very differently.[22] The interpretations of religion and moral, of right and wrong, were in this socio-political-religious landscape diverse; yes, they clashed, and they could be linked to incompatible political goals.

This historical outline of religion in Europe as authority and as protest, as domination and confrontation of domination shows a continuous conflict between orthodoxy and heterodox challenges of the right doctrine. There were entanglement and tension between religious and political authority. There was a continuous conflict about petrification of religious teaching and practices and about return to ascetic and puritan ideals of poverty against the backdrop of amalgamation of riches and luxuriance. The socio-religious protest transmitted a fundamentalist tradition, but ideals of asceticism and poverty became problematic when the working class began to thematize the class issue and claim social security and justice for all. There was a dimension of social protest in the religious protest, but the idealization of poverty was to erode during the second half of the nineteenth century when the social protest under the mantra of progress began to emphasize equality and welfare for all. Poor relief and social care were old Christian ideals based on the parable of the Good Samaritan. They were updated and replaced the ideals of poverty and asceticism in a more social approach of the churches which legitimized emerging conservative imageries of social responsibility under state authority as well as radical political protest movements for more social justice. Pius XI's papal encyclical *Quadragesimo Anno* in 1931 on the ethical implications of the social and economic order, issued against the backdrop of the Great Depression and mass unemployment, forty years after Leo XIII's encyclical *Rerum Novarum* addressing the conditions of the workers around 1890, are cases in point.

Modernity and secularization, social integration and multiculturalism

'Secularization' is one of the most persistent concepts in the discussion of the relationships between religion and modernity. According to the conventional understanding of the secularization thesis, religion loses legitimizing authority when modernity unfolds on the basis of reason and rationalization. Secularization is the consequence of rationalization.

Religion is about what we cannot know, where belief replaces knowledge. Belief creates certainty about what is uncertain in the reflection on transcendence. Reflection on the transcendental can lead to introversion, *Verinnerlichung*, and mysticism, to eremitic isolation from the world in the search for the divine as an individual relationship. Asceticism and ideals of purification accompany the search. This kind of religious practice loses importance with modernity. However, the transcendental reflection can also provoke claims for collective action driven not only by the same religious ideals of asceticism and purification but also by their connection to social protest. The ideals might originally be religious but the secular view considers them to be secular phenomena.

Auguste Comte's outline of positivism told about a growing accumulation of knowledge as an alternative way to transform uncertainty to certainty. His narrative constituted a meta-norm for the secularization thesis. His focus on knowledge production is a somewhat different approach than that of Weber, who concentrated on religion as social movement. Both approaches provided interpretation in the long debate on the nature of religion. Weber used the concept of secularization only at a few occasions. He talked about continuous disenchantment in the wake of the proceeding of modernity. In the communist world Karl Marx was the authority who validated the thesis of secularization in a third version.

Max Weber referred to the development of modes of sociability in modern societies in terms of process. In this context, in his text on the protestant sects, he referred a couple of times to the *Säkularisationsprozeß* or '*Säkularisierungs*'-*Prozeß*.[23] Weber took it for a historical fact that in his capitalist modernity of the early twentieth century, religion had lost much of the cultural value it had had in the past and reflected on how it happened. His view was retrospective from his present. It was not a prognosis for the future. Secularization with general decline of religion was already there as an accompanying dimension of modernity and capitalism.

However, rather than talking about *secularization*, Weber referred to a process of bureaucratization and *disenchantment* leading to a *stahlhartes Gehäuse*, a shell as hard as steel, conventionally somewhat improperly translated as 'iron cage'. He was convinced that the generations after him would not experience flowering summers but 'the polar night of icy darkness and hardship'. On this point he dared a prognosis. The key concept in Weber's world image was disenchantment much more than secularization. At the conceptual level the poet Schiller inspired him with his exposition of the *Entgötterung der Natur*, the de-deification of nature. Schiller's *Entgötterung* became Weber's *Entzauberung*.

Max Weber saw a religious connection in the origin of capitalism, which was the result of a protestant work ethic based on hard work, methodic economic activity, a frugal life and the reinvestment of savings. With the development of capitalism followed both religious and legal rationalization and the two were interconnected. Legal rationalization meant the de-sacralization of law. In the modern secular state law ruled supreme. Religious rationalization meant that the issue of transcendence lost meaning.

Weber finished *Protestant Ethics* with a clear statement on this point: 'The modern man is in general, even with the best will, unable to give religious conscience a significance for the conduct of life, culture and national character which it had [in the past].'[24] People of his time were simply unable to imagine how religious the West had been a few centuries earlier. Weber compared the two moments of the unfolding capitalist modernity: the point of departure for his sociology of religion, the age of 'lived religiosity' in the seventeenth century, and his own Wilhelminian epoch at the beginning of the twentieth century, which made him talk about secularization and general loss of meaning. The later exegetics on the meaning of the protestant ethics have established a causative link between protestantism and capitalism. However, later debates have also rejected the idea of a simple link. The emergence of capitalism, and the meaning of capitalism, is a much more complicated issue as we showed in the previous chapters. The connection to the protestant ethics is just *one* dimension of this emergence.

In the Introduction to *The Economic Ethics of the World Religions* Weber distinguished between knowledge-based rational domination of the natural world and individual, inexpressible, incommunicable mystical experiences, the unspoken content of which stood as 'the last Beyond still possible alongside the de-deified mechanism of the world'. Weber designated the very long period of religious rationalization that Judaism/Christendom underwent in terms of an ethical form of religious devaluation and rejection of this world.

Secularization and disenchantment obviously overlapped but the concepts were not synonymous. For Weber, disenchantment of the world took place in more religious cultures as an essentially religious process beginning with the prophets where the ethical (and monotheistic) religions eliminated the magic as a means of salvation. The early connection to Hellenistic scientific thought reinforced the process. Disenchantment was a process *within* religion, a transformation of religion, as opposed to secularization, which implied abandonment or reduction of religious thought. Disenchantment was the recurrent manifestations of the persecution of sorcerers and witches by prophets and hierocrats, the political-religious repression of the magic. Secularization connoted modernity's cultural battles against religion itself and the rejection of the function of religion for social integration.[25] Weber's view on secularization and disenchantment, rationalization and bureaucratization might look like dystopian teleology, but here one must draw attention to his use of charisma and tradition as alternative methods of legitimization to rational rule. They were not bygone concepts in a three-stage development, but recurring correctives where rational rule failed. And, as emphasized, they were instruments in outlines of past development processes rather than prognoses about the future. One might also read into Weber's world-view the argument that the sorcerers and the witches recurred in new forms continuously.

Comte, Marx and Weber were not the only intellectual authorities who depicted a declining role for religion. Émile Durkheim, with his view on modernity as functional differentiation in industrial societies,[26] Herbert Spencer and Sigmund Freud were other influential voices.

In the 1960s, when the secularization thesis peaked, a genealogy of intellectual thought on secularization provided legitimacy to the view. In the vein of Durkheim, Talcott Parsons had most recently emphasized differentiation as a process where new institutions continuously emerge to guarantee legitimacy when monolithic traditional institutions lose credibility and break up. One of these was religion institutionalized through states and churches.

The paradigm in the 1960s told that religion will gradually lose its social significance as a consequence of the process of modernization. The seminal book to maintain this thesis was Peter L. Berger's *The Sacred Canopy* in 1967.[27] The promises of permanent economic prosperity ('affluent society') underpinned the belief in progress guaranteed by human agency. Religion and transcendental questions seemed to disappear ever more from the public sphere and were at most a private concern if any at all. It goes without saying that wealth and affluence as a point of departure for the secularization thesis made it less relevant outside the rich Western world. The secularization thesis went hand in hand with the master narrative about modernization that emerged in the 1960s. This narrative developed by the American social sciences described how superstition became reason, how backwardness became progress, how absolutism became democracy and how poverty became welfare. They established a development norm which everybody could benefit from in and beyond Europe. The USA was on the top of the development scale constituting both the norm and the goal of economic and political development. Barrington Moore was crucial for the breakthrough of this narrative with his classic on the origin of dictatorship and democracy.[28] A narrative emerged where the final goal of modernization was democracy and welfare. It was now that democracy, as a consequence of the Enlightenment philosophy, not the world wars, became a core dimension of (West) European self-understanding. The modernization researchers built one bridge to the Enlightenment over the gap of the world wars and another between capitalism and democracy, political and economic reason and progress over the gap of the Great Depression and social destitution.

The culmination in the 1960s of the language of functional differentiation and secularization, epitomized under the overall concept of modernization, did not only mean that it peaked but also that the decline of this worldview began. The breakdown in the early 1970s of the international order based on the dollar established after the Second World War (Chapter 9) made the modernization narrative ever less convincing. The consequences of decolonization proved in the 1970s not to be development as the modernization discourse taught in the 1950s and 1960s. The doubts that history was linear progress grew. The secularization paradigm became problematic. It came under attack and a revision began. Peter Berger changed his position entirely. The new world he now saw was, with a few exceptions, as 'furiously religious as it ever was, and in some places more so than ever', he noted.[29] The sociologists of religion began to doubt that the displacement of religion from the public to the private was evidence of a general decline of religion. Drawing on the breakthrough of the term postmodern, sociologists of religion launched the idea of post-secularization with a focus on the capacity of religion to resist the sharp attacks of modernity. They discovered religious practices beyond established institutions and laid out an imagery of religious revivalism, the return of the sacred where, for instance, in Poland and the GDR a religious-communitarian re-energizing of culture and civil society precipitated the end of real socialism. The sociologists of religion referred to New Age spirituality in Western Europe, the growth of religious fundamentalism in the Muslim world, and evangelical revivalism in Latin America.[30] Sociologists of religion began to discover religious activity in what Parsons had referred to as the private sphere, with the implicit assumption that religion was going to lose social interest and influence in that private sphere. Others suggested that it was time to bury the whole secularization thesis.[31] The sociologists of religion talked about New Religious Movements with a growing multiplicity of extra-ecclesiastical, para-ecclesiastical and non-ecclesiastical religious manifestations and groupings. The postmodern society was a post-secular society in this emerging view which gained strength in the 1990s against the backdrop of the end of the Cold War and the expectations in the future as endless openness, although, as Chapter 9 will show, not under the lodestar of material progress through human agency.

The erosion of the secularization paradigm gained new force after the World Trade Center attacks in 2001 and the subsequent resurgence of religious conflicts. The rise of religiosity was the framework of the emergence of moralist motivated neoconservative politics in the USA, culminating in the Iraq War. Neoconservatism was the ideological framework of an emerging Christian fundamentalism, particularly in the USA, but with links to Europe. Its opposite was Islam and Muslims, *pace* Huntington and the imagery of clash of civilizations. The vision of multiculturalism based on community-building through liberal pluralism lost credibility when 'multicultural' proved to be the label for ethnically demarcated immigrant ghettos where ethnicity also had a religious subtext. Religion was back as political ideology in polarized societies. The imagery of multiculturalism aiming at integration of immigrants with different cultural and religious background faded. Under the label of 'post-secular', scholars claimed not only the comeback of religion but also the need to incorporate it into the public sphere.[32]

Against the backdrop of this scholarly wave of 'post-secular' literature the Catholic philosopher Charles Taylor published his seminal *A Secular Age* (2007), a deep analysis of the phenomenon of religion in the modern world. He refers to secularization as a long history of reforms of the Western Christendom beginning in the Middle Ages with the Reformation as one phase among others. The long-term outcome of this movement of continuous reform was disenchantment of religion from magical elements. Religion has become one of several options since different beliefs as well as disbelief are equally acceptable. Modernity has brought gains but also deprived us of spiritual dimension, Taylor concludes.[33]

The trend in the wake of Taylor is that the term post-secular has lost meaning, but that the secularization thesis requires revision and refinement. Craig Calhoun argues for the recognition of religious contributions to public discourse and believes that it is possible to translate these views into a language comprehensible also for non-believers. Rethinking secularism means for him not least to prevent a cleavage between citizen-believers and citizen-nonbelievers.[34] Olivier Roy has in this trend of revision innovatively argued that secularization and globalization have changed religion rather than marginalized it. What is perceived as a religious revivalism is for him a product of secularization. Religion reforms itself in its autonomy provided by secularization and this autonomy, in turn, provides the condition for the expansion of religion.[35]

The postmodern vocabulary proclaimed the end of the modernization narrative. The argument about post-secularization proclaimed that the secularization thesis had collapsed together with the end of modernization theory. The idea of post-modernity followed upon the culmination of modernity as we will see in Chapter 9, a culmination marked by critique of domination and confrontation of authority. Post-modernity was the term to describe the erosion of authority and control. However, like with the term 'post-secular' the debate has developed views which play down the sharp break with the past that the prefix of 'post' suggests. The recent views emphasize the continuities across such divides. However, there remains a lack of conceptual clarity and precision in the debate on what religion is and how it relates to politics and modernity. The religious-political nexus remains ambiguous. Ambiguity is a condition of modernity which cannot be dismissed as post-modernity. Secularization is a condition of modernity which cannot be dismissed as post-secularism. Religion is a remaining condition within modernity, much older than modernity, which cannot be dismissed as post-religion. The history of the religious dimension of modernity is a history where 'modernity' tries to emancipate itself from religion but religion continuously recurs. In a way, the relationship between modernity and religion is a bit like the relationship between the economy and the political in the disembedding-re-embedding dynamics of Polanyi.

A brief note on religion as European value

A recurring argument in the political debate is that Europe is built on a unique value canon and that a core dimension of it is a specific European Christian heritage (in implicit demarcation to Judaism and Islam). The Enlightenment narrative about progress offered various possibilities of interpretation, not only a demarcation but also a connection between modernity and Christendom. The colonial project of the nineteenth century was based on ideas of a supreme Western civilization with values like whiteness and Christianity, and ideals of a civilizing global mission under the motto of white man's burden. The missionaries were key actors of colonialism. The gauge of this project was set in temporal terms of backwardness against progressiveness under the general concept of modernity. Christendom was modernity in this scenario. The Christian civilization project underpinned the idea of a European and later Western progressive development towards mastery of the world. During the era of decolonialism after 1945 this narrative was linked to the politics of development aid.

The issue at stake a quarter of a century after the end of the Cold War is whether Western Christian values are again being mobilized on the side of Good against Evil. The threat is no longer communism but Islam, which is depicted as the source of religious fundamentalism as opposed to European self-understanding based on tolerance and soft Christendom.

The idea of a Christian Western civilization became the main argument for the legitimacy of the wars on terror and on Iraq in response to 9/11 where the self-imagery of tolerance shifted to fundamentalism in the mobilization for the war in the Christian West. The governments of the US, Britain, Spain and Poland referred implicitly or explicitly to Christian values as a cause of war. They avoided to comment on the fact that the cause of war based on a lie about the finding of poison gas and the alleged existence of long-range rockets and other weapons of mass destruction, was a lie incompatible with the canon of Christian values. Nevertheless, the question earlier in this chapter about the Crimean War remains. Were the wars on terror and in Iraq religious wars? Is *jihad*, the Holy War, a religious or a social and political protest? Holy War is a central thought not only in the Koran but also in the Old Testament, but do these sources make the war religious? Were the Crusades, the Reconquista of the Iberian Peninsula in 1492 or the Huguenot wars religious wars? They were obviously violent military power struggles but to what extent were they driven by specific values based on religion?

The claims for fundamentalism in the 2000s, either in its Christian or its Islamic form, emerged against the backdrop of images of cultural relativism shaped during the last third of the twentieth century. The call for cultural relativism in the wake of de-colonization must, in turn, be seen as a critical comment on the power struggle between the West and the East in what was referred to as the under-developed Third World. The earlier anthropological approaches were, in the 1960s, accused of ethnocentrism: cultural relativism seemed to deliver the method that promised to grasp the diversity of different civilizations and cultures, while overcoming the colonialist ideology of a superior Western/European civilization confronting under-developed or even primitive non-Western societies.[36] Cultural relativism ended up, after a few decades of practice, in immigrant ghettos all over Europe with a strong religious, i.e. Islamic, subtext. Autonomy meant at the end social exclusion and political-religious radicalization.

Looking for an alternative value base to the polarizing trend, medieval Andalusia emerges as a contrasting historical point of reference and intellectual refuge. *La Convivencia*, 'the Coexistence', is the period from the Muslim Umayyad conquest of Hispania in the early eighth century until the expulsion of the Jews in 1492, the time and the space where Muslims, Christians and Jews lived in relative peace. It is a European-Oriental immaterial cultural heritage, a European-Oriental legacy. There was an interplay of cultural ideas between the three religious groups based on ideas of religious tolerance. This was the culture that brought the classics of Greek philosophy to Europe through translations to Arabic and Hebrew to Latin. This period of religious diversity differs from later Spanish and Portuguese experiences when Catholicism became the sole religion as a result of expulsions, inquisition, and forced conversions. The assumed intercultural harmony has certainly by many been argued to be a myth and to depend on an undocumented tradition.[37] However, it remains a point of reference and an intellectual asylum even as a myth and, in particular, as a value basis to be activated.[38] It is true: it did come to an end. It was an episode. But still . . . And as a value basis it remains, although not uncontested.

PART THREE

The Great Transformations of European Modernity

8

The First Great Transformation:

Organized Modernity for Welfare and Warfare (1870s–1960s)

The catalysts of the 1870s: Karl Marx and Otto von Bismarck

In the 1870s the optimistic wealth-of-nations scenario of Adam Smith became problematic. It had been challenged early on by alternative views like that of Sismondi in the glut debate in the 1820s and the arguments for protectionism by List in the 1840s as we saw in Chapter 5. The free trade myth that Cobden developed in the 1850s cannot, as we also saw, conceal this fact.

In April 1873, the Austrian *Creditanstalt* feared a speculation bubble and sold off bonds and securities for 20 million guilders. The quotations on the stock markets fell. The collapse of the global stock markets was the result not only of unrestrained speculation. It was also due to rapid increases in production capacity which resulted in falling prices and decreasing profits. The development was at the time experienced as dramatic and at the same time lasting, which soon in the contemporary debate was referred to as the Great Depression. In Germany, for instance, where economic growth in 1872 had been 8 per cent, the growth rate stagnated at around zero, and at a certain point prior to 1879 it was negative. Since the situation was more or less the same on the world markets, exports did not offer a way out. Political power centres came under increasing pressure to provide protection and lock off domestic markets.

Laissez-faire liberalism lost credibility as a political ideal – an ideal that, as we saw in Chapter 5, was never really implemented in political and economic practice – and customs protectionism rose and became in the 1880s a general political instrument which emphasized the crisis of economic liberalism.

However, rather than a depression, 1873 initiated a lengthy period lasting until the mid-1890s of economic stagnation where growing industrial production capacity led to intensified competition with increasing pressures on profits and wages as well as to mass lay-offs of labour, which in the 1880s got a name: unemployment.[1]

Before the economic crisis in the wake of the speculation bubble in 1873, Bismarck's violent unification of Germany in the war against France in 1870–1871 was a tectonic shake-up of the European continent that not only destroyed the French Empire but also initiated the short-lived Paris Commune. The rise of Karl Marx was the other side of the fall of the empire and the rise of the Reich. Whereas the Manifesto with Friedrich Engels in 1848 was soon forgotten, the ruling elites of Europe were convinced that the Commune was the work of Karl Marx and his International as we saw in Chapter 5. Marx became a highly feared man in Europe's establishments and at the same time a much esteemed and respected leader of the working classes, who expected him to lead them towards a better future through revolutionary confrontation of the existing power relationships. Together with his growing reputation as the author of *Capital* (1867), Marx rapidly became known as the great revolutionary architect of 'scientific socialism'.[2]

The social question which we discussed in Chapter 5 transformed into the class question. The louder voices about class struggle in the 1870s alerted the ruling elites and put the question of how to integrate the social protest on the political agenda all over Europe. The social protest was more cohesive and the threat more massive than ever, and the memories of the revolutions in 1830 and 1848 recurred. The Paris Commune was soon crushed but the threat it represented to the ruling elites remained.

The impression of the Commune belonged to the backdrop imagery when a group of German professors of political economy, *Nationalökonomie*, met in 1872 to discuss how to promote state intervention in social issues on the basis of historical-economic investigations. Economic theories with generalizing pretensions did in their view not pay attention to persisting poverty in the wake of the spread of industrial capitalism. Poverty did not disappear, they argued, through some automatic function inherent in the capitalist order, but had to be confronted through politics drawing on historically given institutions and preconditions specific to each nation. In 1873, the professors founded the *Verein für Sozialpolitik*, the Association for Social Policy.

The Association aimed to become a forum in which academic, economic and political-administrative elites could discuss what measures should be taken on the basis of the results of social scientific research. After the national integration, the issue of social integration of the new nation was urgent. There was a pressing need for a public debate. The idea of social politics was based on the conscious insight that state and society necessarily had to be activated in order to establish balance between social interests drifting apart.[3]

In Britain, against the backdrop of the Paris Commune, Disraeli's government programme of social reform in 1874–1875 was another example of conservative reforms to divert revolutionary threats. National integration came to mean social integration of the working classes. The British prime minister had manifested his attention to the social question already in his 1845 novel *Sybil, or the Two Nations* (the rich and the poor), where he referred to 'the only duty of power, the social welfare of the people'. In 1874, his concern became political, with a programme for social reform in housing, savings and labour relations, against slum buildings, and for public health. The Employers and Workmen Act 1875 established equality before the law regarding labour contracts. Other laws allowed peaceful picketing and regulated labour standards in factory work.[4]

The 1870s signalled, against the backdrop of the experiences of economic crisis and the Paris Commune, a new academic-political approach to national integration in Europe. The problem formulation changed dramatically as compared to Adam Smith's outline of the liberal future. The new problem could no longer be formulated within a liberal interpretative framework. The German Association for Social Policy and Disraeli's politics for social integration of the workers marked an ideological shift towards paternalist state responsibility for the integration of the workers, ever more performing as a class, into the nations of Europe.

The programme of the German Association fit hand in glove with Bismarck's programme for social integration of the growing number of industrial workers with ever louder voices. Welfare for social integration followed upon the warfare for national unification. Bismarck developed an alternative solution to the crisis to that of Marx, whom he confronted by trying to circumvent him. Occasionally Bismarck called himself a state socialist as opposed to the class struggle socialism of the workers. Thereby he did not refer to any idea of state ownership of industry but to a general concern about the allegiance of the workers through provision of certain social standards. Bismarck's approach focused on insurance programmes designed to increase productivity, and included sickness insurance, accident insurance, disability insurance, and a retirement pension, none of which were then in existence to any great degree. The long-term imagery of a welfare state, a *Sozialstaat*, emerged around the Bismarckian anti-liberal approach to ward off class struggle socialism. He gradually disarmed the revolutionary threat formulated by Marx linking to liberal, more or less philanthropic, social reforms by local government and social charity, and to social democratic and trade union struggles for better labour and living standards.

Disraeli, Bismarck and the social politics of the moderately conservative German professors were cases in point in a more general development. Inspired by Bismarck, Eduard Taaffe introduced social legislation in Austria in the 1880s.[5] In Italy the so-called *statalisti* among the lawyers and economists – as opposed to the adherents of a liberal economy – tried to emulate the German approach after Italian unification. In Sweden, conservative political science professor Rudolf Kjellén argued for a national socialism in response to class struggle socialism. He was just one in an academic chorus on the need for a nationalism for social integration of the workers in the nation, which was understood as the conservative unification of the people under the king rather than as the emancipation of the subjects to citizens.[6] In France the idea of *solidarisme* emerged, a main interpreter of which was Léon Bourgeois, who was strongly influenced by Durkheim. Bourgeois was a radical statesman and thus not part of the conservative reform trend but as interested as the conservatives in finding alternatives to class struggle socialism. Ever more protagonists found *laissez-faire* unacceptable and promoted reinforced state activity to mitigate the class clash.

In the 1890s, Émile Durkheim became a leading intellectual point of reference in these developments. In *The Division of Labour in Society* he distinguished between mechanical and organic solidarity where mechanical solidarity produced social cohesion and integration in traditional societies with people being connected through similar work, education and religion. Organic solidarity, in contrast, expressed social cohesion transcending the atomization between individuals by emphasizing their dependence on each other in more advanced societies where they perform different tasks and often have different values and interests.[7] Already before Durkheim, German sociologist Ferdinand Tönnies had suggested a parallel dichotomy to describe the social problems and the risk of atomization in the wake of industrial capitalism.[8] He distinguished nostalgically the past as *Gemeinschaft*, a community held together by a common essence, from the ambiguous and more atomized future as *Gesellschaft* society. The workers began in the wake of this conceptualization of organic, functional, interest-based solidarity and society to understand themselves as a cohesive, although oppressed, part of the nation, as a class with class-consciousness. Organic solidarity or *Gesellschaft* worked through institutional ties essential in large-scale modern societies, while mechanical solidarity or *Gemeinschaft* worked through the affective ties associated with the small-scale relationships of traditional society.

The insight grew in the academic-political debate on the social and the class questions since the 1870s that national unification had to build on social integration under the responsibility of the state. Conservative national or state socialism emerged as an alternative to Marx's idea of class struggle socialism. Marx and Bismarck bypassed economic liberalism in a pincer movement.

The development mobilized the state not only as a protector of labour but also as a protector of the crisis-ridden capitalist order. Industry required protection. The movement of German politics in the 1880s towards protectionism is a case in point which was followed in many other European countries. Protectionism also activated a new kind of more aggressive nationalism. The concepts of nation and state increasingly overlapped. They were increasingly seen as the arena where the economic difficulties had to be solved. The national unification involved in the emerging imagery all subjects, including the workers, but as subjects under a social monarch rather than as autonomous citizens.[9] The perspective was top-down not bottom-up. The state was, in this conservative futurist scenario, responsible for the social integration of all subjects through new legislation and institutions for welfare, in particular workers' welfare, and interest mediation. The fiction of the market as an autonomous force transcending national borders through international division of labour was played down. The fiction of the nation-state was mobilized to ward off threats from competitors on the world market and images of a shared capital and labour national interest against other nations were conjured up. The protectionist and nationalistic language fit well with perverted Darwinian biologist metaphors about struggles for the survival of the fittest (where Darwin had argued about evolution and natural selection).

It was also in this context that the concept of 'unemployment' emerged. Unemployment was first recognized in Britain in the late 1880s. The concept was a social construct. It reflected a prescriptive approach closely aligned with a desire to improve industrial performance in the face of increasing competition on foreign markets. The term emerged when an accelerating expansion of the manufacturing industry, based on large-scale concentrations of wage labour and capital, had come to an end. The term connoted suboptimal rational resource mobilization. The Marxist perspective was different. Marx did not see a suboptimal situation but a conscious exploitation of labour by capital. He referred to the industrial reserve army, a term that Friedrich Engels had used in his bestseller *The Condition of the Working Class in England* (1845) and which Marx theorized in *Capital*. The availability of supply of labour to hire and fire according to the market situation was an instrument of profitability. The extended economic stagnation from the 1870s onwards demonstrated how vulnerable the order was irrespective of whether it was seen from the perspective of Marx or from that of the capitalist and political establishment. The economic stagnation shifted the argumentation to the problem of downswing in world markets where the liberal idea of market self-regulation lost credibility. From Britain, the plague of unemployment rapidly spread to other industrializing countries and so did the conceptualization of the plague.[10]

Market liberalism, free trade and the cooperation of capital and labour were up to then the keystones of the imagery of a global system of division of labour (Smith) or exploitation (Marx). In political practice, the universe of the new economy was increasingly from the 1870s to become the fiction of the nation organized as a centralized state. Market freedom required rules that could only be made and implemented by the state. The global division of labour was thus gradually subsumed into national competition on world markets. Liberal theories about universalism fortified national projects in competition or struggle with other national projects. Liberal arguments which previously had connected the imagery of competition to distribution of labour, free trade and peace began to emphasize competition as struggle for survival between nations. The conservative reform approach did not only draw on transformed liberal arguments, however, but developed also a new conservative world-view which transformed paternalist experiences in the old corporate society into imageries of the social state as the basis of national economies. Max Weber postulated in 1895 the ruthless self-assertion of the national *Machtstaat* as the last value of the *Nationalökonomie*. This was the transformation of liberalism into 'organised modernity'.[11]

The next step in this discursive turn towards protectionism and nationalism was the 1890s armaments race, which had positive effects on the economy. The protectionist and nationalistic mix which had emerged since the 1870s exploded in 1914. After a short armistice, it exploded again in the 1930s. The period from the 1870s until the 1940s was an extended crisis of the liberal heuristic framework, but the Marxist interpretations did not manage to establish an alternative hegemony. The most influential answer to the Marxist critique of liberalism was nationalism. This answer did not come from the liberals, however, but from conservative ruling strategies.

The 1870s were a catalyst in the shift of the economic and social paradigm. Against the backdrop of economic stagnation and feelings of crisis, free trade began to shift to protectionism and governments began to intervene with social politics for the integration of the working class and for the de-polarization of the social conflict to which the louder class language drew attention. Ideals of *laissez-faire* were ever more transformed to ideals of state intervention in order to correct social problems in the wake of the spread of industrial capitalism. This is not to say that the ideals of *laissez-faire* disappeared. The case was rather that other approaches confronted these ideals and opened up alternative views. The 1870s were the beginning of a Great Transformation of the capitalist economies and of the labour markets, a transformation which continued in ever new forms, through periods of war and peace during the following century. The Great Transformation meant the demarcation to the liberal imagery outlined by Adam Smith and the classical economists.

Organized labour versus organized capital

The German opening of the road to protectionism became paradigmatic. Most other industrializing states went the same way in the 1880s. Germany provided the model of organized modernity that accompanied the campaign for protectionism. In Germany, the *Centralverband deutscher Industrieller* (Central Federation of German Industrialists, CdI) was established in 1876. The federation represented the whole spectrum of industry and its central idea was the rejection of liberal free trade. It became a powerful lobbying organization. Somewhat later than industry, the agrarian sector ceased to benefit from free trade. Cheap cereals from Canada, the USA and Russia (Ukraine) closed export markets to German agrarian products. The German market also opened to imports from these countries following the reduction of transportation costs. A month after the establishment of the CdI, the *Großagrarier* founded the *Vereinigung der Steuer- und Wirtschaftsreformer*, the Association of the Tax and Economy Reformers, which began to lobby for protection of the German agrarian market. The name shows how the agrarian lobbyists appropriated the term reform to give the campaign for protectionism a progressive connotation shaking off images of reactionary *Junkertum*. One of the core ingredients of organized modernity was centralized interest organizations with political lobbying as a main goal like in the German prototype.

The language of free trade lost its appeal. The one remaining free-trade country was Britain, a nation with good reasons for maintaining its free-trade orientation. British steel and textiles industries dominated the world market. The City of London financed these export industries and organized credit for investments in industry and agriculture abroad. Britain also benefitted from free trade in its shipping and insurance sectors. Significantly, it had the highest share of workers who did not feel threatened by free trade. Britain's *Sonderweg* was a rejection of protectionism, and the British government maintained this stance even when other countries discredited British commodities through import customs.[12]

The capital reaction to the Great Depression went far beyond the lobbying for protectionism. The stagnating economies put a dampener on the lust for speculation, abated the entrepreneurial spirit of risk-taking and promoted the search for long-term yields through planning. The capital owners responded to market stagnation by screwing down the expectations and adjusting to lower levels of profit, making the industry less speculative. The industry began to give priority to predictability and long-term stability. The planning of production and of the labour force became a key instrument when the enterprises expanded their administrative capacities, a process that Weber would describe as bureaucratization. Organization and standardization were key instruments in this response to the Great Depression. The interest grew not least in coming to terms with the industrial conflict about wages and working conditions and with the long-term supply of labour. The institutions for negotiation with the workers in collective forms grew, which meant a recognition of trade unions as legitimate representatives of the interests of the workers. The idea that the trade unions could be used as instruments for the achievement of calculability and predictability grew. Organized capital and organized labour at the local company level built hierarchical organizations at the national level and reinforced one another in what might be called a rationalization of the interest conflict.

The employers began to recommend collective employment agreements with the representatives of the workers as a more efficient way towards predictable labour relations than the old competition among the workers through individual contracts. For ever more employers, collective bargaining with a few representatives of the workers became a more attractive labour relations alternative than individual bargaining with all of them with the aim to keep the workers divided. With growing resources for conflict, for both organized labour and organized capital more was at risk in a conflict. The strike and lockout weapons began to be used with more cautioun. The propensity to look for compromises increased. The solidarity ties came with the centralized and hierarchical organization of the interests ever more to follow national trans-industry lines.[13]

Bismarck's attempt to stop the social democrats by offering them a certain level of state protection did not prevent the social democratic expansion in Germany. The workers and their leaders did certainly not experience an idyll and they were often persecuted in Germany and elsewhere. The authorities confronted the labour movement with both stick and carrot, where policies for social integration went hand in hand with politics of repression. This confrontation modified but did not silence the class struggle language. The revolutionary imagery of Karl Marx drove the labour movements in Europe, despite the fact that it was difficult to discern a revolutionary moment with an imperative to act. The revolution became ever more of a distant goal and a belief than a matter of political practice. As a belief the apocalyptic imagery of revolution and final triumph mobilized the workers and committed them to the building of ever stronger organizations with growing memberships and unionization rates with growing economic resources and conflict capacity. The belief in revolution went in tandem with the reformist approach to day-to-day politics of muddling through, searching for compromises and gradual improvement.

Governments contributed to de-escalation and depolarization of conflict through the expansion of the administration in the new fields of social and labour market policies. They introduced institutions and rules for arbitration and for labour market conflicts. The definition of minimal social and labour standards such as working hours, female work and children's work began. The state administration expanded into new fields and got a more distinct social dimension in addition to the traditional military focus and the new attention in the nineteenth century to politics of communications and commerce. Conflicts did not disappear, of course, and interests continued to be defined in terms of opposition and clash, but the solution to the conflicts went ever more towards the search for compromises.[14] The specialist competence in the state bureaucracies became ever more differentiated and ever more refined. Administrative expansion was based on specialization, professionalization and division of labour. This development characterized also the hierarchical interest organizations.

The development led to centralized interest organizations, hierarchical but with a clear bottom-up profile, which, together with the sectorial specialized state administration, could mediate in the interest conflicts. The old corporate model based on the crafts in the pre-industrial paternalist order came back in new and more centralized forms after having disappeared in the imageries of economic liberalism.

This organization of interests was obviously different from the predictions of Karl Marx. However, the development did not mean that inequalities and exploitation in the new contract-based labour markets of industrial capitalism disappeared. It was rather the matter of new, more organized ways to articulate and highlight them and to an intensified search for solutions. However, there was never any final solution and the articulation of interests continued from new positions where Karl Marx represented continuity in his role as a lodestar for organized labour. He offered a variety of possibilities of interpretation.

The period from the 1870s onwards was the end of political apathy or disinterest, the politicization of the business community, the stagnation of the liberal parties, the regrouping of conservative forces and the upsurge of the social democrats despite Bismarck's model based on the attempt to appropriate socialism from the labour movement by the ruthless combination of stick and carrot, repression and social reform. Core paternalist conservatism with a social profile, and the social democratic struggle for social reforms driven by the class struggle language and the distant imagery of revolution with history on its side, cemented organized modernity.[15]

The growing organizational capacity brought gradually growing economic strength and a shift towards a new kind of industry through capital concentration and production based not only on bureaucracy and planning but also on research and new technological knowledge produced at state universities. The states promoted academic research in sciences and technology. Karl Jaspers, whom we met in Chapter 2, discerned this period as the end of an epoch which had culminated with Goethe and Hegel and the beginning of a post-Kantian age represented by Kierkegaard and Nietzsche, and by positivism and natural science, which could not really be considered as philosophy.[16] Spectacular advances in chemical and physio-electric sciences and the invention of the new mobile source of power, the internal combustion engine, triggered a new wave of knowledge-based industry based on electricity and oil like telephones, automobiles, the chemical industry, and alimentation which began to break through in the 1890s. These developments compensated for the decline in the 1870s of the first wave of steam-based industries such as steel, mechanical engineering and textiles. The Great Depression that began in 1873 ended in economic recovery from the mid-1890s.

However, although the transformation of the industrial relationships towards corporatist centralized bargaining and social compromise – in a

European pattern of diversity – contributed to domestic social peace, the development did not necessarily promote international peace. The contribution of the new set of industrial production to the increasing economic dynamics did not only refer to the products for the civil market but also to expanding markets for armament. The recovery occurred in the framework of growing military orders to industry and growing conflicts between the European powers in the colonies. Capitalism got not only a social face but also an imperialist one. It got both a more military side and a more social side. Wilhelm II engaged Germany in a naval armament race with Britain and Russia about power in the North Sea and the Baltic at the same time as he presented himself as a social monarch.

Political leaders began to canalize domestic frustration towards foreign activism through nationalism and social imperialism. National socialism with ethnic we-they demarcations canalized class struggle socialism in social reform-oriented, but not necessarily peaceful, directions. The language of social imperialism was part of an explosive mix which sought to unify national communities, threatened by disintegration through the class question. It promoted expansion and aggression on other continents. Social imperialism was a refashioning of the old idea of colonial settlements as the solution to domestic poverty and overpopulation (Chapter 5).

The language of social imperialism linked Europe's domestic social problems to the colonial world. Social nationalism and social imperialism reinforced the rivalry between the European nations in Europe and in the colonies and increased the colonial pressures on the native populations. Social nationalism and social imperialism reinforced the crisis of liberalism in the wake of the Great Depression because they had answers to the ever more obvious social problems in the wake of the spread of industrial capitalism and of its crisis since 1873 that liberalism did not have.

Liberalism was squeezed in the struggle for solutions to the social and the class questions. The conservative language of social nationalism and the socialist and social democratic language of class struggle came ever closer to each other with the marginalization of liberal economic world-views.

There were voices who tried to save liberalism by giving it a more social dimension, however. Probably the most prominent of them was J.A. Hobson. Unlike Marx, he did not see the imperial development as the result of some sort of internal logic in capitalism. Indeed, he suggested alternative developments. He suggested the elimination of domestic underconsumption by increasing people's purchasing power as a tool to tame the capitalist lust for imperialist expansion, and a tool for the development of alternative domestic markets for the sale of the products.[17] Half a century later, J.M. Keynes was going to follow up that argument, and before him Henry Ford began to apply the idea in industrial practice with mass production of cars for mass consumption.

One could epitomize the situation in Europe in 1914 in terms of organized modernity. The promises of economic liberalism based on ideals of innovative entrepreneurship and competition did not convince any more. In the new view efficiency and economic growth would instead come through planning and administration, coordination and cooperation, albeit for the masses rather than by the masses. Organization of modernity was also hierarchization. Negotiations between organized labour and organized capital were institutionalized. This development was accompanied by an increase in state power into new areas such as social politics, which was feared by some as restricting the freedom of individuals while others saw it as a social and political possibility. The Austrian-German social democratic and neo-Marxist theoretician Rudolf Hilferding presented his vision of organized labour taking over a state apparatus that organized capital had prepared.[18]

The organization of capital and labour through concentration and hierarchy confirmed a model where authoritarian conservatism with a social face ruled with growing state administrations and centralized hierarchical interest organizations and institutions for social and labour market policies to mitigate the backside of industrial capitalism. The socialist protest and the class language persisted but the revolution was ever less of an immediate threat. A skilful use of concessions consolidated conservative power. Europe in 1914 was not only organized, but also represented conservative modernity based on monarchical power in more or less authoritarian, more or less constitutional forms.[19] However, the developments since the 1870s also meant that the successful imagery of social nationalism got ever more of an ethnic blend. Domestic peace was bought at the price of external friend-enemy imageries with a clear ethnic dimension. The social protest of the workers and their class language was not silenced but it was contained and controlled as well as canalized in new directions by conservative concessions with social and political reforms.

Imperialism connected the organized modernity of Europe to the world and made it global. The British Empire, which had been the global hegemon back in Vienna in 1815, experienced growing competition after 1870 when the USA and Germany emerged as the new world powers, with Germany as the prototype of organized modernity. Europe's organized modernity had a global imperial base and got an Asian imitator when Japan after the Meiji Restoration in 1868 began a powerful economic development emulating the European, in particular the German model, translating it to fit Japanese preconditions. The fact that Japan began to build its own empire in mainland Asia was part of this emulation.

Karl Polanyi and the Great Transformation

When we in this book discern European modernity in terms of two Great Transformations, beginning in the 1870s and the 1970s respectively, we have taken the label from Karl Polanyi, inspired by his approach and conceptualization as a point of departure for our analysis of what happened in these two dynamic decades distinguished by experiences of crisis and great change. By the end of the Second World War, Polanyi in his *The Great Transformation* reflected on the developments that had brought the world to such catastrophe.[20] He described the nineteenth century as a long-term struggle between 'society' trying to 'embed' the market and liberal economic forces trying to escape the straightjacket that the political embedding of a feudal and corporatist order imposed on them. In turn, the successful separation of the political framework and the market by economic forces provoked social protests against their experiences of the negative sides of the economy, which in turn provoked a politics of re-embedding. This was the second wave of major transition, the Great Transformation during the era of the world wars. *The Great Transformation* is one of the most influential analyses of economic transitions.

Polanyi's conceptualization around the key concepts of political embedding of the economy, economic disembedding and social protests for re-embedding underlines the intertwined dynamics and tensions between politics and the economy. Economies are always political economies.[21] Polanyi confronts fictions of self-regulated economies with the 'market' as an autonomous force. Moreover, he does not only emphasize the connection between politics and the economy but also the social dimension with social protests and attempts to respond to the protests as a key dimension of both politics and the economy. Polanyi's perspective is reminiscent of Reinhart Koselleck's critique and crisis dynamics where social critique provokes crisis and politics for response to the crisis through integration of the critique.[22]

However, there is one major problem with Polanyi's interpretation of the past. Paradoxically enough, his neo-Marxist approach ignores the role of class conflict. He conceives, as Sandra Halperin has demonstrated, of society as organic and sociologically undifferentiated, and of state and global structures as sociologically neutral. The protest against economic power comes from society as a united whole.[23] She argues and demonstrates that Polanyi overlooks in his conceptualization the role of social conflicts and imperialist wars during Europe's industrial expansion, when in the nineteenth century a 'new' industrial capitalist class rose to power, a period of economic liberalism and general peace. Halperin argues that the central dynamics were not, as Polanyi pretends, a double movement of protection by and for 'society as a whole' against the expanding liberal market system, but a dualism around the social question *within* society itself. Polanyi is mistaken about the imagery of the long peace of the nineteenth century. Far from being a period of peace gradually overtaken by the contradictions of the unregulated market, the period was born in violence and remained violent throughout. Halperin's appendix records 540 violent domestic social and interstate military conflicts in the nineteenth century.

Our position is somewhere between Halperin and Polanyi. Halperin is right in her argument that Polanyi does not pay due attention to the class clash, but she exaggerates if her argument is that the transformation was mainly class conflict and war. We emphasize the successful conservative counter-strategies for social integration as the instrument against revolutionary threats. The dynamics between disembedding and re-embedding was complex. The economic elites contributed themselves to the re-embedding through the hierarchical organization of what they defined as their interests and the development of a machinery for negotiations with organized labour. The economic elites were not necessarily emancipating themselves from the political elites but rather merged with them in their attempt to ward off the class threat through re-embedding and increased state responsibility for social integration.

Organized modernity and the Second European Thirty Years War

The shift from classical economic liberalism towards organized modernity since the 1870s culminated in 1914. This is not to say that it caused the First World War and the thirty-year period of warfare that followed, with a brief peace interlude in the 1920s. One might say that organized modernity contained a military dimension through the connection of the search for domestic social integration and social peace to ethnic nationalism and imageries of friend-enemy distinctions. However, there was no structural necessity that this dimension would end in a world war. Here is not the place to go further into the complicated question of the causes of the First World War, but the responsibility of human agency must be emphasized. Europe in the summer of 1914 was not a sleep-walk into the war as some authors have argued. Rather it was a matter of gamblers in the military staffs and diplomatic services as well as among the state leaders; gamblers who were ignorant about the consequences of the martial structures that the weapon technology of organized modernity had built up since the 1890s. They continued to believe in the theory of Carl von Clausewitz after the Napoleonic Wars about war as the continuity of politics.[24] Clausewitz was a point of reference for Bismarck, but after the chancellor's resignation in 1890 the weapon technology became much more destructive and the remaining belief that war was just a version of politics became disastrous.

The century between the Vienna Peace in 1815 and the beginning of the First World War in 1914 was obviously not a teleology towards the fulfilment of democracy via constitutionalization of Europe through the binding of royal power and in a second step through parliamentarianism as the conventional view argues (see Chapter 4). The century was a successful conservative ward-off of claims for democracy through concessions and organization. The organization of the social protest in the wake of the spread of industrial capitalism and its crises met with a powerful conservative and authoritarian organization of a counter movement. Democracy did not come as the outcome of a long process towards the final fulfilment of the Enlightenment values of liberty and equality. Instead it was the world war that provided the preconditions for democracy. The war had mobilized all the resources of the European societies for mass killing on the military fronts. The war intensified and cemented neo-corporate structures of organized modernity developed since the 1870s. The war propaganda mobilized the masses with patriotic and ethnic nationalism. The war required the masses in the mobilization for what was a total war that involved the home front and the masses as shapers of politics much more than earlier. The organized modernity became mass-based much more than before. The war imposed discipline on the masses. When the war ended the constraints of the war disciplines eased off. The common denominator in Europe in 1919 was the breakthrough of the masses in politics and the political problem became how to canalize the released energy. Democracy was not the only way in that respect.

The rise of the masses was threat as much as promise. Social revolutions or threats of revolution belonged to the order of the day and the violence frightened. The revolutionary threats polarized. Right-wing extremism of armed *soldateska* masses refusing to demobilize after the war terrorized the societies. The postwar revolutions failed after a few years, however, with the exception of the Russian Revolution. The remaining impact was that political leaders discovered that the masses could be manipulated. The new politics by and for the masses, *could* lead to democracy, but this was as just noted not the only possibility.

A few countries, Britain, France and those that made up Scandinavia managed to establish lasting democracies. The new Weimar Republic was a promising experiment in democracy after centuries of authoritarianism and it was far from doomed from the beginning. However, at the end it succumbed. It had from the beginning a clear democratic potential although it is also true that this potential was fragile. Italy solved the social problems after the war with fascism.

The Second World War was not inherent in the First World War. The peace in Versailles was sharply criticized for its punishment of Germany, and after the rise of Hitler many began to see the peace as the cause of the next war. This is wrong. The US government helped Germany to overcome the hyperinflation which was the response to the severe peace conditions. Versailles became a weapon in the Nazi propaganda but it did not cause the breakdown of the Weimar. In the mid-1920s a new generation of political leaders in Europe such as Aristide Briand in France, Austen Chamberlain in Britain and Gustav Stresemann in Germany committed themselves to reconciliation and signed the Locarno Treaty in 1925.

Amidst the general turmoil and confusion in the immediate postwar years, three kinds of future-oriented modernity approaches emerged: the Western democratic; the Eastern Soviet communist; and the fascist. The

Western democratic and the Eastern communist versions identified a global mission and competed about how to define it: the international of the global state community in the League of Nations making the world safe for democracy against the International of the working class. The latter promised sovereignty of the peoples, and also for the colonies, whereas the League envisaged a world order with colonies. The European postwar modernity of the masses shed its seed also in other continents such as the South African Native National Congress, the black representation in the previously white-only South African communist party, and the Indian National Congress Movement where Gandhi and his young supporters imbued the Congress rank-and-file to combat British rule directly. In China, the 4 May movement against the Versailles peace meant the birth of the communist party there. The breakthrough of the masses went beyond Europe. The protest guided by Enlightenment arguments about freedom and people's sovereignty bounced back on the colonial powers also from without.

Modernity in Europe before 1914 was social integration through conservative national concessions. After 1919 Europe's modernity was protest and mass mobilization where the movement left its entrenchment in the imperial centres and became global. However, the Soviet communist dream of the world revolution soon petered out, as did the Western liberal dream of the League as a world government.

Organized global modernity emerged in the economy. Instead of the contours of a world government, envisaged by the League of Nations, a global capital regime emerged when international cartels in key production areas divided the world markets through secret price and product agreements.[25] This order was a contradictory supplement to the wave of protectionism and nationalism in reaction to the economic depression in the 1930s, a global disembedding of the economic forces in the sense of Polanyi.

The international cartels peaked in the interwar years, but they had a pre-history. They emerged with protectionism, first in Germany and Japan in the 1880s, from where they spread to other countries protecting the expansion of their industries. The new thing in the 1920s was the internationalization of the cartels. Cartels obviously deviated from the theoretical prescriptions of liberal economic theory but they were quite frequent from the 1880s and were generally considered to bring benefits. They helped governments to manage their economies. They were not necessarily contrary to liberal ideas about competition, rather a variation on liberal practices connected to coordination and cooperation, rationalization and standardization of markets and production, as well as technological development. On the eve of the Second World War, cartels controlled 40 per cent of world trade. It was hoped that the founding of the International Steel Cartel in 1926 would pave the way for an overall economic settlement in Western Europe in the framework of the Locarno spirit.

It was a new speculation bubble that finally destroyed the architecture of Versailles and ended the Locarno spirit. The stock-market crash in New

York in October 1929 spread to Europe where the economies collapsed one after the other. Mass unemployment recurred and the voices of the workers grew in strength. The masses were a much more explosive force after the First World War than they had been before 1914. Germany was hardest hit by the economic breakdown after 1929 which soon was called the Great Depression. The economic historians began to refer to the previous version as the Long Depression. The social problems in the wake of the Great Depression paved the way for Hitler. The parties to the right in the Weimar Republic were ignorant about his destructive capacity and the parties on the left were absorbed by internal quarrel about the right way to socialism instead of confronting Hitler's version of socialism in a joint effort. This development was not intrinsic in the economic structures but must be referred to as failure and lack of imagination of human agency. With Hitler, a new form of politics for and/or by the masses supplemented the democratic, fascist and communist versions. It is not so that democracy was the European standard that failed. The political systems in Europe covered the whole scale from totalitarianism in its fascist, Nazi and Stalinist versions to authoritarianism in Central and Eastern Europe and democracy in the West. The language of modernity became with this diversity over-excited and more cacophonic. The futurist promises of art, science and technological knowledge stretched the horizons of expectation at the same time as the Faustian spirit spread threat and fear.

The distance and distinction between these versions of mass politics were much less clear at the time than they would become in the reconstruction of Europe's past after the following war when the European democracies, in the reconstruction of their past, were designed as the standard based on the fulfilment of the Enlightenment promise, against the deviating cases of fascism, Nazism and Stalinism. Roosevelt was, in his struggle for economic recovery from 1931, very interested in Mussolini's corporatist experiment with organized modernity as interest coordination under the auspices of the state. Hitler's solution to mass unemployment through expansive budget politics provoked admiration. Democracy, fascism and Nazism were distant relatives. It was only when Italy and Germany, from 1935, committed themselves to military solutions and war that the differences became visible.[26]

The second half of the 1930s was an economic crisis, which became a political crisis, which became a value crisis. The entanglements of democracy, totalitarianism and authoritarianism in the 1930s did not mean that all politics became entangled in one large mass and that one did not see the alternatives, risks and threats. Ernst Cassirer and Edmund Husserl initiated in Germany a debate with Martin Heidegger about the value crisis they observed.[27] Dutch medievalist Johan Huizinga wrote the bestseller *In the Shadow of Tomorrow*.[28] The book reflected a decennium of growing cultural pessimism, the 'spiritual suffering' as Huizinga formulated it. The book belonged to the same genre as Oswald Spengler's volumes on *The Decline of the West* after the First World War, Ortega y Gasset's book on the riots of the masses and Aldous Huxley's dystopic vision of future in *Brave New World*.[29] Franz Kafka was another name in this trend that connected to the cultural pessimism at the turn of the twentieth century. There was no naïve belief in the superiority of democracy but rather an intellectual concern about the threatening shallowness and superficiality, populism and mob-law in the wake of the breakthrough of mass politics. It was a concern with what the masses could undertake. The organization of modernity since the 1870s became less orchestrated and began to lose its balance between top-down and bottom-up.

In what remained of democracy in Europe after 1933 – except for Czechoslovakia almost all the new states which with democratic fanfares had been erected in 1919 in Central and Eastern Europe shifted to more or less authoritarian regimes – the struggle against the crisis dealt with some form of planned economy as it had been adapted during the First World War or in the corporatist model of fascism. Stalinism developed its specific mix of planning, terror and paranoiac violence.

The search for order in a chaotic world occurred in many versions. In 1933, the Conservative Harold MacMillan, British prime minister from 1957 to 1963, proposed an 'economic form of orderly capitalism' close to the Italian fascism. Oswald Mosley was a conservative aristocrat, intellectual, MP and Labour cabinet minister who became the leader of the British Union of Fascists, which he imagined as the third force in British politics. Mosley wanted to give fascism a respectable British, rather than violent Italian, face. This change of opinion destroyed his friendship with Keynes, but the case demonstrates how fluid the relationships were between what after the Second World War would appear as clear oppositions. It was exactly the most antifascist socialists who argued that they had to learn from the fascists and the national socialists, who had taken over the attributes of youth, vitality, virility, will, struggle and vanguard from the socialists. They had established parties based on and exploiting the masses with the claim of being a transcending synthesis of the mission of the proletariat. The rebels in the French socialist party and the left faction of the British Labour Party agreed that under prevailing circumstances of collapse of capitalist economies fascism and national socialism, despite deformation and perversion, constituted a revolutionary potential.[30]

In the interwar years, the hierarchies of organized modernity broke down and were reshaped. Populism, totalitarianism or authoritarianism were as probable outcomes as democracy of this reshuffling of hierarchies. The Second World War was the culmination of this development where organized at the end had a clear dimension of unorganized, and the idea of plan a dimension of improvisation. In the 1930s organized modernity split up in a variety of responses to the erosion of order. The first version of the Great Depression led to the organized modernity. The second version led to the collapse of organized modernity based on conservative control through concessions.

The postwar reconstruction boom, the Cold War and decolonization: the culmination of organized modernity

The Second World War ceased without a peace treaty and with the nuclear terror balance of the Cold War as a very special form of peace. However, the terror balance imposed discipline, plan and hierarchical organization at the same time as it split Europe in a Western and an Eastern part with alternative forms of organization of modernity. In Eastern Europe under the Soviet umbrella, the five-year plans soon came to demonstrate the ambiguities, contradictions and ironies in the planned attempts to shape the future. Also, the Western reorganization of modernity contained ambiguities and contradictions as the developments in the 1960s and 1970s were going to demonstrate. The post-1945 phase of what might be called reorganized modernity in an Eastern and a Western version was brief: only a couple of decades.

Europe's post-1945 organized modernity in its two versions was global. The competition between the two models took place within the framework of 'decolonization'. The colonized peoples had been part of the total mobilization for the two wars and began, like the masses in Europe, to require democracy and independence. Whereas the weakened European colonial powers retreated from the colonies – voluntarily or having been forced to – Britain tried to keep its former empire together as a commonwealth. Britain and France were in their accommodating or defensive strategies left behind by the two other victors in 1945, the USA and the Soviet Union, who actively supported the movement for decolonialism. They competed for influence in the new decolonized world in the framework of the Cold War. Hence, according to contemporary vocabulary, the 'first' (USA) and the 'second' (the Soviet Union) with their European annexes competed against the backdrop of the Cold War for influence in what became known as the 'third' world. France granted independence to almost all its African colonies in the single year of 1960. Britain abandoned Africa politically more gradually between 1957 and 1965. France tried to hold on to two of its colonies, Vietnam and Algeria, by force, but both attempts failed. Portugal clung to Angola and Mozambique until the fall of the Salazar regime in 1974.

In Western Europe after 1945, Weimar served as a warning example, reinforced by the other warning example, the Stalinist regime in the Soviet Union and its satellite regimes in Central and Eastern Europe, established through coups under the tautological label of people's democracy. The insight in Western Europe was that democracy could be dangerous and therefore had to be controlled. The rule of the people could be the point of departure for politics in very different directions and it could be manipulated. There were after 1945 stable parliamentarian democracies only in Western and Northern Europe and in Italy. Not least the Cold War contributed to the stabilization. In Spain and Portugal there were authoritarian regimes, and Greece suffered from a civil war immediately after the Second World War and a military regime a couple of decades later.

The fragility of democracy was what the fathers of the European integration project – they were all men – wanted to change. They wanted to establish a stable and predictable political order. They wanted democracy based on rational rule instead of the charismatic and traditional leadership during the era of the world wars to stay with Weber's categories. Technocrats were expected to guarantee their rational democracy. Their instrument was welfare for the allegiance of the masses, but differently than in the Third Reich.

The postwar necessity to re-establish a new Europe on its ruins automatically created an expansive demand situation, the reconstruction boom in the 1950s and the 1960s. The emerging economies of growth and welfare with full employment and a reasonable distribution of incomes and fortunes created a basis for the mutually reinforcing dynamics between mass consumption and mass production, demand and supply, under demarcation to the people's democracies in Eastern Europe. The first lesson when the beginning of the (West) European integration project was negotiated in Paris in 1950 against the backdrop of the Korean War was the connection between a strong welfare economy and democracy. The experiences of the economic crisis in the 1930s told how easily democracy could get lost without a strong social commitment. Welfare was the currency to buy political allegiance in the view that emerged in Paris. The economy based on the common market would provide resources for welfare. Through a general distribution of welfare, European leaders created a contrast to the hardships in the Soviet system.

John Maynard Keynes had already in the 1930s demonstrated that austerity was no solution to the economic crisis and mass unemployment, but the crisis politics in the 1930s were much less guided by economic theory than by mass pressures and political intuition. After 1945 the time of Keynes came in Western Europe. It was Keynes who provided the economic theory that gave an interpretative frame for development in Western Europe whereas exegetic expounding and distortions of Marx provided ideological cement and political apathy in the East. Keynes had laid out the ground already in *The General Theory of Employment, Interest and Money* (1936), written in response to the Great Depression, which was a theory for full-employment politics in the industrial economies with a social psychological component emphasizing the importance of confidence in the future. Keynes argued that a new great depression could be avoided through political management of the economy where a key political task was to infuse social feelings of certainty and security as a corrective to his observations of the precariousness and uncertainty of the capitalist system.[31] He argued that the economy is a polity, not the other way round as the strong argument would be half a century later.[32]

It is important to separate this Keynes from the Keynesianism after the Second World War where the technocratic application of his theories made him a mechanic provider of a toolkit for the maintenance of economic growth where growth became permanent through political techniques and Keynes's insistence on uncertainty as the basic precondition of capitalism disappeared behind the imagery of permanent growth. Keynesianism emerged when Keynes's theories were brought together into a macro-economic imagery with a tool box of economic policy instruments that could be put in order to engineer unemployment, inflation and other disturbances to an otherwise smoothly operating economic machinery where demand management by public spending and distribution of the yields of economic growth formed the basis.[33]

The success of the West European economies of growth and full employment confirmed the toolkit, and a permanent solution to economic growth and full employment appeared to be a possibility. The interpretative framework linked the political, the social and the economic in a stable relationship, outlining a postwar utopia of political and social stability as well as progress through continuous economic growth. The German ordoliberal approach to political economy, based on the belief in the legal rather than political regulation of the economy, where the legal rules got a social dimension under the label of social market economy, applied in crucial respects the Keynesian toolkit. The political management of the Western economies under the name of mixed economy underpinned by the postwar interpretation of Keynes provoked dreams of a long-term convergence of the planned economies in the East and the politically managed economies in the West and the end of the Cold War.

The West European model for democracy based on distribution of labour between (Western) Europe and its nation-states lasted for a couple of decades during the reconstruction boom after the war. It was only now that the European nation-states emerged in their strong merging of the two concepts. Earlier there had been nations and states with a shifting degree of overlap but seldom identical. The (West) European nation-states were defined in civic and social rather than ethnic terms, in close cooperation with other nation-states, as national communities of destiny on the basis of welfare and (West) European cooperation ('integration') – and the Cold War.

This (West) European reconstruction order refined the corporatist structures in the negotiation of the distribution of the yields of the economic growth. Tripartite centralized bargaining organizations including governments and employer and employee confederations circumvented the parliamentary decision centres and gave democracies a technocratic dimension.[34]

Still another factor underpinned this development towards technocracy substituting democracy. At the height of what in the booming West European economies of growth was interpreted as permanent affluence, just before radical voices began to claim that it was harvest time, the mainstream parties began to abandon their representation of specific interests, developing a catch-all approach scrambling together votes far beyond their core constituencies, becoming office-seeking apparatuses cutting their ties to interest representation with a basis in the civil society as Peter Mair argued in a posthumously published book.[35]

One might develop Mair's thesis to an argument that politics became professional in a much more technocratic sense than when Weber wrote about politics as *Beruf*, which certainly connotes a dimension of profession but much more of vocation. The latter dimension got more or less lost when vocational interest representation became professional interest mediation.

The 1960s was the peak of organized modernity, as the next chapter will show. New, unexpected challenges waited around the corner. The decline began at the moment of the triumph of the model. As we saw at the beginning of this chapter, the organization of interests in the 1870s was the end of political apathy. After the Second World War the fear of the instability of the high-mobilization polities since the end of the First World War (Weimar) promoted the idea of citizen apathy being important for the stability of inclusive democracy. Technocracy would guarantee democracy. Interest mediation instead of interest organization at first made political apathy come back, before the instability of high-mobilization politics recurred. The next chapter will discuss how more precisely organized modernity, in the shape it had got during a century of European politics for coming to terms with the global economy and with the problem of social integration in its wake, came to an end.

9

The New Great Transformation:

The Dismantling of Organized Modernity and the Search for New Forms of Social 'Self-defence' (1960s to the Present)

The two Great Transformations

Even though it has by now been widely accepted as a fact, the dismantling of organized modernity is not easy to understand. This is so, not least, because organized modernity, and its European version, had been seen as eminently stable in its heyday, the 1950s and 1960s. The period can be compared with the era of Restoration after the Napoleonic Wars: then, a socio-political arrangement that was meant to guarantee peace and stability was introduced after a turbulent quarter-century of revolution and war between 1789 and 1815.[1] Organized modernity, in turn, was the answer, first to the long economic stagnation beginning in the early 1870s, following on the Italian and German wars of unification and accompanied by an ever louder language of class struggle, and then, reformed and reinforced the answer to the Second Thirty Years War (1914–1945), which had also been underpinned by strong political mobilization and revolutionary strivings of various kinds (Chapter 8). In its self-understanding, furthermore, organized modernity in its second reformed and reinforced version after 1945 appeared clearly superior to Restoration Europe because it had done away with some of the latter's most glaring earlier incoherencies: the political unit of organized modernity was the nation-state rather than an empire governing other peoples; this nation-state was democratic in an egalitarian-inclusive way rather than formally restricting political participation to narrow elites;

and rather than letting the laws of market and capitalist competition reign supreme the commitment to social solidarity was generally recognized. On the face of it, there seemed to be no reason why organized modernity should not be a lasting answer to European socio-political questions.

Like Restoration Europe, however, European organized modernity also contained the seeds of its own demise. As we have seen before, the builders of the 1815 Holy Alliance had recognized that they could not just return to the times of the Old Regime. They acknowledged a limited right to liberty, and they expected increasing peace and wealth from the extension of commercial society. Unintendedly, thus, they triggered what has become known as the Great Transformation, or the disembedding of capitalist markets from society. It is important to underline (as we did in Chapter 4) that commercial freedom and market self-regulation never became the only principles that were applied. But they were the guiding ideas for socio-political organization; and it was difficult for the elite actors of the time to identify the limitations of this economic creed and to develop alternative principles and policies. When the first contours of organized modernity were emerging with social policies and concertation at the end of the nineteenth century, they were so tentative and thinly sketched that they could be erased by the more radical and violent alternatives of Nazism and Stalinism.

We have to see the demise of European organized modernity in a similar light. Like Restoration Europe, European organized modernity aimed to combine stable institutional forms with a dynamism of advance in knowledge and of economic growth that should provide the substantive basis for lasting political stability by enhancing the 'mass loyalty' that was necessary under democratic conditions. And like in Restoration Europe, the combined effect of remaining normative institutional incoherencies, which were increasingly exposed to critique, and of the undermining of the institutional framework through the expansionist capitalist economy led to a dismantling of the apparent stability. This is a process that has by now gone on for half a century. It has its own history with sequences of steps and significant comparative variations. It has not ushered into a new arrangement of some degree of stability but is rather marked by a series of crises. We can, therefore, see the dismantling of organized modernity as the beginning of a New Great Transformation, comparable in size and socio-political significance with the one analysed by Karl Polanyi. To some extent, it is analysable in analogy with its historical predecessor, provided that the specificity of current conditions as well as the historical experience with the building of organized modernity are taken into account.

In this light, this chapter is devoted to offering an analysis of the past half-century of European socio-political changes as a New Great Transformation that has not yet found an adequate response. The reasoning will proceed in five steps. First, the self-image of organized modernity will be reconstructed, in European and in global terms. Second, the dynamics that led to the undermining of organized modernity will be retraced. As a core component, thirdly, we will reconstruct the course of the politico-economic reinterpretations from the 1970s to the 1990s in some detail. From this analysis, fourthly, the core contours of the New Great Transformation become visible, in terms of both similarities and differences with its historical predecessor. At the current moment, finally, one can also identify reactions to the New Great Transformation, in analogy to the 'self-defence of society' that Karl Polanyi had diagnosed.

Progress and control: the self-image of organized modernity

How widely the global socio-political constellation at around 1960 was perceived as relatively consolidated, can be gathered from the then widespread use of the three-worlds image: a First World of liberal-democratic capitalism; a Second World of Soviet-style socialism; and a Third World of developing countries (see Chapter 8). This imagery was sociologically conceptualized from the First-World point of view as oneself having reached modernity, the status of 'modern society'; the Second World constituting a deliberate and organized deviation but with trends of convergence of those two worlds; and the Third World still needing to undergo processes of 'modernization and development'.[2] These 'worlds', in turn, were composed of societies as unit elements, each of which, according to the dominant perception, had clearly demarcated borders and a state as a central institution with the effective power of monitoring the borders and organizing social life within the borders according to unified rules.

This imagery of orderliness and control also – in only apparent contradiction – extended to the expectations of future social change, conceived in a rather linear way as progress.[3] The stability of institutions was expected to channel change on predictable paths, making it possible to reap the benefits of progress without running the risks that come with entirely open horizons of the future. Progress of knowledge was expected to be 'endlessly' available for the benefit of society, but at the same time one had the closing of the last 'knowledge gaps' in view, thus ruling out any unpleasant surprises in the further pursuit of new knowledge. Economic progress was similarly to be channelled into predictable paths. Keynesian demand management, socialist planning and the development of a national industrial economy through import substitution policies were the strategies, as suited to one of the three 'worlds' each, by which economic growth could be reached without suffering the cyclical downturns that had marked the earlier history of capitalism. Applying these government techniques, economic progress would not only be steady but also lastingly high, thus providing the material background for also accomplishing social and political progress.

While epistemic and economic progress namely were meant to continue in a controlled way, social and political progress were thought to be completed and consolidated. For social progress, emphasis was placed on inclusion, to be reached with the extension of the welfare state regimes so as to protect all members of society against all conceivable risks, 'from the cradle to the grave', as Winston Churchill put it in 1943. In Europe, comprehensive social inclusion was largely accomplished by the 1960s, both in Western Europe and in socialist Europe, even though by different means. In the USA, it was announced as the core objective of the 'War on Poverty', the key component of President Johnson's 'Great Society' programme. In 'Third World' societies, similar social progress was at best distantly on the horizon. Inclusion within the 'First' and 'Second Worlds' relied on firm boundaries towards the 'Third', adapting the colonial division of labour to post-colonial times by controlling the terms of trade. Significantly, furthermore, social progress through welfare state measures meant a standardization of life-situations and, together with a male bread-winner full-employment economy, of life-courses. Individualization, therefore, was not a central criterion for social progress at the time.

Political progress was conceived in a similar manner, as accomplished in some parts of the world and as accomplishable everywhere, provided that a restricted view on such progress was accepted. Accomplishment was defined as free and equal 'conventional' political participation, through which governments were elected that both had some degree of accountability towards the citizenry and were capable of designing and implementing policy programmes. This was reached in the West European and North American 'First World', had found a particular interpretation in the 'Second', and would be reached through political modernization in the 'Third'. As great as the variety of political forms was, they all aimed at stabilizing the political constellation: by competitive-party democracies based on 'political apathy' (Gabriel Almond and Sidney Verba) rather than high-intensity participation in Western Europe and the USA (see Chapter 4 above); by the imposition of a historical-materialist framework for political action in the Soviet-socialist 'people's republics' in Eastern Europe; by the organization of political life in authoritarian frameworks, through military dictatorships and/or organicistically inspired socio-political organization, in Southern Europe and in Latin America; and by the expectation that former colonies claiming the right to self-determination would follow one of the above political paths. This restricted view entailed that the existing states could be the containers of political progress, and that within them a suitable balance between participation in collective self-determination and effective implementation of the common rules was created, in all situations of doubt giving priority to the latter over the former.

In the light of this brief characterization of expected social change, one can recognize that the ambiguous orientation towards progress in the organized modernity of the post-Second World War period, as both open and known, expressed a novel relation between experience and expectations. The experiences of the first half of the twentieth century, in particular, had suggested that the widely open horizon of expectations permitted the rise of undesirable, even disastrous experiences. The conclusion from those experiences was to narrow the horizon of expectations, through the institutions of organized modernity, without closing it entirely. Or in other words, this was an attempt to select from the wide range of historically generated possibilities the limited number of those that appeared to be both functionally viable and normatively desirable.

With hindsight, one can see that this 'choice' – resulting from decisions of the early postwar political and economic elites – was only temporarily sustainable because of this ambiguity towards change, which led to contradictory orientations. On the one hand, the progressive imaginary created two centuries earlier was now to be taken more seriously as a guide to socio-political practices. In public debate, the existing socio-political constellation was not presented as a power regime in principle equal to others in history, but as a socio-political order subject to normative justifications. Thus, claims based on that imaginary – for individual liberty, collective self-determination, social justice – could not just be suppressed. They had to be addressed, in some way or other; and if they were not, pressure for change was likely to continue.

On the other hand, the particular form that this socio-political order took was shaped by the contingency of the moment. In this contingent context, significantly, the USA was the plausible candidate for taking over the lead of history from Europe for a number of reasons. It had been less directly a source of the disasters of the first half of the twentieth century. It had risen to be an economic power and transformed the economy into mass-consumption capitalism, thus had been successful in addressing the question of material needs. It had a reputation of greater political inclusion than European societies, despite the subjection of the native population and the discrimination of the African-American population. And up to this moment it had had a smaller role in colonial domination than Europe, presenting itself rather as one of the first postcolonial societies. While the US was thus the hegemonic power in the early postwar decades, Europe nevertheless provided the model form of organized modernity because it seemed to have combined freedom, democracy and solidarity in the most coherent and institutionally stable way, in the liberal-democratic Keynesian welfare state.

Challenging the conventions of organized modernity

Highlighting these features of the socio-political constellation of around 1960 helps to understand the dynamics that unsettles this constellation and through its dismantling brings about the core contours of the present. In other words, the main issues that need to be confronted when aiming to understand the present can be identified by reading the conflicts and transformations from the 1960s to the 1990s as challenges to the prevailing interpretations of modernity, in the light of perceived normative and functional deficiencies. Again, we will set the European experience in global context.[4]

We should first underline that the present socio-political constellation did not at all evolve smoothly from the preceding organized modernity; its emergence was neither driven by linear progress towards greater individualization, democratization and inclusion nor by any logic of capital. Rather, the organized modernity of the 1960s – to which some authors today look nostalgically back[5] – was actively contested and exposed to critique on a number of fronts, and often in radical ways 'from below'. In the then so-called Third World, movements for national liberation called for decolonization and collective self-determination, these struggles reaching a high point around 1960. They were initially misconceived as merely a step ahead towards the 'modernization and development' that the 'First World' had already accomplished. In the then so-called First World, the year 1968 marked a climax of workers' and students' contestation, often seen as the combination of a political and cultural revolution. And even though the latter aspect should become dominant,[6] the years of intensified protest at the end of the 1960s and during the early 1970s were much more than a short 'crisis of governability' from which one could easily return to elite government and political apathy as usual. In the wake of 1968, time-honoured issues were returned to the political agenda, with greater force and urgency, also by the feminist movement and the ecological movement.

In socio-economic terms, the accommodating response of elites in many European polities – in contrast to persistence or re-instauration of authoritarian regimes in Latin America, South East Asia and South Africa – restored legitimacy for a moment, but also deepened the fiscal crisis of the Keynesian welfare states. The so-called rise of neoliberalism is best considered as the next step of elite response to the threat of the withering away of profitable production possibilities. It involved the weakening of protective labour legislation and the curtailing of trade union power, but also the 'structural adjustment policies' in what is now often called the global South and the relocation of major sectors of industrial production from the supposedly 'advanced industrial societies' to initially East Asia and now many parts of the globe (as we will discuss in more detail below).

In politico-cultural terms, and despite the intentions of the early protest activists, a major consequence of the movements that started in the 1960s was a weakening of the collective concepts the political use of which had marked the preceding one and a half centuries: nation, class, state, and also society. These collective conventions and regulations had not only stabilized modernity temporarily in the West but also contributed to giving meaning to social life. Their dismantling, both through institutional changes and cultural re-significations, was partly brought about by elites who saw their power endangered. But these conventions and regulations were also under attack by people who experienced them as constraining their liberties and capacities for self-realization. Thus, a double-pronged attack, highly differently motivated, on collective conventions led to the destabilization of European organized modernity. We can identify here a 'double movement' similar to the one Karl Polanyi observed for the late nineteenth century: parts of the elites and parts of the dominated groups, without agreeing on their diagnosis of the problems, joined forces in giving society a new direction. The main difference is that the first Great Transformation was built by means of new and forceful collective institutions, against any strong notion of self-regulation, which was perceived to have failed. In contrast, the New Great Transformation entailed, at least in its first major step, the dismantling of the existing institutions, most of which dated back to the first Transformation. The fall of Soviet socialism in the decade after the rise of the first neoliberal governments to power – in Chile, the United Kingdom and the United States of America – then appeared to confirm the de-collectivizing tendency of recent political change. Globalization, seen in connection with the decline of the nation-state, and individualization, seen as the weakening of the capacity for collective action, became the keywords for describing socio-political change during the 1990s.

In sum, we can state that contestations had a considerable share in what we now recognize as the dismantling of organized modernity. Decolonization dismantled (most of) what had remained of the empires. The women's movement achieved – in many, though not all societies – the abolition of remainders of patriarchal law. Restrictions to information and expression were lifted, partly enabled by new technologies. The party structures, of which political scientists thought that they mirrored lasting social divides, crumbled partly because of the formation of movement parties, partly because of a blurring of those social divides. In other words, and again in very sweeping terms, the contestations proved highly successful, to the degree of bringing about a pronounced social transformation.

The outcomes of many of these occurrences can be described in terms of normative achievements: of recognition, of freedom, of equality. This, precisely, is where the success of contestations can be located. An important qualification needs to be added, however. Other components of organized modernity, namely, were dismantled in parallel, but the normative assessment of these processes is much more ambivalent, to say the least: the capacity of states to direct national economies diminished; commercial and financial flows are increasingly beyond control; the institutional frames for collective self-determination have been weakened, partly deliberately in favour of supranational or global cooperation, partly because of an escape of socio-political phenomena from the view and grasp of political institutions. Most observers keep the two components of the recent social transformations separate: as increasingly successful movements for rights, freedom and democracy, on the one hand; and as a global economic transformation driven by the exploitative and oppressive logic of capital, on the other. We will now take a slightly more detailed look at the politico-economic transformations to show the interconnectedness of these components.

The economic crisis of the 1970s and the neoliberal response

The end of the 1960s brought strains in European full-employment economies as workers radicalized their language in a struggle for a larger share of the economic yield, better working conditions and a reduction in job-related stress. The conflict level grew and the claims for economic democracy accompanied the strikes, sits-ins and lockouts. This occurred at the same time as the growth rates began to stagnate. The stagnating economies disturbed the imagery of affluence ahead, and voices demanding more of the pie and grass-roots democracy disturbed the corporatist centralized bargaining machinery of organized modernity. The claims went beyond the mere issue of wages and developed into a struggle about the work-place more generally, centring on concepts such as co-determination, *autogestion*, *Mitbestimmung*, state ownership and economic democracy. This struggle, in turn, was intertwined with a larger generational revolt which in Europe began in France and spread over Western Europe, but went beyond Europe as a worldwide escalation of social conflicts and peoples' rebellions against militarism and capitalism, bourgeoisie and bureaucracy. The Prague Spring was its East European version. '1968' was also the birth of the environmental and anti-nuclear movements.

However, strains came also most unexpectedly from another direction a few years later. External factors began to undermine Europe's welfare economies during the first half of the 1970s. The first hit was the collapse of the Bretton Woods order around the dollar in 1971. The next blow came with the oil price shock in the autumn of 1973, which initiated the beginning of a new international world order, a decrease in the power for the old European industrial economies and a growing scope of action for those Third World countries producing raw materials. The events showed that Europe and the US could no longer unilaterally determine the global terms of trade in an established neo-colonial way.

The dollar collapse in 1971 must be seen against the backdrop of the Vietnam War, which was one of the triggers of the 1968 revolt, and the financial exhaustion as triggered by the military exhaustion. Warfare rather than welfare eroded the Western model of democratic capitalism around the dollar. (One and a half decades later, similar signs of erosion emerged also in the communist model around the Soviet Union. Here, too, the connection to the financing of the military is obvious. The Vietnam War of the Soviet Union was the Afghanistan War in the 1980s.)

Political radicalization and decline of economic performance occurred in a particular temporal sequence. The outcome was reminiscent of the developments during the 1870s. The upward wage pressures in the wake of the radicalization of workers shifted to a downward pressure on wages and profits when economic growth began to level out. Governments tried to mitigate the consequences through inflationary politics which did not prevent the collapse of key industries like coal, steel and shipbuilding, however, and the emergence of mass unemployment for the first time since the 1930s, a development that generally was considered impossible since the Keynesian interpretative framework provided the toolkit for the management of full-employment economies. The memories of the impact of the social protests in the 1930s on the political system came back and alarmed European governments. The West German Minister of Finance and later Chancellor, Helmut Schmidt, famously declared in the mid-1970s that he preferred 5 per cent inflation to 5 per cent unemployment. Very soon, West Germany had both, and more. Governments intervened with massive subsidy packages to stop or slow down the industrial collapse. The accumulation of massive state debts accelerated inflation under conditions of economic stagnation, a development which ran counter to conventional theoretic economic wisdom. The new phenomenon acquired a new name: stagflation.

Keynesian ideas progressively lost credibility in the wake of accelerating unemployment, growing public budget deficits, and increasing inflation. The imagery of proactive management of the economy shifted to the imagery of political helplessness with only a reactive capacity. A new economic orthodoxy with deep roots in liberal philosophy emerged, prescribing a lesser role to the state and promoting greater market freedom. The market would heal the economies from corporatist sclerosis. A new magic word – *flexibility* – promised a panacea. Like the radicalization of the industrial relations were embedded in a more general wave of social protest ('1968') the neoliberal turn occurred within a larger framework of ideological reorientation.[7] Many of the ideas of '1968' around the theme of de-hierarchization were redefined and the priority of interpretation appropriated by the political right and the employers. The years around 1970 saw a huge conceptual confrontation about the redefinition of key concepts like freedom, equality, solidarity, economic distribution, welfare, state and market.

Only gradually did the horizons and images of a new organization of labour and of the economy as a whole emerge. The new organization of labour was a reaction both to the collapse of the Bretton Woods order and to the workers' radicalization from the end of the 1960s. One early symptom of the demarcation of the old order from the new appeared when management and labour in collapsing industrial enterprises mounted the same barricades in response to having to compete for taxpayers' money with corresponding groups in competing companies. Ties of solidarity between the trade unions, which since the 1870s had developed into a national network, were at first stretched, thereafter severed, in the fight between companies for survival.[8] The overall impact, not only on trade unions and the labour market, but on the whole organization of society, was tremendous. National patterns of class solidarity established over a period of a century began to mutate into company-related habits of identification.

The extent of this transformation varied from society to society, but the trend as such was general. Against the backdrop of persisting mass unemployment, the collapse of the previous Keynesian key concept of 'full employment', and exploding state financial deficits, the locus of employment security moved from the state to the company level. Frequent references to the Japanese myth of life-long employment as a model to emulate underpinned this shift. However, the belief in job security at the company level was brief. The new flexibility language of the 1980s, based on concepts such as 'lean production', 'slimming down', 'the flexible company', 'labour hoarding', 'outsourcing' and so on, showed that a new basis of responsibility and certainty could not be socially constructed on the foundations of the company. The next refuge for disappointed hopes and expectations was to be 'the market'.

The imagery of general employment security mediated by the key concept of 'full employment' disappeared under the new system of labour market demarcation between core and occasional employees. The practices of hiring and firing, the social marginalization and the individual employment contracts from the era previous to organized modernity were updated and recurred in new modernized forms.

In a crucial way, the breakdown of national patterns of solidarity meant that mass unemployment did not represent the same political problem and threat to social stability as was first anticipated in the 1970s. Instead of social revolution, the period witnessed a stabilization through social marginalization and a cultural retreat to old Darwinian metaphors, according to which it became generally accepted that only the stronger could expect to survive in the fight for survival in hardening markets.[9]

The contours of what Wolfgang Streeck has called a market nation (*Marktvolk*) emerged, replacing the old state nation (*Staatsvolk*) built in the nineteenth and twentieth centuries and culminating in the welfare state.[10] Many began to believe that the market with its individual development opportunities constituted the nation instead of the suffocating and tax-burdening state, which choked initiatives and development of creative force. Arguments which had dominated in the period before the beginning of the debate on the social question in the 1830s, to the effect that those who 'failed' in their social careers were uniquely responsible for this themselves, recurred. The emphasis shifted to the symbolic presentation of the state as a problem and a barrier to the realization of creative initiatives. This was to become its default status in an ever more hegemonic economic theory and ideology. The propagation of a powerful neoliberal economic vocabulary went hand in hand with a major ideological shift. Hayek and Chicago replaced Keynes and the 'social market economy' (*soziale Marktwirtschaft*). Flexibility replaced welfare as the key socio-economic concept. The welfare state became the tax and debt state. In the academic underpinning of the conceptual transformation public choice replaced public finance as the field of investigation. This shift in perspective had a name: Margaret Thatcher, the 'Iron Lady' and the instigator of 'Thatcherism', who was British prime minister from 1979 to 1990.

The apparent breakthrough of working-class ideals about work in the late 1960s and early 1970s, with the success of key terms such as 'economic democracy', 'co-determination' and 'state ownership', coupled with the step towards the realization of the Marxist view of industrial society that it signalled, turned out to contain the germs of the dissolution of the working class in its historically established form. The end of industrial society in its centenary established forms and the recurrence of social exclusion was near. State-guaranteed universal social citizenship rights were split up in company-specific welfare arrangements and benefits for core employees and emergency relief for the marginalized part of the labour force with occasional work and pay.

The responses of employers to signs of worker militancy, together with the collapse of the international order around the dollar, broke down corporatist structures as well as class identities and national solidarity patterns established over the course of the century. The argument that the trade unions had become too powerful and that their successful wage politics had resulted in wage levels at which the enterprises could no longer compete accompanied the individualization and stratification of the labour markets in response to the mass unemployment. Collective wage agreements were eroded and individual wage contracts gave substance to the flexibility language. The trade unions lost their reputation, prestige and power. The state subsidies and debts to bridge the breakdown of the industrial labour market order became a field of economist attack, whereas the new neoliberal language prescribed flexibility for the healing of the labour markets, and the recipe for the tax-burdening state was budget rigidity, tax reduction and debt clearing.[11]

The long-term impact of government attempts to rescue the collapsing corporatist structures with subsidy packages and other forms of intervention was an increase in social rivalry and a growing questioning of the role of the state in the wake of growing budget deficits and inflation. This had obvious consequences for historically developed conventions of social responsibility and for the principles of organized modernity. The neoliberal hegemony of the 1980s was about to respond to the worker protests and the massive state interventions of the 1970s.

Leaving now this core example, one can probably say, in general terms, that any major socio-political transformation entails the dismantling of existing institutions, but that this dismantling is often accompanied by building new institutions, or by giving new purpose and meaning to existing institutional containers. The transformation from restricted liberal to organized modernity (discussed in Chapter 8) is a strong example for the building of collective institutions to address problems that restricted liberal modernity had created. The contestations of organized modernity, however, have often had the oppressive, exploiting or excluding nature of existing institutions as their target, and have therefore been aiming at de-institutionalization in the first place. As an unintended side-effect, this orientation has tended to incapacitate collective action: on the one hand, because specific existing institutions are weakened, and on the other, because institutional rebuilding in general is delegitimized in the name of some generic concept of equal individual freedom.

In other words, the contestations of organized modernity contained only a weak image of a constructive reinterpretation of modernity. The key elements of this reinterpretation are: the general idea of equal individual rights, which can be found in the women's movement, the civil rights movement in the USA or the struggle against apartheid; the idea of inclusive collective self-determination, or: democracy, in liberation from colonial rule (including the particular case of South Africa) and from authoritarian rule such as in Southern Europe and Latin America; and the idea of freedom from particular constraints in the forms of commercial freedom, media freedom, freedom of movement, and freedom for self-realization. The question then is if, and in which way, these ideas could guide not only the neoliberal dismantling of organized modernity, as they did, but also the creation of the institutional frames for a new interpretation of modernity beyond neoliberalism.

The contours of the New Great Transformation (1): an emerging hegemonic discourse

There was a moment in this exit from organized modernity, during the 1980s and early 1990s, when this weak image gained stronger contours. At this moment, much public political philosophy – from Francis Fukuyama to Richard Rorty – suggested that an abstract commitment to individual freedom and to collective self-determination was about to be globally and unproblematically implemented. It would be accompanied and underpinned by an idea of economic freedom that suggests that constraints to economic action are both freedom-limiting and dysfunctional for economic performance and thus need to be removed. These politico-philosophical ideas translated into a political discourse about 'human rights and democracy' and an economic discourse about a strong return to market freedoms and free trade, both in temporarily hegemonic positions. Furthermore, these discourses found partial institutional expression in various forms: in the abolition of domestic forms of economic regulation; in the lowering of international barriers to economic exchange; in the introduction of the 'responsibility to protect' principle in international law in tension with the principle of state sovereignty; in elements of the internationalization of penal law; and in the tendency to identify public protest movements with an expression of collective self-determination, among others.

Like the discourses of free trade and market self-regulation in Restoration Europe, these discourses were far from having had the effect of abolishing institutional structures and boundaries of various kinds. Indeed, one can even say that they have rarely been found fully persuasive in continental Western Europe, even though more so in Britain and in formerly socialist Eastern Europe. But they have provided elements for a novel and global reinterpretation of modernity with very characteristic features and an enormous ideological force. As such, they underpinned the first step of what we call here the New Great Transformation. Like the sociological theorem of globalization and individualization, this political discourse suggests that there is (and should be) little, or nothing, between the individual human being and the globe. Every social phenomenon that stands in-between tends to be considered as having freedom-limiting effects. Significantly, the notion of democracy, which presupposes a specific decision-making collectivity and thus appears to stand necessarily in an intermediate position between the individual and the globe, tends to be redefined. Rather than referring to a concrete, historically given collectivity, processes of self-determination are, on the one side, related to social movements without institutional reference, and on the other side, projected to the global level as the coming cosmopolitan democracy. We can characterize this conceptual tendency as the *erasure of space*. In a second step, we can identify a similar tendency towards the *erasure of time*. The individual human beings in question are seen as free and equal, in particular as equally free. Thus, their life-histories and experiences are no longer seen as giving them a particular position in the world from which they speak and act. And political orders are seen as associations of such individuals who enter into a social contract with each other, devoid of any particular history.

Even though the imagery sketched here never became the fully dominant interpretation of modernity, it provided significant orientation for much political action after the exit from organized modernity for some time, in particular during the 1980s and 1990s. Today, the imagery still exists, but it has lost plausibility and persuasiveness to a considerable degree, due to occurrences that have been interpreted as signs of its inadequacy, such as a sequence of economic and financial crises across the world; increasing concern about past injustice impacting on the present; the increased awareness of the consequences of human-induced climate change; regional crises of democracy; and lack of criteria for evaluating international conflicts. But, like in the 'self-defence of society' against the idea of market self-regulation during the historical Great Transformation, it remains difficult to develop an alternative to this imagery.

The contours of the New Great Transformation (2): searching for tools for 'self-defence'

Because Polanyi's book has so often been misread, it is worth recalling that the historical Great Transformation, as Polanyi conceptualized it, was not about the rise of the idea of commercial freedom and market self-regulation; it was about the 'rise and fall of market society'. Polanyi did not see the rise of market self-regulation as inevitable; markets were not for him a generally superior means of economic organization. Rather, he wanted to underline that people will react to market society by defending themselves against its shortcomings. Furthermore, he underlined – in the concluding sections that are rarely referred to today – that such self-defence is difficult because it needs to combine the principles of freedom and solidarity that are often seen as opposed to each other in practice.

The New Great Transformation lets similar questions arise. Since the 1970s, we have witnessed the transformation of a globe, which was composed of a set of consolidated regional, indeed, spatially defined, interpretations of modernity, in which Western European societies were part of the 'First World' and Eastern European ones part of the 'Second World', into a globe with de-structured social relations, expecting the emergence of a boundary-less planet populated by unattached individuals. But the view that our current modernity embraces a global commitment to individual human rights and democracy, partially correct as it is, conceals urgent questions and makes it more difficult to address them: individual rights are not an answer to questions of material deprivation and absence of meaning; and democracy becomes an empty term when there is little of significance a limited collectivity can truly decide upon.

As this recently hegemonic discourse tends to erase time and space, the general response needs to be the reconstitution of historical temporality and meaningful spatiality. As we insisted from the outset, modernity is misunderstood as an abstract philosophical idea or as a determined long-term socio-historical trend. Rather, the modern commitment to autonomy and mastery is always open to interpretation, and any such interpretation will occur in the light of experiences with earlier answers and their sedimentation in institutions. In this sense, there are only situation-specific answers. This insight places the burden on the analysis and interpretation of the situation one finds oneself in. As in earlier periods, socio-political situations today vary considerably between regions. But not only is the degree of interconnectedness today higher than in earlier periods, the current work at reinterpretation also takes place in the context of a common experience, in general terms, of the dismantling of existing institutions and commitments without clear and concise guidance for their rebuilding. More specifically, in the face of the experience of attempted erasure of temporal and spatial significance, the current reinterpretation encounters the need for a high degree of justification for any spatio-temporally specific collective commitments.

Thus, let us briefly add to our look at the recent past some observations on world-interpretations. The coining of the term 'Third World' and the elaboration of the three-world imagery, at the high point of organized modernity, was a Northern conceptualization reserving a particular place for what is today often called the global South, namely carrying specific claims, connecting with the notion of *'tiers état'* preceding the French Revolution, but also relegating the inhabitants of this world to the 'not yet' of modernity. This imposition was responded to, one might say with hindsight, by the active positioning of 'Southern' countries in the Bandung conference of 1955. In turn, the diagnosis of the breaking up of organized modernity has been a key theme of the Trilateral Commission, which held its first meeting in 1973 and soon after published its report on the crisis of democracy. The heyday of globalization has been monitored and interpreted by the World Economic Forum (from 1987, preceded by the European Management Forum) and, as a critical alternative, the World Social Forum (from 2001, preceded by 'encuentros' in Latin America). Whereas the former promoted the erasure of time and space through its discourse on economic globalization, the latter provided a mirror image similarly devoid of specific place and history.

But since the 1990s we have increasingly witnessed attempts at reinterpretation and reconstruction that are consciously situated in social space and acknowledge the historicity of human social life. In some way, the events in Tehran in 1979, often referred to as the Iranian Revolution, are an early example of such reconstruction. As specific as the Iranian circumstances were, they can now be seen as an opening towards a broader understanding of political possibilities in the present, since then intensified not only by the strengthening of political Islam but also by 'emerging' novel political self-understandings reaching from the variety of 'progressivist' political majorities in Latin America to the transformation-oriented post-apartheid polity in South Africa to post-communist China. More recently, the emergence of Brazil, Russia, India, China and South Africa (BRICS) entails a further proposal to reconstitute specific spatiality – the global South – and temporality – rectification of past Western (Northern) domination. The term BRIC was coined in 2001 by a business analyst but has later been appropriated by those to whom it was assigned and used to counter the asymmetries of power and wealth due to historical domination.

Thus, despite all technology-induced space-time compression, often called 'globalization', the earth does not at all become a socially homogeneous space. Rather, we witness intense regional attempts at organizing ways of living together according to specific self-understandings and circumstances, in which the experiences of the past are of present relevance for individuals as well as for collectivities. At the same time, those 'regions' are not homogeneous cultures in which a shared world-interpretation prevails. In contrast to long-prevailing assumptions of the historical and social sciences, 'space', as presumed shared territory, and 'time', as presumed common history, are not determinants of collective identity. There is intense struggle over interpretations within those 'spatio-temporal envelopes' (Bruno Latour) that we here call 'regions'. Rather than determinants of action, lived space and historical time are conditions as well as resources for interpretation with a view to enabling individual and collective agency. These brief observations suggest that one can analyse the present as an ongoing attempt at re-interpreting modernity, with again significant regional varieties against the background of earlier experiences with modernity (but in a context of greater connectedness).

But where is the place of Europe within these global attempts at re-interpreting the world as a response to the New Great Transformation? With hindsight, one can recognize its role already in the building of organized modernity. According to one influential analysis, the creation of the European Coal and Steel Community in 1951 and the European Economic Community in 1957 meant the 'rescue of the nation-state',[12] which was to become the pillar of European organized modernity, in the face of the formation of the USA and Soviet Union as super-powers. During the 1960s and 1970s, it was widely assumed that Europe followed an unstoppable logic of 'ever further integration', which was both normatively desired and functionally required. However, the crisis of the early 1970s, discussed above, put strains on this project. The building of European stateness that would transfer the accomplishments of liberal-democratic Keynesian welfare to the larger level, as seemed to be required by adverse politico-economic tendencies, was resisted by the business community and some nation-state elites. As a consequence, integrationists moved towards enhancing politico-cultural instead of institutional integration, launching the slogan of 'European identity' in 1973.[13] Whatever the merits of this move might have been, it was soon superseded by two events that followed rapidly on each other: the coming to power of Margaret Thatcher in 1979; and the fall of the Berlin Wall in 1989. The European elites reacted to the first event by speeding up market integration. The initiator of this move, Jacques Delors, then President of the European Commission, saw this as an indirect way of achieving political integration and the enhancement of European democracy, overcoming the earlier obstacles. But the success of such a strategy is much in doubt, given the consequences of unleashing market forces. The reaction to the second event, in turn, was a deliberate attempt at enhancing political integration, through the Maastricht Treaty of 1992, with the creation of the European Union and of a common currency, the Euro. The fall of the Soviet Union was seen as requiring not only the accession of the formerly socialist Eastern European states, but also the building of European political structures for the post-Cold War era.[14]

The acceleration of European integration since the Maastricht Treaty, accompanied by intense debates about the European self-understanding, is generally recognized as a major attempt at regionally based world-interpretation. It generated quite some enthusiasm in terms of hinting at a real-world alternative against the Thatcherian notion that 'there is no alternative'. By many, it was hopefully seen as providing an institutional and communicative space in which, if not full-fledged alternatives, then at least moderations and attenuations of the tendencies towards erasing historical time and meaningful space could be achieved. As such, it was seen as a model for emulation in Latin America, in East Asia and to some extent also in Africa. During these years, the concluding years of the twentieth century and the opening ones of the twenty-first, it was at the very least open whether Europe was only getting itself ready for more aggressive global economic competition, thus adapting to the globe as it was, or whether it was preparing an alternative idea of socio-political organization, thus contributing to 'self-defence' against the erasure of time and space in the New Great Transformation.[15]

If the latter was the case, then the last decade has shown how this attempt has been defeated, at least for the time being. European integration, and with it the idea of European modernity that had started to gain contours during the 1990s, suffered one blow after another throwing the whole project ever deeper into crisis. This idea of Europa had found an institutional expression in the constitutional treaty, in particular its Charter of Fundamental Rights. But to have it accepted as the Constitution of the European Union became impossible after the referenda in France and the Netherlands in 2005. The extended economic-financial crisis, triggered in the US by the bankruptcy of Lehman Brothers in 2008, made the deficiencies in the management of the European common currency visible, leading to bank crises and quickly rising state debt in the south of Europe. The acute Greek debt crisis after 2009 turned out to demonstrate the narrow limits of European solidarity, forcing the country into an austerity straightjacket. During the same period, the number of refugees trying to reach Europe increased enormously, many of them dying in the Mediterranean Sea, not least owing to the deteriorating political and economic situations in the Middle East and North Africa that suffer from the consequences of the Second Gulf War, from the failed attempts at reconstituting political institutions after the Arab Spring and, in connection with the two, the rise of fundamentalist violence. In 2015, it was finally recognized that the refugee question needed a European answer, but no convincing such answer has yet been forthcoming. Rather, the United Kingdom referendum in favour of leaving the European Union in June 2016, building on time-honoured British Euro-scepticism, gave another sign of the citizen disaffection with the Europe of today. In contrast to the 'double movement' that Polanyi observed during the first Great Transformation, elites and citizens in the current Europe fail to connect in developing a response to the current transformations that would give a meaning to the term 'self-defence' adequate for our time.

10

From Ambiguity to Disorientation:

European Modernity Derailed

Europe has been both praised and blamed for having developed a concept of modernity meant to guide socio-political transformations and to provide a model for future socio-political organization. Our preceding observations and reflections have suggested that some such concept existed, and that it indeed provided some guidance for action. However, the concept has never been fully coherent and closed, but marked by ambiguity and wide openness to interpretation. Rather than sketching a single trajectory of development, it provided at most a horizon towards which one could move on a variety of paths, and whether one should move into that direction at all could also be contested.

Once one adopts such a broader perspective, it is no longer problematic to maintain that some such core concept of modernity was indeed elaborated in European debates between 1650 and 1800, during the era of the Enlightenment. It was developed in response to the cultural-intellectual and political challenges that the encounter with other, unknown peoples and the breakdown of the unity of Christian cosmology entailed. The last resort in such a crisis situation was the individual: as the subject of certain knowledge, as the source of interests and desires; as the holder of inalienable rights; as the atom with which viable polities could be constructed. All other socio-political phenomena were relegated to secondary status in such individualist ontology: the social contract was drafted and signed by reasonable individuals. Popular sovereignty became to be seen increasingly as the aggregate of individual preferences. The thus constituted polity needed to be distinct from the comprehensive world-views that tied human beings to each other, importantly through religious beliefs (we outlined this model in Chapter 1).

Given the explicitness and radicality of the ways in which the human condition was being rethought in Enlightenment philosophy, the view became widespread that the onset of European modernity – and, in this view, of modernity *tout court* – took place in the eighteenth century, and that it opened the horizon of the futures. The problematic, sometimes outright disastrous experiences with such modernity during the twentieth century re-opened, ironically, the horizon towards the past, allowing for a longer-term and less linear perspective. This rethinking led to a focus on the Axial Age as the plural but interconnected beginnings of human history and, later on, to the notion of multiple modernities being generated from the encounter of crystallized civilizations with European modernity. Rather than entailing a fruitful new view on the origins of modernity, however, we argued, the debates should be seen as leading to the insight that human societies undergo major transformations during which they may adopt radically new societal self-understandings (Chapter 2). The transformation around 1800 then becomes a significant one among several others rather than one that stands out in all respects.

From this broader perspective, furthermore, that which we called above the core concept of modernity can now more easily be recognized as a very particular interpretation of modernity. Even though it was put forward very forcefully in Europe during the eighteenth century, the individualist-instrumentalist model of the human being and of society and polity never went uncontested. Alternative proposals were made in response. That is why it is always somewhat inadequate, even though not entirely wrong, to denounce European individualism-cum-instrumentalism from a critical, postcolonial or decolonial perspective. True, one may want to argue that the alternatives were marked by the fact that they were a response to the strong model concept. When European thought underlined the richness and density of social bonds among human beings, it did so in rejection of individualism and instrumentalism. When the emphasis was placed on meaning-providing communities into which human beings are always embedded, then this was meant to oppose the idea that human collectivities only come into existence through a contract between rational individuals. Nevertheless, these responses brought about a great variety of intra-European self-understandings, many of which integrated underlying religious commitments drawing on Catholic, Protestant and Orthodox Christianity, Judaism and Islam and furthermore reflected on a range of different, and often quite distinct, regional historical experiences. Europe has never been monolithic, and neither has European modernity (Chapter 3).

In the light of this intra-European variety of world-interpretations, furthermore, it is not surprising – but very important for our purposes – to note that the core model of modernity was never applied in European history. This is due, partly, to the fact that it was rejected by elites aiming to preserve their privileges in the face of the revolutionary agenda entailed by the model, and partly because of the incoherence and recognized inadequacy of the model itself. Europeans have never in large numbers been convinced of an individualist ontology – much less, for instance, than the settler descendants in the US. None of its key components – democracy, markets, individual autonomy, separation of religion and politics – was implemented in the way in which the promotors of the model had conceptualized and expected it (Chapters 4 to 7).

Once this is recognized, then the question of European modernity is no longer one about the invention and realization of a model but one of rethinking self-understandings and world-interpretations in the face of the challenges of different historical moments. What we have called here the core model was created in the face of unknown alterity and cosmological divide during the period that Europeans call 'early modernity'. Later transformations are distinct from earlier ones not least by the fact that they take place at a moment when the core model already exists and shapes the discursive space within which reinterpretation occurs. The events that were analysed by Karl Polanyi under the label 'Great Transformation' were thus marked by the imaginary of market self-regulation, in the very centre of Polanyi's own thinking (Chapter 5), and the imaginary of inclusive-egalitarian democracy, much less central in institutional practices, but identified by Alexis de Tocqueville as early as the 1830s (Chapter 4). In both cases, the individual human being assumes a pivotal role (Chapter 6) and comprehensive world-views are relegated to a secondary role (Chapter 7). But this is the case again much more in thought than in practice. Recognizing the fallacies of instrumentalist individualism as well as, often enough, experiencing negative consequences of its partial applications, Europeans tried to elaborate smooth compromises between different commitments, such as the 'solidarisme' of the Third French Republic, or the inter-class alliances in Scandinavia between the world wars. But such arrangements worked under rather favourable circumstances only, and they lacked the conceptual coherence of the core model. Under more conflictive circumstances, Europeans embarked on radical reinterpretations, such as the supremacist racial oppression, exploitation of colonialism and the 'collective essentialisms' of fascism, Nazism and Stalinism (Chapter 8).

Based on the experience with the earlier trials, both the positive ones and the disastrous ones, it seemed that a stable institutional compromise could be reached after the end of Nazism and the Second World War. This was the liberal-democratic Keynesian welfare and nation-state set in a context of increasing European integration. However, this arrangement crumbled, and Europeans have lost their bearings in the new global context that we characterized as a New Great Transformation (Chapter 9). Europe seemed to be ready to spell out, in the proper name of Europe, the core principles of its particular interpretation of modernity when it elaborated its own Charter of Fundamental Rights, proclaimed in the year 2000 and acquiring legal force with the Lisbon Treaty of 2009. This Charter commits the European Union and its member states to individual rights, democracy, solidarity and justice; and beyond binding itself, Europe aims at portraying itself globally as the leading defender of these principles. But at the same time, it easily recedes from these commitments in the face of problems such as the post-2008 recession with rising unemployment and public deficits and the recent refugee crisis. Importantly, it becomes increasingly clear that Europe lacks criteria for applying these principles. Europe is abstractly committed to democracy but has developed little sense of the requirements for democratic deliberation and decision-making. On the inside, there is no self-understanding of the EU as a polity with boundaries enabling collective self-determination. Towards the outside, the rhetoric welcoming apparent 'democratization' through movements such as in North Africa, the Middle East and Eastern Europe replaces reflection about conditions for viable democracy. Similarly, Europe appears to be leading trade-policy negotiations, such as the Transatlantic Trade and Investment Partnership (TTIP) with the USA, as if it had remained blindly committed to the idea of the enhancement of peace and the increase of the wealth of nations by expanding commerce without any consideration for negative social and environmental consequences.

Europe is caught in the abstractness of the formulae for 'human rights and democracy' and the boundary-less extension of freedoms without being able to give them meaning in the concrete place and time of the present. It has fallen into the trap of hegemonic discourse. And, thus, two historical shortcomings have become clear today. In cultural-intellectual terms, first, Europeans have never determined their relation to the individualist ontology promoted in the Enlightenment: is it the foundation for the normative claims on which a new and better society can be built, or is it an erroneous exaggeration of concerns arising in a situation of strife and radical doubt? This cultural-intellectual ambiguity, secondly, became dangerous in political terms: the calls for freedom and self-determination derived from Enlightenment ontology could be adopted by elites for their purposes arguing against existing constraints, as freedom of commerce, as freedom to buy labour-power, as freedom to transform the earth. And even though this ontology also served the dominated groups – women, workers, the colonized – to make their claims for liberation and recognition, in their resistance to elites their political proposals could turn anti-liberal.

The socio-political transformations over the past two centuries can largely be read in the light of those tensions and ambiguities. The current situation, in turn, is still marked by the conviction that the post-Second World War arrangement had finally resolved those tensions: the European liberal-democratic Keynesian welfare and nation-state was seen – and to some extent experienced – as the optimum combination of individual liberty, competitive-party democracy, social solidarity, and national belonging and community. This conviction led to a complacency that makes it difficult to confront the challenges of the present.

When internal and external shocks to this 'model' emerged from the late 1960s and through the 1970s, the general assumption was that adaptation was possible without major problems, in particular in the forms of greater individual liberty (later captured as 'individualization') and greater openness to the outside (later captured as 'globalization'). It was little recognized that these changes, as justifiable as they may partly be in normative terms, undermined the bases of the socio-political arrangement. In particular, they undermined democracy by de-specifying the collectivity that self-determines its rules (no longer the nation, but neither Europe nor the globe) and weakening the bonds between the members of a polity; and they undermined social solidarity by withdrawing resources from the polity through fiscal and legal competition.

At the current moment, thus, the tensions and ambiguities within the normative commitments have re-emerged in strong terms, but the capacity to recognize and address them has decreased, and this again for the same kinds of reasons. In cultural-intellectual terms, the commitment to 'human rights and democracy' leaves today less space for doubt than ever, and therefore the consequences of an overly abstract conception of such commitment are more difficult to recognize and accept than at earlier historical moments. In political terms, the 'thirty glorious years' of the postwar era had created the conviction that a viable compromise between different normative commitments was not only possible but had actually been reached in Europe. Thus, it proves difficult now to see this as a merely temporary achievement under very particular, unrepeatable, historical circumstances.

Dismantling this European organized modernity may have been unavoidable for a number of reasons (briefly discussed in Chapter 9). But the dismantling happened without any guidance for re-instituting European modernity in a more adequate way. The destruction of the institutions of organized modernity largely happened in the name of freedom, be it the freedom for personal self-realization hailed by '1968' or be it the freedom of the entrepreneur. But, as Michel Foucault recognized, 'the affirmation or the empty dream of freedom' leads into misconceived 'projects that claim to be global or radical', without being so. The new horizons of individualization and globalization, in sociological terms, or of human rights and democracy, in political terms, have left Europe without orientation. They do not provide for a place for Europe, which needs to be specific, circumscribed in social space and rooted in historical time, without being narrow-minded with regard to others or determined by its past.[1]

Thus, there is a strong tension between abstract normative commitments and the requirements of the current situation, which though is barely recognized. We can make it more visible by briefly addressing two questions that will need to be central for any reinterpretation of modernity for our time – of European modernity in particular, but for modernity in other parts of the globe as well. These are the questions of: (1) historical injustice; and (2) of the need to give form to processes of collective self-determination.

Across the nineteenth century, as shown above, the notion that Europe had developed universal commitments that would be applied across the globe became widespread, not least as a consequence of actual European global domination. During the first half of the twentieth century, this notion was strongly shaken and widely abandoned. After Nazism and the Second World War, a self-critical view on one's own collective memory was developed, to some extent pioneered, in many European societies, in contrast to earlier notions of national pride.[2] One can even say that European polities re-constituted themselves in the face of historical injustices experienced and committed in the past. By the 1970s and 1980s, however, this focus on self-criticism gave way increasingly to the notion that the problematic past had been overcome and could now be settled. The apparent success of European integration created the basis for a new kind of collective pride. The 'transitions' from authoritarian rule in Southern Europe and later the exit from Soviet-style socialism and the reconstitution of polities in former Yugoslavia were strongly guided by the idea that the past needed to be quickly overcome and settled to open the path for a better future.[3] Similarly, the European sense of responsibility for the former colonies, still dominant in a paternalistic way during the 1970s, gave way to a view of cooperation on equal terms with everyone responsible for oneself.[4] In other words, the idea that socio-political organization and cooperation in the present should be based on formal equality and on a 'veil of ignorance' cast over past experience became more widespread. Europeans see themselves as committed to values of freedom and equality, but they behave as if everyone on the globe could act as equally free without being conditioned in the present by the consequences of past injustice.

After the Second World War, as discussed earlier, Europe had developed a commitment to democracy that was both firm and contained. The nation was the unquestioned site of popular sovereignty, and at the same time European integration and postcolonial cooperation were emerging forms of inter-polity coordination. Within the polity, the egalitarian-inclusive commitment to free and universal suffrage was no longer in doubt, even though political mobilization outside institutional channels was discouraged and radical political views outlawed or marginalized. On these assumptions, democracy seemed stable.[5] From the late 1960s onwards, however, the scenario became much more unstable both internationally and domestically. Internationally, the terms of trade turned more unfavourable towards the 'advanced industrial economies', and at the same time increasing international trade permitted less Keynesian-style control of the national economy. Furthermore, more radical political alternatives emerged in Latin America and in decolonization struggles in the name of democracy. Domestically, 'unconventional political participation' increased and raised concerns about a 'crisis of governability'. By the end of the twentieth century, these tensions had found a 'solution' that satisfied the elites for a while: intensified democratic participation was accepted while at the same time collective self-determination was emptied of substance because of global interconnectedness and interdependencies.[6] Here, again, an abstract normative commitment is applied without regard for the specific circumstances. Thus, such 'solution' cannot be stable: because of increasing dissatisfaction, governments are regularly voted out of office; but since incoming governments continue to pursue the same policies both citizen disaffection and populist leanings increase. European politics is facing an explosive situation, with ever more cases of extreme political instability and, at the same time, an inability to create new avenues of collective action through deliberation in the public sphere.

What is to be done? The preceding observations and analyses are not meant to provide recipes for action. But if taken seriously they might contribute to bring about an overdue leap in European consciousness that, in turn, is a precondition for more adequate collective action. Over the past half century, namely, the impression was created – or re-created – that Europe and Europeans are on the winning side of history: other societies were inclined to copy the 'European model' or at least parts of it; or they aimed to join 'Europe' as a collectivity or polity when they had some claim to be European; or people tried – and still try – to reach Europe and settle there in the search for a better life, even risking and often losing their lives. This undeniable attractiveness of Europe has led to a high degree of complacency among Europeans, among elites as well as across society at large. It was – and often still is – widely assumed that Europeans had got it right, whereas others still tended to get it wrong and thus had to orient themselves towards Europe. But this is an enormous misconception of the history of Europe and of world-history. This view tends to separate Europe from other world-regions and situate it on a higher plane. Instead, however, the orientations of other societies and peoples towards Europe need to be understood as expressions of Europe's embeddedness in a global setting, in the two senses that we have emphasized across this book. On the one hand, much of the 'rise of Europe' is a consequence of past European domination and of injustice inflicted on others. While the era of domination is largely over, the consequences are still present and cannot be ignored.[7] And on the other hand, there has never been a European model of modernity that has generally provided a superior mode of socio-political organization, but a particular, contingent trajectory of historical experiences and interpretations derived from them, not separated from but closely entangled with the rest of the world. Such insight entails the need to enquire into the possibility that those particular circumstances may have changed for good.

The required leap in European consciousness touches on all core aspects of the European self-understanding: European democracy is not consolidated at all. It has lost its proclaimed, though rarely well practised, historical nexus of nation and people and has not built any other ground to stand on. The current fear of populism is another version of the historical hesitations about democracy among European elites; and it is an indicator that no strong culture of democracy has developed in Europe during the times of formally democratic institutions. In contrast, the way to go is to overcome the notion of democracy as an institutional regime and strengthen a democratic culture that is capable of self-transformation in the light of new challenges.

In economic terms, Europe did develop a sense of the embedding of markets in institutional frameworks of solidarity and democracy. But it has lost the confidence in being able to keep up such frameworks under changed circumstances and has largely abandoned them without replacement. True, sustaining such frameworks requires their competent monitoring and the continuous judgement of their adequacy. But instead of at least trying to do so, states have left the direction of economic development to the use of indicators that are manipulated at will by self-enriching business elites. It is of great urgency to restore the political capacity to frame economic action.

Among other elements, the abandoning of political capacity was also motivated by a misconceived notion of individual freedom. As a consequence of historical experiences with oppression and restrictions to personal freedom, on the one hand, and of the increasing entanglement of different intra-European self-understandings, on the other, the prevailing concept of freedom has thinned out and turned increasingly individualistic. Alternative notions that see freedom thriving only in connection with democracy and solidarity do exist, but the need for them to be supported by institutions rarely finds consensus any longer.

And something similar, finally, happened to public religion. Historically, Europeans have contributed to the liberal insight that notions of revealed truth cannot be imposed on people. Often they have done so in a half-hearted way, keeping the majority religion in institutional connection with the state, and such arrangements have increasingly been criticized in recent years. However, rather little emphasis has been given to considering the question of religion as connected to the need for meaningful self-interpretation of the situation one finds oneself in – something that cannot be done individualistically but only by mobilizing collectively available sources of meaning.

The leap in European consciousness, to which this book aims to contribute, is a first step in a necessary reinterpretation of European modernity, based on experiences in both an earlier and the more recent past. The second step would need to be future-oriented. It would require a Europe-wide public conversation about democracy, the economy, freedom and meaning in our current time. Such a conversation is already taking place in many sites, in Europe and elsewhere. But it needs to acquire momentum and focus so as to allow reorientation of public affairs. The current state of Europe does not offer much hope that this will happen soon. But it rather should.

NOTES

Chapter 1

1 For a philosophical and historical work that tries to overcome both forms of overemphasis while retaining the critical perspective, see Dipesh Chakrabarty, *Provincializing Europe: Postcolonial Thought and Historical Difference* (Princeton, NJ: Princeton University Press, 2000).

2 For related recent works, see Gerard Delanty, *Formations of European Modernity* (London: Palgrave-Macmillan, 2013); and Gerard Delanty and Chris Rumford, *Rethinking Europe* (London: Routledge, 2005).

3 See, for instance, Kenichi Mishima, 'The long shadow of European self-interpretation in another modernity', *Social Imaginaries* 2, no. 2 (2016).

4 Such as Kenneth Pomeranz, *The Great Divergence: China, Europe, and the Making of the Modern World Economy* (Princeton, NJ: Princeton University Press, 2000); Christopher Alan Bayly, *The Birth of the Modern World, 1780–1914* (Oxford: Blackwell, 2004); Jürgen Osterhammel, *Die Verwandlung der Welt* (Munich: Beck, 2008) (translated by Patrick Camiller as *The Transformation of the World: A Global History of the Nineteenth Century*, Princeton, NJ: Princeton University Press, 2014).

5 Arno Mayer, *The Persistence of the Old Regime* (London: Croom Helm, 1981); Sandra Halperin, *War and Social Change in Europe: The Great Transformation Revisited* (Cambridge: Cambridge University Press, 2004); Bo Stråth, *Europe's Utopias of Peace* (London: Bloomsbury, 2016).

6 Reinhart Koselleck, *Futures Past: On the Semantics of Historical Time* (Cambridge, MA: MIT Press, 1985). Originally published as *Vergangene Zukunft* (Frankfurt/Main: Suhrkamp, 1979).

7 Peter Wagner, *A Sociology of Modernity* (London: Routledge, 1994).

8 For a recent exploration of this topic, see Nathalie Karagiannis, 'Democratic surplus and democracy-in-failing: On ancient and modern self-cancellation of democracy', in *The Trouble with Democracy*, ed. Gerard Rosich and Peter Wagner (Edinburgh: Edinburgh University Press, 2016).

9 On transformations in the notion of progress, see Peter Wagner, *Progress: A Reconstruction* (Cambridge: Polity Press, 2016).

10 See Angela Lorena Fuster Peiró and Gerard Rosich, 'The limits of recognition: History, otherness and autonomy', in *African, American and European Trajectories of Modernity*, ed. Peter Wagner (Edinburgh: Edinburgh University Press, 2015), 42–53; Peter Wagner, *Theorizing Modernity* (London: Sage,

2001), ch. 1; Peter Wagner, *Modernity as Experience and Interpretation* (Cambridge: Polity, 2008), ch. 9.

11 See for some such argument recently Gunnar Skirrbek, 'Alternative processes of modernization?', in *Nordic Paths to Modernity*, ed. Johann Arnason and Björn Wittrock (Oxford: Berghahn, 2012), 167–189.

12 Cornelius Castoriadis, 'Pouvoir, politique, autonomie', in *Le monde morcelé. Les carrefours du labyrinthe*, vol. 3 (Paris: Seuil, 1990), 113–139, and elsewhere.

13 See William H. Sewell, Jr, *Work and Revolution in France* (Cambridge: Cambridge University Press, 1980), for a detailed analysis.

14 Next to Sewell, see Jacques Donzelot, *L'Invention de la société* (Paris: Fayard, 1984); Giovanna Procacci, *Gouverner la misère: la question sociale en France, 1789–1848* (Paris: Seuil, 1993); and Peter Wagner, 'Freedom and solidarity: Retrieving the European political tradition of non-individualist liberalism', in *European Solidarity*, ed. Nathalie Karagiannis (Liverpool: Liverpool University Press, 2007), as well as Chapter 4 below.

15 Alain Touraine, *Critique de la modernité* (Paris: Fayard, 1992).

16 Johann Arnason, 'The imaginary institution of modernity', *Revue Européenne des Sciences Sociales* 27, no. 86 (1989): 323–337; Wagner, *A Sociology of Modernity*.

17 Maybe even at the conceptual centre, as often argued. For a recent contribution, see Johann Arnason, 'The religio-political nexus: Historical and comparative reflections', in *Religion and Politics: European and Global Perspectives*, Annual of European and Global Studies, vol. 3, ed. Johann Arnason and Pawel Karolewski (Edinburgh: Edinburgh University Press, 2016), 8–36; and Suzi Adams, 'On Johann Arnason and the religio-political nexus', *Social Imaginaries* 2, no. 2 (2016).

18 See Göran Therborn, *European Modernity and Beyond* (London: Sage, 1995). For recent sociological analyses of Europe, see further, William Outhwaite, *European Society* (Cambridge: Polity, 2008); William Outhwaite, *Europe since 1989: Transitions and Transformations* (Abingdon: Routledge, 2016).

Chapter 2

1 Another example from recent history is the notion of manifest destiny applied to the USA. We return to imaginations of North America in relation to Europe in Chapter 3.

2 Karl Jaspers, *Vom Ursprung und Ziel der Geschichte* (Munich: Piper, 1949). Quotes from this work below are from the English translation: *The Origin and Goal of History* (Forge Village, MA: Yale University Press, 1965); see also Henning Trüper, Dipesh Chakrabarty and Sanjay Subrahmanyan, eds, *Historical Teleologies in the Modern World* (London: Bloomsbury, 2015).

3 For a recent comprehensive reassessment, see Johann Arnason, Shmuel Eisenstadt and Björn Wittrock, eds, *Axial Civilizations and World-History* (Leiden: Brill, 2005).

4 Historical materialism gives similar importance to the late-eighteenth-century transformations, seen as the rise of bourgeois-capitalist society, with the important qualification that these are not seen as the last, but as the penultimate major socio-political transformation in human history, to be followed by the proletarian revolution.

5 We need to mention briefly a third way of starting European history as well as a mode of writing European history, a fourth way, so to say, that can do without a clearly delimited starting-point. Less direction-driven and more empirically-oriented accounts of history tend to locate the origins of Europe in that time, during which a large-scale socio-cultural phenomenon emerges that has roughly the contours of contemporary Europe and comes to be known under this name. This is the period of the transformation of the Roman Empire – long referred to as its 'decline' – reaching some kind of conclusion with the crowning of Charlemagne as emperor in 800 CE (see, for instance, Michael Mann, *The Sources of Social Power*, vol. 1, Cambridge: Cambridge University Press, 1983). From a civilizational perspective, this entails identifying Europe with Western Christianity and demarcating it from Orthodox Christianity (Eastern Rome) and from Islam, all of which are in some way successor civilizations to the Roman one (see Garth Fowden, *Before and after Muhammad: The First Millennium Refocused*, Princeton, NJ: Princeton University Press, 2014). We will discuss in Chapter 3 the changing spatial contours of Europe and the variety of discourses that identify Europe with certain spaces. Taking a more 'bottom-up' perspective (or, in other words, taking more seriously Mann's maxim of looking at the actual extension of social relations than Mann himself does), one can also identify the emergence of Europe with the creation of dense and stable networks of connections stretching across the space of what is known as Europe. Even though we do not pursue it in detail in this volume, such an approach also underlies our reconstruction of European modernity (see for such an approach, the book series *Making Europe*, edited by Johan Schott and Phil Scranton).

6 See Shmuel N. Eisenstadt, 'Multiple modernities', *Daedalus* 129, no.1 (Winter 2000): 1–29.

7 See Johann Arnason, 'The Axial Age and its interpreters: Reopening a debate', in Arnason, Eisenstadt and Wittrock, *Axial Civilizations*. For an account of world-history in terms of struggle for 'liberation', see Enrique Dussel, *Política de la liberación* (Madrid: Trotta, 2007). Inspired by liberation theology, this account locates 'origins' in early Christianity and argues against 'Hellenocentrism', the emergence of which in European self-understanding we trace at the beginning of Chapter 3.

8 Arnason, 'The Axial Age'.

9 'Extra-European' not necessarily in a territorial, but in a temporal sense, referring to intellectual developments before the birth of Europe; see Jan Patočka, *Heretical Essays in the Philosophy of History* (Chicago, IL: Open Court, 1996), e.g. 83, 109, for a historico-philosophical account of the rise of Europe, and Rémi Brague, *Europe, la voie romaine* (Paris: Criterion, 1992; Paris: Gallimard, 1999), for a masterful portrait of Europe's 'secondarity', i.e. its reliance on sources for its identity that stem from outside itself – more on this below.

10 This way of formulating the issue relates closely to the first three items in Björn Wittrock's summary ('The meaning of the Axial Age', in Arnason, Eisenstadt and Wittrock, *Axial Civilizations*) of the key contentions of the Axial Age hypothesis: reflexivity, historicity and agentiality. For reasons that will become clearer in the course of the argument, we define these three concepts as follows. Reflexivity refers here to the human ability to, by means of imagination, step out of the immediate present and to imagine other possible worlds, or partial worlds. Historicity refers to the translation of such imagination into time, by means of which the present can be distinguished from a past that was different and from a future that may be different. Agentiality refers to the belief that human action may contribute to bring a particular different future about.

11 As impressively documented in Arnason, Eisenstadt and Wittrock, *Axial Civilizations*.

12 Koselleck, *Futures Past*.

13 See Johannes Fabian, *Time and the Other* (New York: Columbia University Press, 1983), and Chakrabarty, *Provincializing Europe*, as two key examples – even though Sheldon Pollock's call for further caution ('Axialism and empire', in Arnason, Eisenstadt and Wittrock, *Axial Civilizations*) may still be needed.

14 Nelson Goodman, *Ways of Worldmaking* (Indianapolis, IN: Hackett, 1978), or better, 'mises en forme du monde', using Johann Arnason's and Claude Lefort's references to Maurice Merleau-Ponty. See also Nathalie Karagiannis and Peter Wagner, eds, *Varieties of World-Making* (Liverpool: Liverpool University Press, 2007).

15 Cornelius Castoriadis, *L'institution imaginaire de la société* (Paris: Seuil, 1977), and elsewhere.

16 Jan Assmann, 'Axial "breakthroughs" and semantic "relocations" in ancient Egypt and Israel', in Arnason, Eisenstadt and Wittrock, *Axial Civilizations*.

17 Jan Assmann, 'Große Texte ohne eine Große Tradition. Ägypten als eine vorachsenzeitliche Kultur', in *Kulturen der Achsenzeit II. Ihre institutionelle und kulturelle Dynamik*, Teil 3, ed. Shmuel N. Eisenstadt (Frankfurt/Main: Suhrkamp, 1992), 245–280. Also Marcel Detienne, *Les Grecs et nous* (Paris: Perrin, 2009)

18 This is the main gist of the second series of volumes on the Axial Age published under the mentorship of Shmuel Eisenstadt: those that deal with the 'institutional and cultural dynamics' of Axial Age cultures and, more often than not, suggest that Axial Age cultures were sustained until they encountered modernity; see *Kulturen der Achsenzeit*, vols 1–3, ed. Shmuel N. Eisenstadt (Frankfurt/Main: Suhrkamp, 1992), especially volumes 1 and 3.

19 Such overemphasis was evident in Jaspers's work, though much less so in Eisenstadt's where the focus is more on intellectual elites. On the issue of cultural transmission in general, a key text is Jan Assmann, *Das kulturelle Gedächtnis. Schrift, Erinnerung und politische Identität in frühen Hochkulturen* (Munich: Beck, 1999).

20 Such a look is provided by the contributors to Arnason, Eisenstadt and Wittrock, *Axial Civilizations*.

21 See also Eric Voegelin, *In Search of Order*, vol. 5 of *Order and History* (Baton Rouge, LA: Louisiana State University Press, 1987), 38 on 'imagination': 'Imagination offers imagining man escapes from a sort of reality by which it is governed.' Voegelin then goes on to discuss German idealism.

22 Kurt Raaflaub, *The Discovery of Freedom in Ancient Greece* (Chicago, IL: University of Chicago Press, 2004).

23 Jan Assmann, 'Große Texte', 246–247; Aleida Assmann, 'Einheit und Vielfalt in der Geschichte. Jaspers' Begriff der Achsenzeit neu betrachtet', in *Kulturen der Achsenzeit II. Ihre institutionelle und kulturelle Dynamik*, Teil 3, ed. Shmuel N. Eisenstadt (Frankfurt/Main: Suhrkamp, 1992), 338, for the term 'sociology of tradition'; the term 'social labour' is adapted from Luc Boltanski (e.g. *L'amour et la justice comme compétences*, Paris: Métailié, 1990); see also Peter Wagner, 'As intellectual history meets historical sociology: Historical sociology after the linguistic turn', in *Handbook of Historical Sociology*, ed. Gerard Delanty and Engin Isin (London: Sage, 2003), 168–179. Recent research on 'cultural heritage' and 'cultural memory' goes in this direction.

24 For a critical discussion of empire formation in the wake of the Axial Age, see Pollock, 'Axialism and empire'.

25 For discussions about transformations of contemporary polities in related terms, see Peter Wagner, 'Crises of modernity: Political sociology in historical contexts', in *Social Theory and Sociology: The Classics and Beyond*, ed. Stephen P. Turner (Cambridge, MA: Basil Blackwell, 1996), 97–115. For a related discussion in early social science, see Robert von Mohl, 'Gesellschafts-Wissenschaften und Staats-Wissenschaften', *Zeitschrift für die gesammte Staatswissenschaft* 2 (1851), 3–71; for a discussion of the concept of culture in contemporary social theory, see Peter Wagner, *A History and Theory of the Social Sciences* (London: Sage, 2001).

26 More detail on the spatial configuration of Europe will be provided in Chapter 3.

27 See, e.g., Johann Arnason, *The Peripheral Centre. Essays on Japanese History and Civilization* (Melbourne: Trans Pacific Press, 2001) for Japan, and Shin Jong-Hwa, 'The historical formation of modernity in Korea: Events, issues and actors' (PhD thesis, University of Warwick, 2002) for Korea.

28 This section focuses on the historical and temporal understanding of modernity, whereas the following section focuses on the conceptual and substantive aspects.

29 For a Greek view of Europe at the time: 'Those who live in a cold climate and in Europe are full of spirit, but wanting in intelligence and skill; and therefore they retain comparative freedom, but have no political organization, and are incapable of ruling over others' (Aristotle, *Politics*, 1327b24–32, trans. Jonathan Barnes, CUP edition)

30 Shmuel N. Eisenstadt, 'Kurzer Ausblick auf die westliche Kultur', in *Kulturen der Achsenzeit II. Ihre institutionelle und kulturelle Dynamik*, Teil 3, ed. Shmuel N. Eisenstadt (Frankfurt/Main: Suhrkamp, 1992), 283, observes that the connectedness to antiquity is precisely one of the characteristics of Europe.

31 Brague, *Europe*.

32 We return to Brague at the beginning of Chapter 3 to show how his reasoning cautiously and ultimately indecisively tries to move beyond the search for the origins of Europe.
33 Robert Ian Moore, *The First European Revolution* (Oxford: Blackwell, 2000).
34 As in the theory of path dependency in contemporary social science.
35 Presumably such a statement about an intellectual ambit is not objectionable despite the fact that the residence or citizenship of some key contributors is not European.
36 As Jaspers, *Origin and Goal*, 5 put it: 'The age that saw all these developments [. . .] cannot be regarded as a simple upward movement. [. . .] When the age lost its creativeness, a process of dogmatic fixation and levelling-down took place.'
37 Raaflaub, *Discovery of Freedom*, for instance, rightly insists on such learning for the Greek transformation – but also on better grounds than one could for other axial experiences (see also Johann Arnason, 'Autonomy and axiality: Comparative perspectives on the Greek breakthrough', in *Agon, Logos, Polis: The Greek Achievement and its Aftermath*, ed. Johann Arnason and Peter Murphy (Stuttgart: Steiner, 2001), 155–206. Jan Assmann, 'Große Texte', allows for different degrees of generalizability of key concepts, without accepting the idea of a breakthrough to universalism.
38 See Wagner, *Theorizing Modernity*, chapters 1 and 2 for a general such argument.
39 See Stråth, *Europe's Utopias*.
40 Immanuel Kant, 'Beantwortung der Frage: Was ist Aufklärung?' in *Politische Schriften* (1784; Köln: Westdeutscher Verlag, 1965), 1–8; Michel Foucault, 'What is Enlightenment?', in *The Foucault Reader*, ed. Paul Rabinow (London: Penguin, 1984), 32–50.

Chapter 3

1 Johann Arnason and Peter Murphy, eds, *Agon, Logos, Polis: The Greek Achievement and its Aftermath* (Stuttgart: Steiner, 2001).
2 Christian Meier, 'The Greeks: The political revolution in world history', in Arnason and Murphy, *Agon, Logos, Polis*.
3 Johann Arnason and Peter Murphy, 'Introduction', in Arnason and Murphy, *Agon, Logos, Polis*.
4 Karl-Joachim Hölkeskamp and Elke Stein-Hölkeskamp, eds, *Die griechische Welt. Erinnerungsorte der Antike* (Munich: C.H. Beck, 2010).
5 Rémi Brague, *Europe*; Rémi Brague, *Eccentric Culture: A Theory of Western Civilisation* (South Bend, IN: St. Augustine's Press, 2002).
6 Rome was in this respect a kind of predecessor of Japan after the Meiji Revolution, although Brague does not make this comparison.
7 Brague, *Eccentric Culture*, 111.
8 Brague, *Eccentric Culture*, 146.

9 Fowden, *Before and After Muhammad*.
10 'Definierbar ist nur das was keine Geschichte hat.' Friedrich Nietzsche, *Zur Genealogie der Moral. Eine Streitschrift*, Bd IV. Zweite Abhandlung: *Schuld, schlechtes Gewissen und Verwandtes* (Leipzig: C.G. Naumann, 1887; Munich: Carl Hanser, 1980), 820.
11 Bo Stråth, 'Introduction: Europe as a discourse', in *Europe and the Other and Europe as the Other*, ed. Bo Stråth (2000; repr., Brussels: P.I.E.-Peter Lang, 2010).
12 Stråth, *Europe's Utopias*; Volker Sellin, *Das Jahrhundert der Restauration. 1814–1906* (Munich: De Gruyter, 2014). See Chapter 4.
13 Stråth, *Europe's Utopias*, 63.
14 Larry Wolff, *Inventing Eastern Europe: The Map of Civilisation on the Mind of the Enlightenment* (Stanford, CA: Stanford University Press, 1994); Wolff, 'British travellers and Russian orthodoxy in the Age of Enlightenment: The religious features of philosophic geography', in *Unravelling Civilisation: European Travel and Travel Writing*, ed. Hagen Schulz-Forberg (Brusels: P.I.E.-Peter Lang, 2005), 129–142.
15 Katiana Orluc, 'A Wilhelmine legacy, Coudenhove-Kalergi's Pan-Europe and the crisis of European modernity, 1922–1932', in *Wilhelminism and its Legacies: German Modernities and the Meanings of Reform, 1890–1930*, ed. Geoff Eley and James Retallack (New York: Berghahn, 2003), 219–234; Katiana Orluc, 'Europe between past and future: Transnational networks and the transformation of the Pan-European idea in the interwar years' (PhD thesis, European University Institute, Florence/History Dept, 2005).
16 'Prewar' in the 1930s meant also the attempt to build an alternative European unification to that of Pan-Europe based on military violence with Hitler as its main architect.
17 Stråth, *Europe's Utopias*.
18 See, for instance, Jacques Derrida, *La Dissémination* (Paris: Seuil, 1972); Jacques Derrida, *L'écriture et la différence* (Paris: Seuil, 1979) (translated as *Writing and Difference*, Chicago, IL: University of Chicago Press, 1978). Cf. Jonathan Rutherford, 'A place called home: Identity and the cultural politics of difference', in *Identity: Community, Culture, Difference*, ed. Jonathan Rutherford (London: Lawrence & Wishart, 1990), 9–27.
19 John A. Hobson, *Imperialism: A Study* (London: James Nisbet, 1902).
20 Chakrabarty, *Provincializing Europe*; Dipesh Chakrabarty, 'In defence of provincializing Europe: A response to Carola Dietze', *History and Theory* 47 (Feb 2008): 85–96; and Rochona Majumdar, *Writing Postcolonial History* (London: Bloomsbury Academic, 2010), epitomize the debate.
21 *L'Observateur* 14 Aug 1952. Alfred Sauvy, *Théorie générale de la population*, (Paris: PUF, 1963), 270. The original text reads (p. 270): 'Car enfin ce Tiers Monde ignoré, exploité, méprisé comme le Tiers Etat, veut, lui aussi, être quelque chose.'
22 Erik Tängerstad, '"The Third World" as an element in the collective construction of a post-colonial European identity', in *Europe and the Other*

and Europe as the Other, ed. Bo Stråth (Brussels: P.I.E.-Peter Lang, 2000), 157–193.

23 Frantz Fanon, *Les damnés de la terre* (Paris: Maspero, 1961). Translated by Constance Farrington as *The Wretched of the Earth* (Harmondsworth: Penguin Books, 1970).

24 Gunnar Myrdal, *Economic Theory and Under-developed Regions* (London: Duckworth, 1956). The discussion of Myrdal builds on Tängerstad, 'Third World'.

25 Myrdal, *Economic Theory*, 60–61. Quoted from Tängerstad, 'Third World'.

26 Robert Nisbet, 'Hannah Arendt and the American Revolution', *Social Research* (The New School) 44, no.1 (1977): 63–79.

27 John Locke, *The Second Treatise of Government* (1689; Oxford: Blackwell, 1966). See Peter Wagner, 'The resistance that modernity constantly provokes: Europe, America and social theory', *Thesis Eleven* 58 (Aug 1999): 35–58.

28 Alexis de Tocqueville, *De la démocratie en Amérique*, 2 vols (1835, 1840; Paris: Gallimard: 1951) (translated by George Lawrence as *Democracy in America*, ed. J. P. Mayer, New York: Harper & Row, 1969 and later editions).

29 Leopold von Ranke, *The Theory and Practice of History*, ed. Georg Iggers (London: Routledge, 2011), xxxix.

30 For the argument that the French Revolution extinguished the importance of the American Revolution from European memory, see Manfred Henningsen, *Der Fall Amerika. Zur Sozial- und Bewußtseinsgeschichte einer Verdrängung* (Munich: List, 1974). However, as we show, with reference to de Tocqueville and Ranke, before the 1850s this was hardly the case.

31 Reinhart Koselleck, *Kritik und Krise. Eine Studie zur Pathogenese der bürgerlichen Welt* (Freiburg: Alber, 1959; Frankfurt/Main: Suhrkamp, 1992), 148–154 (translated as *Critique and Crisis: Enlightenment and the Pathogenesis of Modern Society*, Oxford: Berg, 1988).

32 Shmuel N. Eisenstadt, *Fundamentalism, Sectarianism, Revolution* (Cambridge: Cambridge University Press, 1999).

33 Bo Stråth, 'Multiple Europes: Integration, identity and demarcation to the other', in Stråth, *Europe and the Other*.

34 Stråth, 'Multiple Europes'.

35 Antoine Panaïoti, *Nietzsche and Buddhist Philosophy* (Cambridge: Cambridge University Press, 2013).

36 See the recent reconstruction by Robin Derrincourt, *Inventing Africa: History, Archaeology, Ideas* (London: Pluto Press, 2011).

37 Edward Said, *Orientalism: Western Conceptions of the Orient* (London: Routledge, 1978).

38 See now Mishima, 'The long shadow'.

39 Jacques Derrida, *Writing and Difference* (Chicago, IL: University of Chicago Press, 1978); Dipesh Chakrabarty, *Provincializing Europe*.

40 Michel Foucault, *Les mots et les choses: Une archéologie des sciences humaines*

(Paris: Gallimard, 1966) and Foucault, *L'archéologie du savoir* (Paris: Gallimard, 1969).

41 L.S. Senghor, *Nation et voie africaine du socialisme* (Paris: Présence Africaine, 1961); L.S. Senghor, *Liberté 1: Négritude et humanisme* (Paris: Éditions du Seuil, 1964); F. Fanon, *Les damnés de la terre*; P. Hountondji, *Sur la 'philosophie africaine'* (Paris: Maspéro, 1976).

42 Cf. Bo Stråth, '*Ujamaa*: The evasive translation of an elusive concept', in *Doing Conceptual History in Africa*, ed. Axel Fleisch and Rhiannon Stephens (New York and Oxford: Berghahn, 2016).

43 Sergei Prozorow, 'Reclaiming European universalism: What does the "promised land" really promise?', in *Playing Second Fiddle? Contending Visions of Europe's Development*, ed. Hans-Åke Persson, Bo Petersson and Cecilie Stokholm Banke (Malmö: Universus Academic Press, 2015) and Jens Bartelson, *Visions of World Community* (Cambridge: Cambridge University Press, 2009).

44 Max Weber, *Wirtschaft und Gesellschaft. Grundrisse der verstehenden Soziologie*, 5th rev. ed. (1922; Tübingen: J.C.B. Mohr, 1980).

45 Koselleck, *Kritik und Krise*.

46 Zygmunt Bauman, *Modernity and Ambivalence* (Cambridge: Polity Press, 1991).

Chapter 4

1 Detienne, *Les Grecs et nous*, 146. Unless otherwise indicated, translations are our own.

2 Christian Meier, *Athen. Ein Neubeginn der Weltgeschichte* (Berlin: Siedler, 1993), 33. The idea is that a victory of the Persians over the Athenians – of 'Asia' over 'Europe', to recall the spatial imaginations from the previous chapter – could have blocked the path for freedom and democracy. See now Johann Arnason, 'Exploring the Greek needle's eye: Civilizational and political transformations', in *The Greek Polis and the Invention of Democracy*, ed. Johann Arnason, Kurt Raaflaub and Peter Wagner (Oxford: Blackwell, 2013).

3 Christian Meier, *Kultur, um der Freiheit willen. Griechische Anfänge – Anfang Europas?* (Berlin: Siedler, 2009), 43; see also Christian Meier, *Von Athen bis Auschwitz* (Munich: Beck, 2002).

4 Quentin Skinner, 'Some problems in the analysis of political thought and action', *Political Theory* 2, no. 3 (Aug 1974): 277–303.

5 Christian Meier, *The Greek Discovery of Politics* (Cambridge, MA: Harvard University Press, 1990) in particular; see also Moses I. Finley, *Democracy Ancient and Modern* (New Brunswick, NJ: Rutgers University Press, 1973); for Cornelius Castoriadis see, among other writings: 'La *polis* grecque et la création de la démocratie', in *Domaines de l'homme. Les carrefours du labyrinthe* vol. 2 (Paris: Seuil, 1977), 261–306; 'Pouvoir, politique, autonomie'; 'La démocratie athénienne: Fausses et vraies questions' and 'Imaginaire politique grec et moderne', both in *La montée de l'insignifiance. Les Carrefours*

du Labyrinthe, IV (Paris: Seuil, 1996), 183–93; *Ce qui fait la Grèce,* vol. 2, *La cité et les lois* (Paris: Seuil, 2008); see also Kurt Raaflaub, 'Perfecting the "political creature": Equality and "the political" in the evolution of Greek democracy', in Arnason, Raaflaub and Wagner, *The Greek Polis.* But see also our contextualization of this thinking in Chapter 3 above.

6 For some examples in the present context, see Cornelius Castoriadis, 'La démocratie comme procédure et comme régime', in *La montée de l'insignifiance. Les Carrefours du Labyrinthe,* vol. 4 (Paris: Seuil, 1996), 221–241; here: 221–226; Meier, *The Greek Discovery.*

7 For recent analyses, see the contributions to Arnason, Raaflaub and Wagner, *The Greek Polis.*

8 Detienne, *Les Grecs,* ch. 6.

9 Raaflaub, *Discovery of Freedom.*

10 Thus the emergence of politics in reflection and common action is closely related to the idea of self-government, that is, democracy in a very general sense of the term; see Castoriadis, 'Power', 125–129.

11 Plato, in particular, together with 'his' Socrates, should be seen as a master in generating radical political ideas rather than as a provider of blueprints for organizing a polity.

12 For more detail on the notion of *problématique,* see Wagner, *Modernity as Experience.*

13 R.R. Palmer, *The Age of the Democratic Revolution: A Political History of Europe and America, 1760–1800,* vol. 1: *The Challenge* (Princeton, NJ: Princeton University Press, 1959).

14 From an extensive literature, see most recently Wilfried Nippel, *Antike oder moderne Freiheit? Die Begründung der Demokratie in Athen und in der Neuzeit* (Frankfurt/Main: Fischer, 2008); Pierre Vidal-Naquet, 'Tradition de la démocratie grecque', introduction to M.I. Finley, *Démocratie antique et démocratie moderne* (Paris: Payot, 2009), 9–44; Nicole Loraux and Pierre Vidal-Naquet, 'La formation de l'Athènes bourgeoise: essai d'historiographie 1750–1850', in Vidal-Naquet, *La démocratie grecque vue d'ailleurs* (Paris: Flammarion, 2009), 161–209.

15 Hans Maier, in Werner Conze et al., 'Demokratie', in *Geschichtliche Grundbegriffe. Historisches Lexikon zur politisch-sozialen Sprache in Deutschland,* vol. 1, ed. Otto Brunner, Werner Conze and Reinhart Koselleck (Stuttgart: Klett-Cotta, 1972), 848.

16 Jean-Jacques Rousseau, *Letters Written from the Mountain,* quoted after Vidal-Naquet, *La démocratie grecque,* 213.

17 Benjamin Constant, 'De la liberté des anciens comparée à celle des modernes', in *Ecrits politiques,* ed. Marcel Gauchet (1819; Paris: Gallimard, 1997), 589–619. The historico-conceptual relations between ancient and modern liberty are discussed in Nathalie Karagiannis and Peter Wagner, 'The liberty of the ancients compared to the liberty of the moderns', in Arnason, Raaflaub and Wagner, *The Greek Polis.* We have touched on the question of freedom in the preceding chapter (see pp. 62–3), and the place of individual autonomy in European history will be analysed in Chapter 6.

18 Quentin Skinner, *Liberty before Liberalism* (Cambridge: Cambridge University Press, 1998), and elsewhere.

19 Maurizio Viroli, *From Politics to Reason of State: The Acquisition and Transformation of the Language of Politics, 1250–1600* (Cambridge: Cambridge University Press, 1992), 78.

20 Josaiah Ober, *Political Dissent in Democratic Athens: Intellectual Critics of Popular Rule* (Princeton, NJ: Princeton University Press, 1998).

21 The major lasting exception – despite all qualifications that would need to be added here, too – were the United States of America, the only large society about which a significant analysis guided by the concept of 'democracy' was written before the late nineteenth century, namely Alexis de Tocqueville's *Democracy in America*, first published in 1835/40.

22 See Charles Taylor, *Sources of the Self* (Cambridge, MA: Harvard University Press, 1989), for the first notion, and for the second, Albert O. Hirschman, *The Passions and the Interests* (Princeton, NJ: Princeton University Press, 1977). The notion of freedom as collective self-determination has – significantly – not yet been equally comprehensively reconstructed. For an important step, see Gerard Rosich, *Autonomy in and between Polities* (London: Bloomsbury, forthcoming).

23 Isaiah Berlin, *Four Essays on Liberty* (Oxford: Oxford University Press, 1971).

24 A more detailed account would make distinctions between different societies because the Greek example was always used as an argument in specific political settings and in the framework of the respective political languages. Nadia Urbinati, *Mill on Democracy: From the Athenian Polis to Representative Government* (Chicago, IL: University of Chicago Press, 2002), ch.1, discusses British and French usage in comparison; for the US, see R.R. Palmer, 'Notes on the use of the word "democracy"', *Political Science Quarterly* 68, no. 2 (1953): 203–226; for the German language sphere with some comparative remarks, see Conze et al., 'Demokratie'.

25 G. Grote, *A History of Greece*, vol. 5 (London, 1851); see Vidal-Naquet, 'Tradition de la démocratie grecque', 37, 169.

26 On 'bourgeois Athens,' see Loraux and Vidal-Naquet, 'La formation de l'Athènes bourgeoise'.

27 Nadia Urbinati, *Mill on Democracy: From the Athenian Polis to Representative Government* (Chicago, IL: University of Chicago Press, 2002).

28 Quoted after Conze, in Conze et al., 'Demokratie', 884.

29 This even permitted the connection of democracy with monarchy, on the assumption that absolute monarchs reduced the privileges of the aristocracy and made all subjects of a polity more equal (thus the Prussian reformer Hardenberg in 1807; see Koselleck, in Conze et al., 'Demokratie', 853).

30 Koselleck, in Conze et al., 'Demokratie', 850.

31 Vilfredo Pareto, *Trasformazione della Democrazia* (Milan: Corbaccio, 1921; Rome: Editori Riuniti, 1999).

32 Karl Mannheim, *Man and Society in an Age of Reconstruction* (London: Routledge, 1940) (originally published as *Mensch und Gesellschaft im Zeitalter des Umbaus*. Leiden: A.W. Sijthoff's Uitgeversmaatschappij N.V., 1935). See

Eckart Bolsinger, *The Autonomy of the Political: Vladimir Lenin's and Carl Schmitt's Political Realism* (Santa Barbara, CA: Praeger, 2001), for a comparative study of Vladimir I. Lenin and Carl Schmitt; and Tracy B. Strong, *Politics Without Vision: Thinking Without a Banister in the Twentieth Century* (Chicago, IL: University of Chicago Press, 2012), for a broader analysis of European political thought in the first half of the twentieth century.

33 The Declaration maintains (article 21, par. 3): 'The will of the people shall be the basis of the authority of government; this will shall be expressed in periodic and genuine elections which shall be by universal and equal suffrage and shall be held by secret vote or by equivalent free voting procedures.'

34 See Leonardo Avritzer, 'Modes of democratic deliberation: Participatory budgeting in Brazil', in *Democratizing Democracy*, ed. Boaventura de Sousa Santos (London: Verso, 2007), 377–404; Wagner, *A Sociology of Modernity*, ch.6.

35 Hannah Arendt, *The Human Condition* (Chicago, IL: Harcourt, Brace, Jovanovich, 1958); for a critical discussion of philosophy and politics, see Hannah Arendt, *The Life of the Mind* (Chicago, IL: Harcourt, Brace, Jovanovich, 1975); for Castoriadis, see the references in note 5 above.

36 During early European modernity, the term 'democracy' was descriptively used for small self-governing polities only. Martin Luther, for instance, used it in 1539 for Switzerland and Dithmarschen, a small peasant republic in Northern Germany (Maier, in Conze et al., 'Demokratie', 845).

37 Wagner, *A Sociology of Modernity*, chs 3 and 4.

38 For the argument in comparison with ancient Greece, see Finley, *Democracy Ancient and Modern*; for the term 'liberal oligarchy', see Cornelius Castoriadis, 'Fait et à faire', in *Fait et à faire. Les carrefours du labyrinthe*, vol. 5 (Paris: Seuil, 1997), 64 and elsewhere.

39 See Nathalie Karagiannis, 'Democratic surplus'.

40 The Grote-Mill interpretation of Athenian politics, mentioned above, suggests less opposition between antiquity and modernity. Some understanding of countervailing mechanisms to 'pure democracy' certainly existed in Athens. A distinction by degree is nevertheless valid – and necessary to understand key developments in political thought.

41 To recall Hannah Arendt's term, as recently retrieved by Strong, *Politics Without Vision*.

42 To be more precise, Greek democracy was radically autonomous with regard to political matters. Economic matters were determined by needs and as such exempt from political deliberation. We return to this issue in the following chapter.

43 Marx's expression 'dictatorship of the proletariat' referred to a form of 'tyranny of the majority', with the important qualification that Marx's philosophy of history suggested that the proletariat had become the 'universal class' whose interests coincided with a well-understood common good.

44 See, e.g., Axel Honneth, 'Das Gewebe der Gerechtigkeit. Über die Grenzen des zeitgenössischen Prozeduralismus', *Westend. Neue Zeitschrift für Sozialforschung* 6, no. 2 (2009): 3–22.

45 Boaventura de Sousa Santos, 'Human rights as an emancipatory script? Cultural and political conditions', in *Another Knowledge is Possible: Beyond Northern Epistemologies*, ed. Boaventura de Sousa Santos (London: Verso, 2007), 16–21.

46 See, e.g., Richard Bellamy and Dario Castiglione, 'Legitimising the Euro-polity and its regime: The normative turn in EU studies', *European Journal of Political Theory* 2, no. 1 (2003): 7–34.

47 A contemporary of Grote, but in striking contrast to the former, Heinrich von Treitschke referred to democratic Athens as a 'mass aristocracy', with the citizens ruling over the slaves (quoted after Conze, in Conze et al., 'Demokratie', 893).

48 Aldo Schiavone, *La storia spezzata. Roma antica e Occidente moderno* (Bari: Laterza, 1996).

49 Wagner, *Modernity as Experience*, ch. 5; Arendt, *The Human Condition*, developed a similar interpretation. In *Politics*, Aristotle discusses slavery by nature and by law and makes recourse to characteristics of persons to justify slavery. Due to the interweaving of normative and empirical issues as well as to the conceptual and societal context of the distinction between freedom and needs, however, these passages remain open to interpretation.

50 David Casassas, *La ciudad en llamas. La vigencia del republicanismo comercial de Adam Smith* (Mataró: Montesinos, 2010).

51 See Michel Crozier, Samuel Huntington and Joji Watanuki, *The Crisis of Democracy: Report on the Governability of Democracies to the Trilateral Commission* (New York: New York University Press, 1975); Jürgen Habermas, *Legitimationsprobleme im Spätkapitalismus* (Frankfurt/Main: Suhrkamp, 1973).

Chapter 5

1 David Landes, *The Unbound Prometheus: Technological Change and Industrial Development in Western Europe from 1750 to the Present* (Cambridge: Cambridge University Press, 1969). Cf. in the same vein David Landes, *Wealth and Poverty of Nations* (New York: W. W. Norton, 1998) and Eric L. Jones, *The European Miracle* (Cambridge: Cambridge University Press, 1981).

2 Landes, *Unbound Prometheus*, ch. 1.

3 Immanuel Wallerstein, *The Modern World System*, 3 vols (New York: Academic Press, 1974, 1980, 1989); cf. review essay by Peer Vries, 'The California School and beyond: How to study the great divergence', *History Compass* 8, no. 7 (2010): 730–751.

4 Vries, 'The California School', 732.

5 Pomeranz, *The Great Divergence*; cf. Patrick O'Brien, 'Ten years of debate on the origin of the great divergence', *Reviews in History* 1008, no. 30 (Nov 2010), http://www.history.ac.uk/reviews/review/1008; and Patrick O'Brien, 'The formation of states and transitions to modern economies: England,

Europe, and Asia compared', in *The Cambridge History of Capitalism*, vol. 1, *The Rise of Capitalism: From Ancient Origins to 1848*, ed. Larry Neal and Jeffrey G. Williamson (Cambridge: Cambridge University Press, 2014), 357–402. Roman Studer, *The Great Divergence Reconsidered: Europe, India, and the Rise of Global Economic Power* (Cambridge: Cambridge University Press, 2015), argues that the thesis of Pomeranz is based on fragile empirical evidence and that it draws general conclusions from an investigation that is limited to China. Studer has compared the Indian and the intra-European trade arrangements and found that intra-European trade, at least since 1700, was superior to that of India, which he takes as an argument for inherent European factors behind the later industrial take-off. Obviously, the thesis of Pomeranz about the Great Divergence around 1800 needs more empirical underpinning for China, but also, and in particular, for other parts of the world outside Europe. However, the existence of early well-developed continental European commercial networks is not as such opposed to the insight that the transatlantic trade became much more decisive for the industrial capitalist take-off after 1800. This transatlantic trade on mainly British keels, as well as British colonialism, triggered the Industrial Revolution much more than the early existence of developed trade structures in continental Europe.

6 Jack Goldstone, *Why Europe? The Rise of the West in World History, 1500–1850* (New York: McGraw Hill, 2008).

7 André Gunder Frank, *ReOrient: Global Economy in the Asian Age* (Berkeley, CA: University of California Press, 1998); the quotation on p.259 is from Vries, 'The California School', 733.

8 O'Brien, 'Formation of states'.

9 Vries, 'The California School', 733.

10 C. Knick Harley, 'British and European industrialisation', in Neal and Williamson, *Cambridge History of Capitalism*, 491–493.

11 O'Brien, 'Formation of states'.

12 Edward L. Dreyer, *Zheng He: China and the Oceans in the Early Ming Dynasty, 1405–1433* (New York: Longman, 2007).

13 Vries, 'The California School', 237

14 Gareth Austin, 'Capitalism and the colonies', in Neal and Williamson, *Cambridge History of Capitalism*, 301–303.

15 Before the wave of decolonization in the wake of the Second World War the historians interested in the slave trade, primarily British, saw the abolition movement uncritically. They saw the decrease in the slave trade as the consequence of religious and human rights arguments. In 1944 West Indian historian Eric Williams argued, in a book positioned against this mainstream historical opinion, that the petering out of the slave trade was the result of economic rationalities without any morality. Around 1800 the West Indian colonies lost economic and political importance for Britain, and the slave system became an economic burden. His argument was not only academic but also a contribution to the independence movement in the Caribbean colonies. Later research has revised the strong economism of Williams and

re-emphasized the role of moral factors, but also underlined that for an understanding of how the slave trade came to an end, the influence of moral reasoning must be connected to economic and political factors. Works on the profitability of the slave trade tend to discredit Williams, without rehabilitating the rosy moralist view of previous historians. Eric Williams, *Capitalism and Slavery* (1944; Chapel Hill, NC: University of North Carolina Press, 1994); Seymour Drescher, *From Slavery to Freedom: Comparative Studies in the Rise and Fall of Atlantic Slavery* (London: Macmillan, 1999), and Seymour Drescher, *Abolition: A History of Slavery and Antislavery* (Cambridge: Cambridge University Press, 2009); Christopher Leslie Brown, *Moral Capital: Foundations of British Abolitionism* (Chapel Hill, NC: University of North Carolina Press, 2000).

16 Sven Beckert, *Empire of Cotton: A New History of Global Capitalism* (London: Allen Lane, 2014).

17 Martti Koskenniemi, *The Gentle Civiliser of Nations: The Rise and Fall of International Law, 1870–1960* (Cambridge: Cambridge University Press, 2001).

18 Koskenniemi, *Gentle Civiliser of Nations*, 112–113.

19 Laura Benton, *A Search for Sovereignty: Law and Geography in European Empires, 1400–1900* (Cambridge: Cambridge University Press, 2010).

20 Benton, *Search for Sovereignty*, 179–280.

21 Martti Koskenniemi, 'Ruling the world by law(s): The view from around 1850', in *Europe 1815–1914: Creating Community and Ordering the World: The European Shadow of the Past and Future of the Present*, ed. Martti Koskenniemi and Bo Stråth (Report from the Research Project 'Europe between Restoration and Revolution, National Constitutions and International Law: An Alternative View on the Century 1815–1914', financed by the European Research Council, 2009–2014, University of Helsinki, Dept. of World Cultures/CENS and Faculty of Law/ECI) (Helsinki: University of Helsinki, 2014), 31–32.

22 Beckert, *Empire of Cotton*, 441.

23 Eric Hobsbawm, *The Age of Empire: 1875–1914* (London: Weidenfeld & Nicolson, 1987).

24 Eric Hobsbawm, *The Pelican Economic History of Britain*, vol. 3, *Industry and Empire: From 1750 to the Present Day* (London: Weidenfeld & Nicolson, 1968), 34–40.

25 Hobsbawm, *Industry and Empire*, 53–54.

26 Bayly, *Birth of the Modern World*, 473–475; Jan de Vries, *The Dutch Rural Economy in the Golden Age, 1500–1700* (New Haven, CT: Yale University Press, 1974).

27 Bayly, *Birth of the Modern World*, 476.

28 Gareth Stedman Jones, *An End to Poverty? A Historical Debate* (London: Profile, 2004), 104–105. Historians generally suggest that Malthus softened his attitude in the second edition of *Principles of Population* in 1803. Jones demonstrates that this is only half true. On the question of social security and

the rights of the poor, Malthus not only adopted a harsher tone, but presented an alarmist, even apocalyptic scenario.

29 T.J. Hatton and J.G. Williamson, *Global Migration and the World Economy: Two Centuries of Policy and Performance* (Cambridge, MA: MIT Press, 2008), 179–181, and J. Oltmer, *Migration im Kontext von Globalisierung, Kolonialismus und Weltkriegen. WBG Weltgeschichte. Eine Globale Geschichte von den Anfängen bis ins 21. Jahrhundert. Bd VI. Globalisierung 1880 bis heute* (Darmstadt: Wissenschaftliche Buchgesellschaft, 2010), 177–221, here 17–19.

30 Hatton and Williamson, *Global Migration*, 181.

31 Hatton and Williamson, *Global Migration*, 180–181.

32 Hatton and Williamson, *Global Migration*, 180–181.

33 John Locke, *Two Treaties of Government* (1689), quoted from Werner Conze, 'Arbeit', in *Geschichte Grundbegriffe. Historische Lexikon zur Politisch-sozialen Sprache in Deutschland*, Bd 1: A-D, ed. Otto Brunner, Werner Conze and Reinhart Koselleck (Stuttgart: Klett-Cotta, 1979).

34 Jean-Charles-Léonard Simonde de Sismondi, *Nouveaux principes d'économie* (Paris: Delaunay, 1819). See also Procacci, *Gouverner la misère*.

35 Thomas Hopkins, 'Sismondi on the problems and promise of international trade', in *Actes de Colloque Sismondi, 'Travaux et Recherches de l'Institut Benjamin Constant'*, ed. Béla Kapossy and Pascal Bridel (Lausanne: Institut Benjamin Constant, 2014).

36 Bernhard Semmel, *The Rise of Free Trade Imperialism: Classical Political Economy, the Empire of Free Trade, and Imperialism 1750–1850* (Cambridge: Cambridge University Press, 1970), 207–208.

37 Peter Wagner, *Sozialwissenschaften und Staat. Frankreich, Italien, Deutschland 1870–1980* (Frankfurt/Main: Campus, 1990), 157–158.

38 Lars Magnusson and Bo Stråth, *A Brief History of Political Economy: Tales of Marx, Keynes and Hayek* (London: Elgar, 2016).

39 Bo Stråth, 'The concept of work in the construction of community', in *After Full Employment: European Discourses on Work and Flexibility*, ed. Bo Stråth (Brussels: PIE-Peter Lang, 2000). Commodification of labour was not new. Slaves, for instance, were treated as commodities. What was new was the imagery of the sellers of labour as individuals free to agree and sign a contract with buyers on the terms of labour. This imagery ignored the uneven power relationships between buyers and sellers and freed on principle the buyer from responsibilities beyond the workplace, which was not the case in the slave system or in the paternalist relationships of the corporate guild order.

40 Wagner, *Sozialwissenschaften und Staat*, 155–156.

41 Wagner, *Sozialwissenschaften und Staat*, 116–117.

42 Gareth Stedman Jones, 'The young Hegelians, Marx and Engels', in *The Cambridge History of Nineteenth Century Political Thought*, ed. Gareth Stedman Jones and Gregory Clayes (Cambridge: Cambridge University Press, 2011), 556–600.

43 Gustav Schmoller, *The Mercantile System and its Historical Significance* (New York: MacMillan, 1967 [1897]), 57. Quoted from O'Brien, 'Formation of states', 357.

44 Edwin Van de Haar, 'The liberal divide over trade, peace and war', *International Relations* 24, no. 2 (2010): 132–154.

45 Herbert Heaton, *Economic History of Europe*, 2nd edn (New York: Harper and Row, 1964), 641.

46 Thomas Hopkins, 'The limits of "cosmopolitical economy": Smith, List and the paradox of peace through trade', in *Paradoxes of Peace in 19th Century Europe*, ed. Thomas Hippler and Miloš Vec (Oxford: Oxford University Press, 2014).

47 Thomas Hopkins, 'Adam Smith on American economic development and the future of the European Atlantic empires', in *The Political Economy of Empire in the Early Modern World*, ed. Sophus Reinert and Pernille Røge (London: Palgrave, 2013).

Chapter 6

1 Taylor, *Sources of the Self*, 305.

2 Taylor, *Sources of the Self*, 305.

3 See Johann Arnason, *Civilizations in Dispute: Historical Questions and Theoretical Traditions* (Leiden: Brill, 2003), 122–124, for a discussion of the thesis initially advanced by Franz Borkenau.

4 See Colin Morris, *The Discovery of the Individual, 1050–1200* (Toronto: University of Toronto Press, 1972), for a strong version of the latter argument.

5 Olive Schreiner, *The Story of an African Farm* (1883; Project Gutenberg, 2008), first published 1883 under the pseudonym Ralph Iron, http://www.gutenberg.org/files/1441/1441.txt

6 Reinhart Koselleck, 'The historical-political asymmetrics of political counter-concepts', in *Futures Past: On the Semantics of Historical Time* (Cambridge, MA: MIT Press, 1985), 155–191. Modernity meant for Koselleck that histories in the plural became progressive history in the singular with a direction and a subject in itself (*pace* Hegel). A new time began when history could no longer serve as *magistra vitae*. Space of experiences and horizons of expectations broke up and opened a gap. The dynamic asymmetric counter-concepts of Christian and Heathen, indicating a civilizing mission, followed by the annihilating Human-Nonhuman, replaced the older static opposition of Hellene and Barbarian. The civilizing quest around the opposition between human and nonhuman would in the wake of the possibilities offered by the technology of industrial capitalism produce much more destructive dynamics than in the attempts to define natives in the Americas in the sixteenth-century Valladolid-Salamanca debates.

7 For a forceful attempt at extending the conceptual history of modernity to the early sixteenth century and to the Iberian and indigenous American contributions, see Dussel, *Política de la liberación*.

8 For such a contextual understanding, see Stephen Toulmin, *Cosmopolis: The Hidden Agenda of Modernity* (Chicago, IL: University of Chicago Press, 1990).
9 For some of our reflections, see Wagner, *Theorizing Modernity*.
10 John Dewey, *The quest for certainty*, in *The Later Works 1925–1953*, vol. 4 (New York: Minton, Balch and Company, 1929; Carbondale, IL: Southern Illinois University Press, 1984), 195.
11 Ludwig Wittgenstein, *Philosophische Untersuchungen*, in *Werkausgabe*, vol. 1, *Tractatus logicus-philosophicus* (Frankfurt/Main: Suhrkamp, 1969), par. 458. The German original plays with the double meaning of *Grund*, namely both ground and reason; a more appropriate translation thus may be: 'one doubts for specific reasons'.
12 Wittgenstein, *Philosophische Untersuchungen*, par. 456.
13 Wittgenstein, *Philosophische Untersuchungen*, par. 454.
14 On knowledge generation through distancing in space, see Aurea Mota, 'Displacements and absences in the modern spatial imaginary', in *The Moral Mappings of South and North*, vol. 4, ed. Peter Wagner (Edinburgh: Edinburgh University Press, forthcoming).
15 John Locke, *The Second Treatise of Government* (1689; Oxford: Blackwell, 1966).
16 Michael Walzer, *Thick and Thin* (Notre Dame: University of Notre Dame Press, 1994).
17 Berlin, *Four Essays on Liberty* (the core essay dates from 1958).
18 Charles Taylor, 'Cross-purposes: The Liberal-Communitarian debate', in *Philosophical Arguments* (Cambridge, MA: Harvard University Press, 1995), has proposed a distinction between questions of social ontology and those of political philosophy when discussing the merits or shortcomings of individualism.
19 We have discussed the ramifications of this issue in Chapter 4.
20 Albert O. Hirschman, *The Passions and the Interests* (Princeton, NJ: Princeton University Press, 1977).
21 We have discussed the economic reasoning in detail in Chapter 5.
22 Axel Honneth, *Freedom's Right* (New York: Columbia University Press, 2014), 15.
23 Axel Honneth, *Die Idee des Sozialismus* (Berlin: Suhrkamp, 2015), 9.
24 For more detail on the following reasoning, see Wagner, 'Freedom and solidarity'.
25 It may be worth noting that Honneth's conceptualization is one that Berlin explicitly argued against. Without following Berlin in detail, it may indeed be questioned whether it is most fruitful to use a socially redefined principle of freedom as the sole core value of modern society, and thus make solidarity and democracy derivative of it, as Honneth does, or whether solidarity and democracy should not be seen as accompanying freedom as core values. In some contrast to de Tocqueville and Lefort, Honneth elaborates a social philosophy rather than a political philosophy. For this reason, democracy is more an outcome than a starting-point.

Chapter 7

1. See, in particular, Samuel Huntington, *The Clash of Civilisations and the Remaking of World Order* (New York: Simon and Schuster, 1996) for the former view.
2. Johann P Arnason, 'The religio-political nexus: Historical and comparative reflections' in Arnason and Karolowski, *Religion and Politics*.
3. Almut Höfert, *Kaisertum und Kalifat. Der imperiale Monotheismus im Früh- und Hochmittelalter* (Frankfurt/Main: Campus, 2015).
4. Arnason, 'The religio-political nexus', 35.
5. Jan Assmann, *Moses der Ägypter* (München: Carl Hanser, 1998) and *Exodus. Die Revolution der Alten Welt* (München: Beck, 2015).
6. Peter Sloterdijk, *God's Zeal: The Battle of the Three Monotheisms* (Cambridge: Polity Press, 2009).
7. Alessandro Pizzorno, 'Politics unbounded', in *Changing Boundaries of the Political*, ed. C. S. Maier (Cambridge: Cambridge University Press, 1987), 27, quoted from Said Amir Arjomand, 'Introduction', in *The Political Dimension of Religion*, ed. Said Amir Arjomand (New York: State University of New York Press, 1993), 1.
8. Shmuel N. Eisenstadt, 'Religion and the civilisational dimensions of politics', in Arjomand, *The Political Dimension of Religion*. Cf. Arjomand, 'Introduction'; Said Amir Arjomand, *The Shadow of God and the Hidden Imam: Religion, Political Order and Societal Change in Shi'ite Iran from the Beginning to 1890* (Chicago, IL: University of Chicago Press, 1984), 18–19.
9. Bo Stråth, 'Introduction: Myth, memory and history in the construction of community', in *Myth and Memory in the Construction of Community, Historical Patterns in Europe and Beyond*, ed. Bo Stråth (Brussels: P.I.E.-Peter Lang, 2000).
10. This text is reprinted in Walter Benjamin, *Selected Writings*, vol. 1, ed. Marcus Bullock and Michael W. Jennings (Cambridge, MA: Harvard University Press, 1996), 288. Cf. Daniel Weidner, 'Thinking beyond secularization: Walter Benjamin, the "religious turn," and the poetics of theory', *New German Critique* 111, vol. 37, no. 3 (Autumn 2010): 131–148 and Dirk Baecker, ed., *Kapitalismus als Religion* (Berlin: Kadmos, 2003).
11. Alexander Herzen, *My Past and Thoughts: The Memoirs of Alexander Herzen*, trans. Constance Garnett, rev. Humphrey Higgens, introd. Isaiah Berlin (1924–1927; London: Chatto and Windus, 1968).
12. Magnusson and Stråth, *Brief History*; Martti Koskenniemi, *From Apology to Utopia: The Structure of International Legal Argument* (Helsinki: Lakimiesliiton Kustannus, 1989; Cambridge: Cambridge University Press, 2005); Stråth, *Europe's Utopias*.
13. Eisenstadt, 'Religion and the civilisational dimensions of politics'; Eisenstadt, *Kulturen der Achsenzeit*.
14. H.E.J. Cowdrey, *The Cluniacs and the Gregorian Reform* (Oxford: Clarendon Press, 1970).

15 Malcom Barber, *The Cathars: Dualist Heretics in the High Middle Age* (Edinburgh: Pearson Education, 2000); Elaine Graham-Leigh, *The Southern French Nobility and the Albigensian Crusade* (Woodbridge: Boydell, 2005); Emmanuel LeRoy Ladurie, *Montaillou, an Occitan Village, 1294–1324* (Paris: Gallimard, 1975; London: Penguin, 1978).

16 Stephen E. Lahey, *John Wyclif* (Oxford: Oxford University Press, 2009).

17 Thomas A. Fudge, *Jan Hus: Religious Reform and Social Revolution in Bohemia* (London: I.B. Tauris, 2010) and Thomas A. Fudge, *The Trial of Jan Hus: Medieval Heresy and Criminal Procedure* (Oxford: Oxford University Press, 2013).

18 Donald Weinstein, *Savonarola: The Rise and Fall of a Renaissance Prophet* (New Haven, CT: Yale University Press, 2012).

19 See for this view Lucian Hölscher, ed., *Das Jenseits: Facetten eines religiösen Begriffs in der Neuzeit* (Göttingen: Wallstein, 2007).

20 Thomas Hobbes, *Leviathan* (1651; London: Penguin, 1985).

21 Koselleck, *Kritik und Krise*.

22 Bo Stråth and Øystein Sørensen, eds, *The Cultural Construction of Norden* (Oslo: Universitetsforlaget, 1995).

23 Max Weber, 'Die protestantischen Sekten und der Geist des Kapitalismus', in Max Weber, *Gesammelte Aufsätze zur Religionssoziologie*, vol. 1 (1920; Tübingen: J.C.B. Mohr, 1988), 212, 217.

24 Max Weber, 'Die protestantische Ethik und der Geist des Kapitalismus', in Max Weber, *Gesammelte Aufsätze zur Religionssoziologie*, vol. 1 (1920; Tübingen: J.C.B. Mohr, 1988), 205.

25 For the distinction between secularisation and disenchantment we draw on Antônio Flávio Pierucci's insightful reading of Weber in his 'Secularisation in Max Weber: On current usefulness of re-accessing that old meaning', *Brazilian Review of Social Sciences*, special issue 1 (Oct 2000): 129–158, here 130–131.

26 Émile Durkheim, *The Elementary Forms of the Religious Life* (1912; New York: Free Press 1995)

27 Peter Berger, *The Sacred Canopy* (Garden City, NY: Doubleday, 1967).

28 Barrington Moore, *Social Origins of Dictatorship and Democracy: Lord and Peasant in the Making of the Modern World* (Boston, MA: Beacon Press, 1966).

29 Peter Berger, ed., *The Desecularisation of the World* (Washington, DC: Ethics and Public Policy Center, 1999).

30 Ronald Inglehart and Pippa Norris, *Sacred and Secular: Religion and Politics Worldwide* (Cambridge: Cambridge University Press, 2004); Franco Crespi, 'La fine della Secolarizzazione: Dalla Sociologia del Progresso alla Sociologia dell'Esistenza', *Studi di Sociologia* 26 (1988): 33–42 and Pierucci, 'Secularisation in Max Weber'.

31 Rodney Stark and Roger Finke, *Acts of Faith* (Berkeley, CA: University of California Press, 2000) quoted from Inglehart and Norris, *Sacred and Secular*. See also Pierucci, 'Secularisation in Max Weber', who draws on, among others, Giacomo Marramao, *Potere e secolarizzazione: Le categorie del Tempo* (Rome:

Editori Riuniti, 1983) and Stefano Martelli, *A religião na sociedade pós-moderna: entre secularização e dessecularização* (São Paolo: Paulinas, 1995).

32 For a survey of the paradigm shift from secularisation to post-secular, see Michał Matlak, 'Beyond post-secularism: Religion in political analysis', in Arnason and Karolewski, *Religion and Politics*. See also Gilles Kepel, *The Revenge of God: The Resurgence of Islam, Christianity and Judaism in the Modern World* (University Park, PA: Pennsylvania State University Press, 1994); José Casanova, *Public Religions in the Modern World* (Chicago, IL: Chicago University Press, 1994); John Rawls, 'The idea of public reason revisited', *University of Chicago Law Review* 64, no. 3 (1997): 767–807; Jürgen Habermas, 'On the relations between the secular liberal state and religion', in Hent de Vries and Lawrence E. Sullivan, eds, *Political Theologies: Public Religions in a Post-secular World* (New York: Fordham University Press, 2006).

33 Charles Taylor, *A Secular Age* (Cambridge, MA: Harvard University Press, 2007). Cf. Matlak, 'Beyond post-secularism'.

34 Craig Calhoun, 'Secularism, citizenship and the public sphere', in Craig Calhoun, Mark Juergensmeyer and Jonathan van Antwerpen, eds, *Rethinking Secularism* (Oxford: Oxford University Press, 2011). Cf. Matlak, 'Beyond post-secularism'.

35 Olivier Roy, *Holy Ignorance: When Religion and Culture Part Ways* (New York: Columbia University Press, 2010). Cf. Matlak, 'Beyond post-secularism'.

36 Almut Höfert and Armando Salvatore, 'Beyond the clash of civilisations: Transcultural politics between Europe and Islam', in *Between Europe and Islam: Shaping Modernity in a Transcultural Space*, ed. Almut Höfert and Armando Salvatore (Brussels: P.I.E.-Peter Lang, 2000). They quote (p. 13) G.R. Garrett, 'Cultural relativity vs. ethnocentrism', in *International Encyclopedia of Sociology*, vol. 1, ed. F.N. Magill (London and Chicago, IL: Fritzray Dearborn, 1995), 283: 'Cultural relativism refers both to an attitude that one should avoid judging the ways of other people without first understanding their culture and to a doctrine that prohibits the judging of another culture under any circumstances. Ethnocentrism is an attitude that the values, beliefs, and norms of other cultures can be used to evaluate cultures and behaviours of other peoples.'

37 Mark R. Cohen, *Under Crescent and Cross* (Princeton, NJ: Princeton University Press, 1995); Daniel J. Lasker, 'Review of *Under Crescent and Cross: The Jews in the Middle Ages* by Mark R. Cohen', *The Jewish Quarterly Review* 88, nos 1/2 (1997): 76–78.

38 Cf. on myth Stråth, 'Myth, memory and history'.

Chapter 8

1 Christian Topalov, *Naissance du chômeur 1890–1940* (Paris: Albin Michel, 1994). Cf. Bo Stråth, 'The concept of work'.

2 Gareth Stedman Jones, 'Introduction', in Karl Marx and Friedrich Engels, *The Communist Manifesto*, ed. Gareth Stedman Jones (London: Penguin Classics, 2002), 17–24.

3 Wagner, *Sozialwissenschaften und Staat*, 80–81. See also Gottfried Eisermann, *Die Grundlagen des Historismus in der deutschen Nationalökonomie* (Stuttgart: F. Enke, 1956), 231–242 and Harald Winkel, *Die deutsche Nationalökonomie im 19. Jahrhundert* (Darmstadt: Wissenschaftliche Buchgesellschaft, 1977).

4 E.P. Hennock, *The Origin of the British Welfare State: Society, State and Social Welfare in England and Wales 1800–1945* (London: Palgrave, 2004); David Englander, *Poverty and Poor Law Reform in Nineteenth Century Britain, 1834–1914: From Chadwick to Booth* (London: Longman, 1998).

5 Robert Grandl, *Die Geschichte der Sozialgesetzverwaltung in Österreich. Von den Anfängen bis 1918* (Vienna: Verlag des österreichischen Gewerkschaftsbundes, 2004).

6 Wagner, *Sozialwissenschaften und Staat* and Wagner, *A Sociology of Modernity*; Stråth, *Europe's Utopias*.

7 Emile Durkheim, *The Division of Labor in Society* (1893; New York: Free Press, 1997).

8 Ferdinand Tönnies, *Gemeinschaft und Gesellschaft. Grundbegriffe der Reinen Soziologie* (1887; Darmstadt: Wissenschafliches Buchgesellschaft, 1991).

9 The concept of social monarch was coined by Lorenz Stein, *Das Königtum, die Republik und die Souveränitat der französischen Gesellschaft seit der Februarrevolution 1848*, vol. 3, *Geschichte der Sozialen Bewegung in Frankreich von 1789 bis auf unsere Tage*, 2nd edn (Leipzig: Wiegand, 1855).

10 Topalov, *Naissance du chômeur*, 13–35.

11 Wagner, *Sozialwissenschaften und Staat* and Wagner, *A Sociology of Modernity*.

12 Stråth, *Europe's Utopias*, ch. 2.

13 Bo Stråth, *The Organisation of Labour Markets: Governance, Culture and Modernity in Germany, Sweden, Britain and Japan* (London: Routledge, 1996).

14 Stråth, *Organisation of Labour Markets*.

15 Stråth, *Organisation of Labour Markets*.

16 Karl Jaspers, *The Great Philosophers. The Disturbers: Descartes, Pascal, Lessing, Kierkegaard, Nietzsche / Philosophers in Other Realms: Einstein, Weber, Marx*, ed. Hannah Arendt (New York: Harcourt, 1995). Kant nevertheless remained Jaspers's main philosopher.

17 Hobson, *Imperialism: A Study*.

18 Rudolf Hilferding, 'Das Finanzkapital', *Marx-Studien. Blätter zur Theorie und Politik des wissenschaftlichen Sozialismus*, V-477 (Vienna, 1906).

19 Sellin, *Das Jahrhundert der Restauration*; Sellin, *Gewalt und Legitimität: die europäische Monarchie im Zeitalter der Revolutionen* (München: Oldenbourg, 2011); Mayer, *Persistence of the Old Regime*.

20 Karl Polanyi, *The Great Transformation: The Political and Economic Origins of Our Time* (New York: Farrar & Rinehart, 1944; Boston, MA: Beacon Press, 2001).

21 See Peter Wagner, 'Introduction: The political constitutions of contemporary capitalism', in *The Economy as a Polity: The Political Constitution of Contemporary Capitalism*, ed. Peter Wagner, Bo Stråth and Christian Joerges (London: Cavendish Press, 2005).

22 Koselleck, *Kritik und Krise*.
23 Halperin, *War and Social Change*.
24 For the sleep-walker metaphor, see Christopher Clark, *The Sleepwalkers: How Europe Went to War in 1914* (London: Allen Lane, 2012). Carl von Clausewitz, *Vom Kriege*, Bd 1–3 (Berlin: Ferdinand Dümmler, 1833–1834). Cf. Stråth, *Europe's Utopias*, ch. 3.
25 Gary Gerstle and John Milton Cooper, *Reconsidering Woodrow Wilson: Progressivism, Internationalism, War, and Peace* (Washington, DC: Woodrow Wilson International Center for Scholars, 2008); John Gillingham, *Coal, Steel, and the Rebirth of Europe, 1945–1955: The Germans and French from Ruhr Conflict to Economic Community* (Cambridge: Cambridge University Press, 1991).
26 Wolfgang Schivelbusch, *Entfernte Verwandtschaft. Faschismus, Nationalsozialismus, New Deal, 1933–1939* (München: Carl Hanser, 2005). See also Jan-Werner Müller, *Contesting Democracy: Political Ideas in Twentieth-Century Europe* (New Haven, CT: Yale University Press, 2011) and Dylan Riley, 'Civic associations and authoritarian regimes in interwar Europe: Italy and Spain in comparative perspective', *American Sociological Review* 70 (2005): 288–310 and Dylan Riley, *The Civic Foundation of Fascism in Europe: Italy, Spain and Romania 1870–1945* (Baltimore, MD: Johns Hopkins University Press, 2010).
27 Edmund Husserl, *Die Krise der europäischen Wissenschaften und die transzendentale Phänomenologie: eine Einleitung in die phänomenologische Philosophie* (1936; The Hague: Martinus Nijhoff, 1954); Barry Smith and David Woodruff Smith, eds, *The Cambridge Companion to Husserl* (Cambridge: Cambridge University Press, 1995); Ernst Cassirer, 'Zur Logik der Kulturwissenschaften', in *Göteborgs Högskolas Årsskrift*, vol. 48 (Göteborg: Göteborgs Högskola, 1942).
28 Johan Huizinga, *In the Shadow of Tomorrow: A Diagnosis of the Spiritual Distemper of Our Time* (London: Heinemann, 1936). Originally published as *In de schaduwen van morgen: een diagnose van het geestelijk lijden van onzen tijd* (Haarlem: H.D. Tjeenk Willink & Zoon, 1935).
29 Oswald Spengler, *The Decline of the West*, 2 vols (London: Allen & Unwin, 1922). Originally published as *Der Untergang des Abendlandes* (Leipzig: Wilhelm Braumuller, 1918–1923). José Ortega y Gasset, *La rebelión de las masas* (Madrid: Revista de Occidente, 1930); Aldous Huxley, *Brave New World* (London: Chatto & Windus, 1932).
30 Schivelbusch, *Entfernte Verwandtschaft*.
31 There is an immense literature on Keynes and Keynesianism. The ones we have found most useful are Roger E. Bachouse and Bradley W. Bateman, *Capitalist Revolutionary* (Cambridge, MA: Harvard University Press, 2011) and Robert Skidelsky, *The Return of the Master* (London: Allen Lane, 2009). Cf. Magnusson and Stråth, *Brief History*, ch. 2.
32 Wagner, Stråth and Joerges, *The Economy as a Polity*.
33 See for example Peter Clarke, *The Keynesian Revolution and its Economic Consequences* (Cheltenham: Edward Elgar, 1998), ch. 10 and Magnusson and Stråth, *Brief History*, ch. 2.

34 Phillipe Schmitter, 'Still the century of corporatism?', *Review of Politics* 36 (1974).
35 Peter Mair, *Ruling the Void: The Hollowing of Western Democracy* (London: Verso, 2013).

Chapter 9

1 Stråth, *Europe's Utopias*; see also Chapter 4.
2 From a current point of view, the comparative analysis needs to be made more nuanced and symmetric by reconsidering the situation around 1960 as a co-existing variety of regional interpretations of modernity. Several steps towards this reconsideration have already been done: in the contemporary, today largely forgotten attempts at a socio-historical mapping of the existing constellation and its historical trajectory (Louis Hartz, *The Founding of New Societies*, New York: Harcourt, Brace, Jovanovich, 1964; Darcy Ribeiro, *The Americas and Civilization*, New York: Dutton, 1971); in the distinction between varieties of Atlantic modernity (North America, South America, sub-Saharan Africa, Europe), see the contributions to Wagner, *African, American and European Trajectories*; in the comparison of varieties of modernity within the BRICS countries see José Mauricio Domingues, *Global Modernity, Development, and Contemporary Civilization* (London: Routledge, 2012); in the on-going work at characterizing in detail the Brazilian, South African and European interpretations of modernity see Jacob Dlamini, Aurea Mota and Peter Wagner, *Possible Futures: The Brazilian, South African and European Trajectories of Modernity Compared* (in preparation). The current book adds to such nuanced comparison by proposing a view of the specificity of European organized modernity, as one regional interpretation among others rather than as a model towards which other world-regions need to aspire.
3 For more detail on what follows, see Wagner, *Progress: A Reconstruction*.
4 A first attempt at analysing the exit from organized modernity was provided in Wagner, *A Sociology of Modernity*. This attempt, however, was limited to Western Europe with a brief glimpse at the USA and historically existing socialism. Furthermore, the sequences of changes in debates and practices were much less visible then than they are now.
5 For two very different forms of nostalgia see Jacob Dlamini, *Native Nostalgia* (Johannesburg: Jacana, 2009); Claus Offe, 'Was (falls überhaupt etwas) können wir uns heute unter politischem "Fortschritt" vorstellen?', *Westend. Neue Zeitschrift fuer Sozialforschung* 7, no. 2 (2010): 3–14.
6 Peter Wagner, 'The project of emancipation and the possibility of politics, or, what's wrong with post-1968 individualism?', *Thesis Eleven* 68 (2002): 31–45.
7 Luc Boltanski and Eve Chiapello, *Le nouvel esprit du capitalisme* (Paris: Gallimard, 1999).
8 For a case study of the shipbuilding industry which demonstrates this development, see Bo Stråth, *The Politics of Deindustrialization* (London: Croom Helm, 1987). For details around the transformation of the labour markets

in the 1970s, the breakdown of Keynesianism and the emergence of the Hayekian neoliberalism, see Stråth, *Europe's Utopias*, ch. 6.

9. See the contributions to Stråth, *After Full Employment*, and especially Peter Wagner's contribution, 'The exit from organised modernity: "Flexibility" in social thought and in historical perspective'.

10. Wolfgang Streeck, *Gekaufte Zeit. Die vertagte Krise des demokratischen Kapitalismus* (Berlin: Suhrkamp, 2013); Wolfgang Streeck, 'Was nun, Europa?', *Blätter für deutsche und internationale Politik* (April 2013): 97–132.

11. Stråth, *After Full Employment*.

12. Alan S. Milward, *The European Rescue of the Nation-state* (Berkeley, CA: University of California Press, 1992).

13. Bo Stråth, 'A European identity: To the historical limits of a concept', *European Journal of Social Theory* 5, no. 4 (Nov 2002): 387–401 (special issue edited by Gerard Delanty); Bo Stråth, 'Identity and social solidarity: An ignored connection. A historical perspective on the state of Europe and its nations', *Nations and Nationalism* 1 (2017).

14. Hagen Schulz-Vorberg and Bo Stråth, *The Political History of European Integration* (London: Routledge, 2010).

15. It seems worthy to note that one of the authors of this book, Peter Wagner, tended to share the hopes of this moment, while the other, Bo Stråth, has always been more sceptical.

Chapter 10

1. For a similar argument regarding Latin America, see Manuel Antonio Garretón, 'Political modernity, democracy and state–society relations in Latin America: A new socio-historical problématique?' in Rosich and Wagner, *The Trouble with Democracy*.

2. See Wagner, *Modernity as Experience*, ch. 11.

3. Svjetlana Nedimović, 'An unsettled past as a political resource', in Wagner, *African, American and European Trajectories*, 197–218.

4. Nathalie Karagiannis, *Avoiding Responsibility* (London: Pluto Press, 2004).

5. It seemed even exportable in this form when Northern European political actors tried to guide the 'democratization' in Southern Europe towards this model.

6. Rosich, *Autonomy in and between Polities*.

7. We explore the question of a debt of Europe towards 'the South' in an ongoing research project, together with other colleagues, called 'The debt: Historicizing Europe's relations with "the South"', funded by the consortium Humanities in the European Research Area (HERA) within the Joint Research Programme 'Uses of the past' (2016–2019).

BIBLIOGRAPHY

Adams, Suzi. 'On Johann Arnason and the religio-political nexus'. *Social Imaginaries* 2, no. 2 (2016).
Arendt, Hannah. *The Human Condition*. Chicago, IL: Harcourt, Brace, Jovanovich, 1958.
Arendt, Hannah. *The Life of the Mind*. Chicago, IL: Harcourt, Brace, Jovanovich, 1975.
Aristotle. *Politics*. Translated by Jonathan Barnes. CUP edition.
Arjomand, Said Amir. *The Shadow of God and the Hidden Imam: Religion, Political Order and Societal Change in Shiíte Iran from the Beginning to 1890*. Chicago, IL: University of Chicago Press, 1984.
Arjomand, Said Amir. 'Introduction'. In *The Political Dimension of Religion*, edited by Said Amir Arjomand. New York: State University of New York Press, 1993.
Arnason, Johann, and Peter Murphy, eds. *Agon, Logos, Polis: The Greek Achievement and Its Aftermath*. Stuttgart: Steiner, 2001.
Arnason, Johann, and Peter Murphy. 'Introduction'. In *Agon, Logos, Polis: The Greek Achievement and Its Aftermath*, edited by Johann Arnason and Peter Murthy. Stuttgart: Steiner, 2001.
Arnason, Johann, Shmuel Eisenstadt, and Björn Wittrock, eds. *Axial Civilizations and World-History*. Leiden: Brill, 2005.
Arnason, Johann. 'The imaginary institution of modernity'. *Revue Européenne des Sciences Sociales* 27, no. 86 (1989): 323–337.
Arnason, Johann. 'Autonomy and axiality: Comparative perspectives on the Greek breakthrough'. In *Agon, Logos, Polis: The Greek Achievement and Its Aftermath*, edited by Johann P. Arnason and Peter Murphy, 155–206. Stuttgart: Steiner, 2001.
Arnason, Johann. *The Peripheral Centre: Essays on Japanese History and Civilization*. Melbourne: Trans Pacific Press, 2001.
Arnason, Johann. *Civilizations in Dispute: Historical Questions and Theoretical Traditions*. Leiden: Brill, 2003.
Arnason, Johann. 'The Axial Age and its interpretors: Reopening a debate'. In *Axial Civilizations and World-History*, edited by Johann Arnason, Shmuel Eisenstadt and Björn Wittrock. Leiden: Brill, 2005.
Arnason, Johann. 'Exploring the Greek needle's eye: Civilizational and political transformations'. In *The Greek Polis and the Invention of Democracy*, edited by Johann Arnason, Kurt Raaflaub, and Peter Wagner. Oxford: Blackwell, 2013.
Arnason, Johann. 'The religio-political nexus: Historical and comparative reflections'. In *Religion and Politics: European and Global Perspectives. Annual of European and Global Studies*, vol. 3, edited by Johann Arnason and Pawel Karolewski, 8–36. Edinburgh: Edinburgh University Press, 2016.

Assmann, Aleida. 'Einheit und Vielfalt in der Geschichte. Jaspers' Begriff der Achsenzeit neu betrachtet'. In *Kulturen der Achsenzeit II. Ihre institutionelle und kulturelle Dynamik*, Teil 3, edited by Shmuel N. Eisenstadt, 330–340. Frankfurt/Main: Suhrkamp, 1992.

Assmann, Jan. 'Große Texte ohne eine Große Tradition. Ägypten als eine vorachsenzeitliche Kultur'. In *Kulturen der Achsenzeit II. Ihre institutionelle und kulturelle Dynamik*, Teil 3, edited by Shmuel N. Eisenstadt, 245–280. Frankfurt/Main: Suhrkamp, 1992.

Assmann, Jan. *Moses der Ägypter*. Munich: Carl Hanser, 1998.

Assmann, Jan. *Das kulturelle Gedächtnis. Schrift, Erinnerung und politische Identität in frühen Hochkulturen*. Munich: Beck, 1999.

Assmann, Jan. *Exodus. Die Revolution der Alten Welt*. Munich: Beck, 2015.

Austin, Gareth. 'Capitalism and the colonies'. In *The Rise of Capitalism: From Ancient Origins to 1848*. Vol. 1 of *The Cambridge History of Capitalism*, edited by Larry Neal and Jeffrey G. Williamson, 301–347. Cambridge: Cambridge University Press, 2014.

Avritzer, Leonardo. 'Modes of democratic deliberation: Participatory budgeting in Brazil'. In *Democratizing Democracy*, edited by Boaventura de Sousa Santos, 377–404. London: Verso, 2007.

Bachouse, Roger E., and Bradley W. Bateman. *Capitalist Revolutionary*. Cambridge, MA: Harvard University Press, 2011.

Baecker, Dirk, ed. *Kapitalismus als Religion*. Berlin: Kadmos, 2003.

Barber, Malcom. *The Cathars: Dualist Heretics in the High Middle Age*. Edinburgh: Pearson Education, 2000.

Bartelson, Jens. *Visions of World Community*. Cambridge: Cambridge University Press, 2009.

Bauman, Zygmunt. *Modernity and Ambivalence*. Cambridge: Polity Press, 1991.

Bayly, Christopher Alan. *The Birth of the Modern World, 1780–1914*. Oxford: Blackwell, 2004.

Beckert, Sven. *Empire of Cotton: A New History of Global Capitalism*. London: Allen Lane, 2014.

Bellamy, Richard, and Dario Castiglione. 'Legitimising the Euro-polity and its regime: the normative turn in EU studies'. *European Journal of Political Theory* 2, no.1 (2003): 7–34.

Benjamin, Walter. *Selected Writings*, vol. 1, edited by Marcus Bullock and Michael W. Jennings. Cambridge, MA: Harvard University Press, 1996.

Benton, Laura. *A Search for Sovereignty: Law and Geography in European Empires, 1400–1900*. Cambridge: Cambridge University Press, 2010.

Berger, Peter, ed. *The Desecularisation of the World*. Washington, DC: Ethics and Public Policy Center, 1999.

Berger, Peter. *The Sacred Canopy*. Garden City, NY: Doubleday, 1967.

Berlin, Isaiah. *Four Essays on Liberty*. Oxford: Oxford University Press, 1971.

Bolsinger, Eckart. *The Autonomy of the Political: Vladimir Lenin's and Carl Schmitt's Political Realism*. Santa Barbara, CA: Praeger, 2001.

Boltanski, Luc. *L'amour et la justice comme compétences*. Paris: Métailié, 1990.

Boltanski, Luc, and Eve Chiapello. *Le nouvel esprit du capitalisme*. Paris: Gallimard, 1999.

Brague, Rémi. *Europe, la voie romaine*. Paris: Gallimard, 1999. First published 1992 by Criterion.

Brague, Rémi. *Eccentric Culture: A Theory of Western Civilisation.* South Bend, IN: St. Augustine's Press, 2002.
Brown, Christopher Leslie. *Moral Capital: Foundations of British Abolitionism.* Chapel Hill, NC: University of North Carolina Press, 2000.
Calhoun, Craig. 'Secularism, citizenship and the public sphere'. In *Rethinking Secularism*, edited by Craig Calhoun, Mark Juergensmeyer and Jonathan van Antwerpen. Oxford: Oxford University Press, 2011.
Casanova, José. *Public Religions in the Modern World.* Chicago, IL: Chicago University Press, 1994.
Casassas, David. *La ciudad en llamas. La vigencia del republicanismo comercial de Adam Smith.* Mataró: Montesinos, 2010.
Cassirer, Ernst. 'Zur Logik der Kulturwissenschaften'. In *Göteborgs Högskolas Årsskrift*, vol. 48. Göteborg: Göteborgs Högskola, 1942.
Castoriadis, Cornelius. 'La *polis* grecque et la création de la démocratie'. In *Domaines de l'homme*. Vol. 2 of *Les Carrefours du Labyrinthe*, 261–306. Paris: Seuil, 1977.
Castoriadis, Cornelius. *L'institution imaginaire de la société.* Paris: Seuil, 1977.
Castoriadis, Cornelius. 'Pouvoir, politique, autonomie'. In *Le monde morcelé.* Vol. 3 of *Les Carrefours du Labyrinthe*, 113–139. Paris: Seuil, 1990.
Castoriadis, Cornelius. 'Imaginaire politique grec et moderne'. In *La montée de l'insignifiance*. Vol. 4 of *Les Carrefours du Labyrinthe*. Paris: Seuil, 1996.
Castoriadis, Cornelius. 'La démocratie athénienne: Fausses et vraies questions'. In *La montée de l'insignifiance*. Vol. 4 of *Les Carrefours du Labyrinthe*. Paris: Seuil, 1996.
Castoriadis, Cornelius. 'La démocratie comme procédure et comme régime'. In *La montée de l'insignifiance* . Vol. 4 of *Les Carrefours du Labyrinthe*, 221–241. Paris: Seuil, 1996.
Castoriadis, Cornelius. 'Fait et à faire'. In *Fait et à faire*. Vol. 5 of *Les Carrefours du Labyrinthe*. Paris: Seuil, 1997.
Castoriadis, Cornelius. *La cité et les lois.* Vol. 2 of *Ce qui fait la Grèce*. Paris: Seuil, 2008.
Chakrabarty, Dipesh. *Provincializing Europe: Postcolonial Thought and Historical Difference.* Princeton, NJ: Princeton University Press, 2000.
Chakrabarty, Dipesh. 'In defence of provincializing Europe: A response to Carola Dietze'. *History and Theory* 47 (Feb 2008): 85–96.
Clark, Christopher. *The Sleepwalkers: How Europe went to War in 1914.* London: Allen Lane, 2012.
Clarke, Peter. *The Keynesian Revolution and its Economic Consequences.* Cheltenham: Edward Elgar, 1998.
Clausewitz, Carl von. *Vom Kriege*, Bd 1–3. Berlin: Ferdinand Dümmler, 1833–1834.
Cohen, Mark R. *Under Crescent and Cross.* Princeton, NJ: Princeton University Press, 1995.
Constant, Benjamin. 'De la liberté des anciens comparée à celle des modernes'. In *Ecrits politiques*, edited by Marcel Gauchet, 589–619. Paris: Gallimard, 1997. First published 1819.
Conze, Werner. 'Arbeit'. In *Geschichte Grundbegriffe. Historische Lexikon zur Politisch-sozialen Sprache in Deutschland*, Bd 1: A–D, edited by Otto Brunner, Werner Conze and Reinhart Koselleck. Stuttgart: Klett-Cotta, 1979.

Cowdrey, H.E.J. *The Cluniacs and the Gregorian Reform*. Oxford: Clarendon Press, 1970.
Crespi, Franco. 'La fine della Secolarizzazione: Dalla Sociology del Progresso alla Sociology dell'Esistenza'. *Studi di Sociologia* 26 (1988).
Crozier, Michel, Samuel Huntington and Joji Watanuki. *The Crisis of Democracy: Report on the Governability of Democracies to the Trilateral Commission*. New York: New York University Press, 1975.
De Sousa Santos, Boaventura. 'Human rights as an emancipatory script? Cultural and political conditions'. In *Another Knowledge is Possible: Beyond Northern Epistemologies*, edited by Boaventura de Sousa Santos, 3–40. London: Verso, 2007.
Delanty, Gerard. *Formations of European Modernity*. London: Palgrave-Macmillan, 2013.
Delanty, Gerard, and Chris Rumford. *Rethinking Europe*. London: Routledge, 2005.
Derrida, Jacques. *La Dissémination*. Paris: Seuil, 1972.
Derrida, Jacques. *L'écriture et la différence*. Paris: Seuil, 1979.
Derrincourt, Robin. *Inventing Africa: History, Archaeology, Ideas*. London: Pluto Press, 2011.
Detienne, Marcel. *Les Grecs et nous*. Paris: Perrin, 2009.
Dewey, John. *The quest for certainty*. In *The Later Works 1925–1953*, vol. 4. Carbondale, IL: Southern Illinois University Press, 1984. First published 1929 by Minton, Balch and Company.
Dlamini, Jacob. *Native Nostalgia*. Johannesburg: Jacana, 2009.
Dlamini, Jacob, Aurea Mota, and Peter Wagner. *Possible Futures: The Brazilian, South African and European Trajectories of Modernity Compared*. In preparation.
Domingues, José Mauricio. *Global Modernity, Development, and Contemporary Civilization*. London: Routledge, 2012.
Donzelot, Jacques. *L'Invention de la société*. Paris: Fayard, 1984.
Drescher, Seymour. *From Slavery to Freedom: Comparative Studies in the Rise and Fall of Atlantic Slavery*. London: Macmillan, 1999.
Drescher, Seymour. *Abolition: A History of Slavery and Antislavery*. Cambridge: Cambridge University Press, 2009.
Dreyer, Edward L. *Zheng He: China and the Oceans in the Early Ming Dynasty, 1405–1433*. New York: Longman, 2007.
Durkheim, Émile. *The Elementary Forms of the Religious Life*. New York: Free Press, 1995. Originally published as *Les formes élémentaires de la vie religieuse* (Paris: Librairie Félix Alcan, 1912).
Durkheim, Émile. *The Division of Labor in Society*. New York: Free Press, 1997. Originally published as *De la division du travail social* (Paris: Alcan, 1893).
Dussel, Enrique. *Politica de la liberación*. Madrid: Trotta, 2007.
Eisenstadt, Shmuel N. 'Kurzer Ausblick auf die westliche Kultur'. In *Kulturen der Achsenzeit II. Ihre institutionelle und kulturelle Dynamik*, Teil 3, edited by Shmuel N. Eisenstadt. Frankfurt/Main: Suhrkamp, 1992.
Eisenstadt, Shmuel N., ed. *Kulturen der Achsenzeit*, vols 1–3. Frankfurt/Main: Suhrkamp, 1992.
Eisenstadt, Shmuel N. 'Religion and the Civilisational dimensions of politics'. In *The Political Dimension of Religion*, edited by Said Amir Arjomand. New York: State University of New York Press, 1993.

Eisenstadt, Shmuel N. *Fundamentalism, Sectarianism, Revolution*. Cambridge: Cambridge University Press, 1999.
Eisenstadt, Shmuel N. 'Multiple modernities'. *Daedalus* 129, no. 1 (Winter 2000): 1–29.
Eisermann, Gottfried. *Die Grundlagen des Historismus in der deutschen Nationalokonomie*. Stuttgart: F. Enke, 1956.
Englander, David. *Poverty and Poor Law Reform in Nineteenth Century Britain, 1834–1914: From Chadwick to Booth*. London: Longman, 1998.
Fabian, Johannes. *Time and the Other*. New York: Columbia University Press, 1983.
Fanon, Frantz. *Les damnés de la terre*. Paris: Maspero, 1961.
Finley, Moses I. *Democracy Ancient and Modern*. New Brunswick, NJ: Rutgers University Press, 1973.
Foucault, Michel. *Les mots et les choses: Une archéologie des sciences humaines*. Gallimard: Paris, 1966.
Foucault, Michel. *L'archéologie du savoir*. Gallimard: Paris, 1969.
Foucault, Michel. 'What is Enlightenment?' In *The Foucault Reader*, edited by Paul Rabinow, 32–50. London: Penguin, 1984.
Fowden, Garth. *Before and After Muhammad: The First Millennium Refocused*. Princeton, NJ: Princeton University Press, 2014.
Frank, André Gunder. *ReOrient: Global Economy in the Asian Age*. Berkeley? CA: University of California Press, 1998.
Fudge, Thomas A. *Jan Hus: Religious Reform and Social Revolution in Bohemia*. London: I.B. Tauris, 2010.
Fudge, Thomas A. *The Trial of Jan Hus: Medieval Heresy and Criminal Procedure*. Oxford: Oxford University Press, 2013.
Fuster Peiró, Angela Lorena, and Gerard Rosich. 'The limits of recognition: History, otherness and autonomy'. In *African, American and European Trajectories of Modernity*, edited by Peter Wagner, 42–63. Edinburgh: Edinburgh University Press, 2015.
Garretón, Manuel Antonio. 'Political modernity, democracy and state–society relations in Latin America: A new socio-historical problématique?' In *The Trouble with Democracy*, edited by Gerard Rosich and Peter Wagner. Edinburgh: Edinburgh University Press, 2016.
Gerstle, Gary, and John Milton Cooper. *Reconsidering Woodrow Wilson: Progressivism, Internationalism, War, and Peace*. Washington, DC: Woodrow Wilson International Center for Scholars, 2008.
Gillingham, John. *Coal, Steel, and the Rebirth of Europe, 1945–1955: The Germans and French from Ruhr Conflict to Economic Community*. Cambridge: Cambridge University Press, 1991.
Goldstone, Jack. *Why Europe? The Rise of the West in World History, 1500–1850*. New York: McGraw Hill, 2008.
Goodman, Nelson. *Ways of Worldmaking*. Indianapolis, IN: Hackett, 1978.
Graham-Leigh, Elaine. *The Southern French Nobility and the Albigensian Crusade*. Woodbridge: Boydell, 2005.
Grandl, Robert. *Die Geschichte der Sozialgesetzverwaltung in Österreich. Von den Anfängen bis 1918*. Vienna: Verlag des österreichischen Gewerkschaftsbundes, 2004.
Grote, G. *A History of Greece*, vol. 5. London, 1851.

Haar, Edwin van de. 'The liberal divide over trade, peace and war'. *International Relations* 24, no. 2 (2010): 132–154.

Habermas, Jürgen. *Legitimationsprobleme im Spätkapitalismus*. Frankfurt/Main: Suhrkamp, 1973.

Habermas, Jürgen. 'On the relations between the secular liberal state and religion'. In *Political Theologies: Public Religions in a Post-secular World*, edited by Hent de Vries and Lawrence E. Sullivan. New York: Fordham University Press, 2006.

Halperin, Sandra. *War and Social Change in Europe: The Great Transformation Revisited*. Cambridge: Cambridge University Press, 2004.

Harley, C. Knick. 'British and European industrialisation'. In *The Rise of Capitalism: From Ancient Origins to 1848*. Vol. 1 of *The Cambridge History of Capitalism*, edited by Larry Neal and Jeffrey G. Williamson. Cambridge: Cambridge University Press, 2014.

Hartz, Louis. *The Founding of New Societies*. New York: Harcourt, Brace, Jovanovich, 1964.

Hatton, T.J., and J.G. Williamson. *Global Migration and the World Economy: Two Centuries of Policy and Performance*. Cambridge, MA: MIT Press, 2008.

Heaton, Herbert. *Economic History of Europe*, 2nd ed. New York: Harper and Row, 1964.

Henningsen, Manfred. *Der Fall Amerika. Zur Sozial- und Bewußtseinsgeschichte einer Verdrängung*. Munich: List, 1974.

Hennock, E.P. *The Origin of the British Welfare State: Society, State and Social Welfare in England and Wales 1800–1945*. London: Palgrave, 2004.

Herzen, Alexander. *My Past and Thoughts: The Memoirs of Alexander Herzen*, translated by Constance Garnett, revised by Humphrey Higgens, introduction by Isaiah Berlin. London: Chatto and Windus, 1968. First published 1924–1927 in Russian.

Hilferding, Rudolf. 'Das Finanzkapital'. *Marx-Studien. Blätter zur Theorie und Politik des wissenschaftlichen Sozialismus*, V-477. Vienna, 1906.

Hirschman, Albert O. *The Passions and the Interests*. Princeton, NJ: Princeton University Press, 1977.

Hobbes, Thomas. *Leviathan*. London: Penguin, 1985. First published 1651.

Hobsbawm, Eric. *Industry and Empire: From 1750 to the Present Day*. Vol. 3 of *The Pelican Economic History of Britain*. London: Weidenfeld & Nicolson, 1968.

Hobsbawm, Eric. *The Age of Empire: 1875–1914*. London: Weidenfeld & Nicolson, 1987.

Hobson, John A. *Imperialism: A Study*. London: James Nisbet, 1902.

Höfert, Almut. *Kaisertum und Kalifat. Der imperiale Monotheismus im Früh- und Hochmittelalter*. Frankfurt/Main: Campus, 2015.

Höfert, Almut, and Armando Salvatore. 'Beyond the clash of civilisations: Transcultural politics between Europe and Islam'. In *Between Europe and Islam: Shaping Modernity in a Transcultural Space*, edited by Almut Höfert and Armando Salvatore. Brussels: P.I.E.-Peter Lang, 2000.

Hölkeskamp, Karl-Joachim, and Elke Stein-Hölkeskamp, eds. *Die griechische Welt. Erinnerungsorte der Antike*. Munich: C.H. Beck, 2010.

Hölscher, Lucian, ed. *Das Jenseits: Facetten eines religiösen Begriffs in der Neuzeit*. Göttingen: Wallstein, 2007.

Honneth, Axel. 'Das Gewebe der Gerechtigkeit. Über die Grenzen des zeitgenössischen Prozeduralismus'. *Westend. Neue Zeitschrift für Sozialforschung* 6, no. 2 (2009): 3–22.
Honneth, Axel. *Freedom's right*. New York: Columbia University Press, 2014.
Honneth, Axel. *Die Idee des Sozialismus*. Berlin: Suhrkamp, 2015.
Hopkins, Thomas. 'Adam Smith on American economic development and the future of the European Atlantic empires'. In *The Political Economy of Empire in the Early Modern World*, edited by Sophus Reinert and Pernille Røge. London: Palgrave, 2013.
Hopkins, Thomas. 'Sismondi on the problems and promise of international trade'. In *Actes de Colloque Sismondi, 'Travaux et Recherches de l'Institut Benjamin Constant'*, edited by Béla Kapossy and Pascal Bridel. Lausanne: Institut Benjamin Constant, 2014.
Hopkins, Thomas. 'The limits of "cosmopolitical economy": Smith, List and the paradox of peace through trade'. In *Paradoxes of Peace in 19th Century Europe*, edited by Thomas Hippler and Miloš Vec. Oxford: Oxford University Press, 2014.
Hountondji, P. *Sur la 'philosophie africaine'*. Paris: Maspéro, 1976.
Huizinga, Johan. *In the Shadow of Tomorrow: A Diagnosis of the Spiritual Distemper of Our Time*. London: Heinemann, 1936. Originally published as *In de schaduwen van morgen: een diagnose van het geestelijk lijden van onzen tijd* (Haarlem: H.D. Tjeenk Willink & Zoon, 1935).
Huntington, Samuel. *The Clash of Civilisations and the Remaking of World Order*. New York: Simon and Schuster, 1996.
Husserl, Edmund. *Die Krise der europäischen Wissenschaften und die transzendentale Phänomenologie: eine Einleitung in die phänomenologische Philosophie*, edited by W. Biemiel. The Hague: Martinus Nijhoff, 1954. Originally published as '*Die Krise der europäischen Wissenschaften und die transzendentale Phänomenologie: eine Einleitung in die phänomenologische Philosophie*' (*Philosophia* 1, 1936: 77–176).
Huxley, Aldous. *Brave New World*. London: Chatto & Windus, 1932.
Inglehart, Ronald, and Pippa Norris. *Sacred and Secular: Religion and Politics Worldwide*. Cambridge: Cambridge University Press, 2004.
Jaspers, Karl. *The Great Philosophers. The Disturbers: Descartes, Pascal, Lessing, Kierkegaard, Nietzsche / Philosophers in Other Realms: Einstein, Weber, Marx*, edited by Hannah Arendt. New York: Harcourt, 1995.
Jaspers, Karl. *Vom Ursprung und Ziel der Geschichte*. Munich: Piper, 1949.
Jones, Eric L. *The European Miracle*. Cambridge: Cambridge University Press, 1981.
Kant, Immanuel. 'Beantwortung der Frage: Was ist Aufklärung?' In *Politische Schriften*. Köln: Westdeutscher Verlag, 1965. First published 1784.
Karagiannis, Nathalie. *Avoiding Responsibility*. London: Pluto Press, 2004.
Karagiannis, Nathalie. 'Democratic surplus and democracy-in-failing: On ancient and modern self-cancellation of democracy'. In *The Trouble with Democracy*, edited by Gerard Rosich and Peter Wagner. Edinburgh: Edinburgh University Press, 2016.
Karagiannis, Nathalie, and Peter Wagner, eds. *Varieties of World-Making*. Liverpool: Liverpool University Press, 2007.
Karagiannis, Nathalie, and Peter Wagner. 'The liberty of the ancients compared to the liberty of the moderns'. In *The Greek Polis and the Invention of Democracy*,

edited by Johann Arnason, Kurt Raaflaub and Peter Wagner. Oxford: Blackwell, 2013.

Kepel, Gilles. *The Revenge of God: The Resurgence of Islam, Christianity and Judaism in the Modern World*. University Park, PA: Pennsylvania State University Press, 1994.

Koselleck, Reinhart. 'The historical-political asymmetries of political counter-concepts'. In *Futures Past: On the Semantics of Historical Time*, 155–191. Cambridge, MA: MIT Press, 1985. Originally published as *Vergangene Zukunft* (Frankfurt/Main: Suhrkamp, 1979).

Koselleck, Reinhart. *Kritik und Krise. Eine Studie zur Pathogenese der bürgerlichen Welt*. Frankfurt/Main: Suhrkamp, 1992. First published 1959 by Alber.

Koskenniemi, Martti. *The Gentle Civiliser of Nations: The Rise and Fall of International Law, 1870–1960*. Cambridge: Cambridge University Press, 2001.

Koskenniemi, Martti. *From Apology to Utopia: The Structure of International Legal Argument*. Cambridge: Cambridge University Press, 2005. First published 1989 by Lakimiesliiton Kustannus.

Koskenniemi, Martti. 'Ruling the world by law(s): The view from around 1850'. In *Europe 1815–1914: Creating Community and Ordering the World: The European Shadow of the Past and Future of the Present*, edited by Martti Koskenniemi and Bo Stråth. Report from the Research Project 'Europe between Restoration and Revolution, National Constitutions and International Law: An Alternative View on the Century 1815–1914', financed by the European Research Council, 2009–2014, University of Helsinki, Dept. of World Cultures/CENS and Faculty of Law/ECI. Helsinki: University of Helsinki, 2014.

Ladurie, Emmanuel LeRoy. *Montaillou, an Occitan Village, 1294–1324*. London: Penguin, 1978. Originally published as *Montaillou, village occitan de 1294 à 1324* (Paris: Gallimard, 1975).

Lahey, Stephen E. *John Wyclif*. Oxford: Oxford University Press, 2009.

Landes, David. *The Unbound Prometheus: Technological Change and Industrial Development in Western Europe from 1750 to the Present*. Cambridge: Cambridge University Press, 1969.

Landes, David. *Wealth and Poverty of Nations*. New York: W.W. Norton, 1998.

Lasker, Daniel J. 'Review of *Under Crescent and Cross: The Jews in the Middle Ages* by Mark R Cohen'. *The Jewish Quarterly Review* 88, nos 1/2 (1997).

Locke, John. *The Second Treatise of Government*. Oxford: Blackwell, 1966. First published 1689.

Loraux, Nicole, and Pierre Vidal-Naquet. 'La formation de l'Athènes bourgeoise: essai d'historiographie 1750–1850'. In P. Vidal-Naquet, *La démocratie grecque vue d'ailleurs*, 161–209. Paris: Flammarion, 2009.

Magnusson, Lars, and Bo Stråth. *A Brief History of Political Economy: Tales of Marx, Keynes and Hayek*. London: Elgar, 2016.

Maier, Hans. 'Demokratie'. In *Geschichtliche Grundbegriffe. Historisches Lexikon zur politisch-sozialen Sprache in Deutschland*, vol. 1, edited by Otto Brunner, Werner Conze and Reinhart Koselleck. Stuttgart: Klett-Cotta, 1972.

Mair, Peter. *Ruling the Void: The Hollowing of Western Democracy*. London: Verso, 2013.

Majumdar, Rochona. *Writing Postcolonial History*. London and New York: Bloomsbury Academic, 2010.

Mann, Michael. *The Sources of Social Power*, vol. 1. Cambridge: Cambridge University Press, 1983.
Mannheim, Karl. *Man and Society in an Age of Reconstruction*. London: Routledge, 1940.
Matlak, Michał. 'Beyond post-secularism: Religion in political analysis'. In *Religion and Politics: European and Global Perspectives. Annual of European and Global Studies*, vol. 3, edited by Johann Arnason and Pawel Karolewski. Edinburgh: Edinburgh University Press, 2016.
Mayer, Arno J. *The Persistence of the Old Regime: Europe to the Great War*. London: Croom Helm, 1981.
Mazower, Mark, *Dark Continent: Europe's Twentieth Century*, London: Lane, 1998.
Meier, Christian. *The Greek Discovery of Politics*. Cambridge, MA: Harvard University Press, 1990.
Meier, Christian. 'The Greeks: The political revolution in world history'. In *Agon, Logos, Polis: The Greek Achievement and Its Aftermath*, edited by Johann Arnason and Peter Murthy. Stuttgart: Steiner, 2001.
Meier, Christian. *Athen. Ein Neubeginn der Weltgeschichte*. Berlin: Siedler, 1993.
Meier, Christian. *Von Athen bis Auschwitz*. Munich: Beck, 2002.
Meier, Christian. *Kultur, um der Freiheit willen. Griechische Anfänge – Anfang Europas?* Berlin: Siedler, 2009.
Mignolo, Walter, *The Darker Side of Western Modernity*, Durham, NC: Duke University Press, 2011.
Milward, Alan S. *The European Rescue of the Nation-state*. Berkeley, CA: University of California Press, 1992.
Mishima, Kenichi. 'The long shadow of European self-interpretation in another modernity'. *Social Imaginaries* 2, no. 2 (2016).
Mohl, Robert von. 'Gesellschafts-Wissenschaften und Staats-Wissenschaften'. *Zeitschrift für die gesammte Staatswissenschaft* 2 (1851): 3–71.
Moore, Barrington. *Social Origins of Dictatorship and Democracy: Lord and Peasant in the Making of the Modern World*. Boston, MA: Beacon Press, 1966.
Moore, Robert Ian. *The First European Revolution*. Oxford: Blackwell, 2000.
Morris, Colin. *The Discovery of the Individual, 1050–1200*. Toronto: University of Toronto Press, 1972.
Mota, Aurea. 'Displacements and absences in the modern spatial imaginary'. In *North – South, Annual of European and Global Studies*, vol. 4, edited by Peter Wagner. Edinburgh: Edinburgh University Press, in preparation.
Müller, Jan-Werner. *Contesting Democracy: Political Ideas in Twentieth-Century Europe*. New Haven, CT: Yale University Press, 2011.
Myrdal, Gunnar. *Economic Theory and Under-developed Regions*. London: Duckworth, 1956.
Nedimović, Svjetlana. 'An unsettled past as a political resource'. In *African, American and European Trajectories of Modernity*, edited by Peter Wagner, 197–218. Edinburgh: Edinburgh University Press, 2015.
Nietzsche, Friedrich. *Zur Genealogie der Moral. Eine Streitschrift*. Bd IV. Zweite Abhandlung: *Schuld, schlechtes Gewissen und Verwandtes*. Munich: Carl Hanser, 1980. First published 1887 by C.G. Naumann.
Nippel, Wilfried. *Antike oder moderne Freiheit? Die Begründung der Demokratie in Athen und in der Neuzeit*. Frankfurt/Main: Fischer, 2008.

Nisbet, Robert. 'Hannah Arendt and the American Revolution'. *Social Research* (The New School) 44, no.1 (1977): 63–79.

Ober, Josaiah. *Political Dissent in Democratic Athens: Intellectual Critics of Popular Rule*. Princeton, NJ: Princeton University Press, 1998.

O'Brien, Patrick. 'Ten years of debate on the origin of the great divergence'. *Reviews in History* 1008, no. 30 (Nov 2010). Available from http://www.history.ac.uk/reviews/review/1008 [accessed 17 October 2016].

O'Brien, Patrick. 'The formation of states and transitions to modern economies: England, Europe, and Asia compared'. In *The Rise of Capitalism: From Ancient Origins to 1848*. Vol. 1 of *The Cambridge History of Capitalism*, edited by Larry Neal and Jeffrey G. Williamson, 357–402. Cambridge: Cambridge University Press, 2014.

Offe, Claus. 'Was (falls überhaupt etwas) können wir uns heute unter politischem "Fortschritt" vorstellen?' *Westend. Neue Zeitschrift fuer Sozialforschung* 7, no. 2 (2010): 3–14.

Oltmer, J. *Migration im Kontext von Globalisierung, Kolonialismus und Weltkriegen. WBG Weltgeschichte. Eine Globale Geschichte von den Anfängen bis ins 21. Jahrhundert. Bd VI. Globalisierung 1880 bis heute*, 177–221. Darmstadt: Wissenschaftliche Buchgesellschaft, 2010.

Orluc, Katiana. 'A Wilhelmine legacy, Coudenhove-Kalergi's Pan-Europe and the crisis of European modernity, 1922–1932'. In *Wilhelminism and its Legacies: German Modernities and the Meanings of Reform, 1890–1930*, edited by Geoff Eley and James Retallack, 219–234. New York: Berghahn, 2003.

Orluc, Katiana. 'Europe between past and future: transnational networks and the transformation of the Pan-European idea in the interwar years'. PhD thesis, European University Institute, Florence/History Dept, 2005.

Ortega y Gasset, José. *La rebelión de las masas*. Madrid: Revista de Occidente, 1930.

Osterhammel, Jürgen. *Die Verwandlung der Welt*. Munich: Beck, 2008.

Outhwaite, William. *European Society*. Cambridge: Polity, 2008.

Outhwaite, William. *Europe since 1989: Transitions and Transformations*. Abingdon: Routledge, 2016.

Palmer, R.R. 'Notes on the use of the word "democracy"'. *Political Science Quarterly* 68, no. 2 (1953): 203–226.

Palmer, R.R. *The Challenge*. Vol. 1 of *The Age of the Democratic Revolution: A Political History of Europe and America, 1760–1800*. Princeton, NJ: Princeton University Press, 1959.

Panaïoti, Antoine. *Nietzsche and Buddhist Philosophy*. Cambridge: Cambridge University Press, 2013.

Pareto, Vilfredo. *Trasformazione della Democrazia*. Rome: Editori Riuniti, 1999. First published 1921 by Corbaccio.

Patočka, Jan. *Heretical Essays in the Philosophy of History*. Chicago, IL: Open Court, 1996.

Pierucci, Antônio Flávio. 'Secularisation in Max Weber: On current usefulness of re-accessing that old meaning'. *Brazilian Review of Social Sciences*, special issue 1 (Oct 2000): 129–158.

Polanyi, Karl. *The Great Transformation: The Political and Economic Origins of Our Time*. Boston, MA: Beacon Press, 2001. First published 1944 by Farrar & Rinehart.

Pollock, Sheldon. 'Axialism and empire'. In *Axial Civilizations and World-History*, edited by Johann Arnason, Shmuel Eisenstadt and Björn Wittrock. Leiden: Brill, 2005.
Pomeranz, Kenneth. *The Great Divergence: China, Europe, and the Making of the Modern World Economy*. Princeton, NJ: Princeton University Press, 2000.
Procacci, Giovanna. *Gouverner la misère: la question sociale en France 1789–1848*. Paris: Seuil, 1993.
Prozorow, Sergei. 'Reclaiming European universalism: What does the "promised land" really promise?' In *Playing Second Fiddle? Contending Visions of Europe's Development*, edited by Hans-Åke Persson, Bo Petersson and Cecilie Stokholm Banke. Malmö: Universus Academic Press, 2015.
Raaflaub, Kurt. *The Discovery of Freedom in Ancient Greece*. Chicago, IL: University of Chicago Press, 2004.
Raaflaub, Kurt. 'Perfecting the "political creature": Equality and "the political" in the evolution of Greek democracy'. In *The Greek Polis and the Invention of Democracy*, edited by Johann Arnason, Kurt Raaflaub and Peter Wagner. Oxford: Blackwell, 2013.
Ranke, Leopold von. *The Theory and Practice of History*. Edited by Georg Iggers. London: Routledge, 2011.
Rawls, John. 'The idea of public reason revisited'. *University of Chicago Law Review* 64, no. 3 (1997): 767–807.
Ribeiro, Darcy. *The Americas and Civilization*. New York: Dutton, 1971.
Riley, Dylan. 'Civic associations and authoritarian regimes in interwar Europe: Italy and Spain in comparative perspective'. *American Sociological Review* 70 (2005): 288–310.
Riley, Dylan. *The Civic Foundation of Fascism in Europe: Italy, Spain and Romania 1870–1945*. Baltimore, MD: Johns Hopkins University Press, 2010.
Rosich, Gerard. *Autonomy in and between Polities*. London: Bloomsbury, forthcoming.
Roy, Olivier. *Holy Ignorance: When Religion and Culture Part Ways*. New York: Columbia University Press, 2010.
Rutherford, Jonathan. 'A place called home: Identity and the cultural politics of difference'. In *Identity: Community, Culture, Difference*, edited by Jonathan Rutherford, 9–27. London: Lawrence & Wishart, 1990.
Said, Edward. *Orientalism: Western Conceptions of the Orient*. London: Routledge, 1978.
Sauvy, Alfred. *Théorie générale de la population*. Paris: PUF, 1963.
Schiavone, Aldo. *La storia spezzata. Roma antica e Occidente moderno*. Bari: Laterza, 1996.
Schivelbusch, Wolfgang. *Entfernte Verwandtschaft. Faschismus. Nationalsozialismus, New Deal, 1933–1939*. Munich: Carl Hanser, 2005.
Schmitter, Phillipe. 'Still the century of corporatism?' *Review of Politics* 36 (1974).
Schreiner, Olive. *The Story of an African Farm*. Project Gutenberg, 2008. First published 1883 under the pseudonym Ralph Iron. Available at http://www.gutenberg.org/files/1441/1441.txt [accessed 17 October 2016].
Schulz-Vorberg, Hagen, and Bo Stråth. *The Political History of European Integration*. London: Routledge, 2010.
Sellin, Volker. *Gewalt und Legitimität: die europäische Monarchie im Zeitalter der Revolutionen*. Munich: Oldenbourg, 2011.

Sellin, Volker. *Das Jahrhundert der Restauration. 1814–1906*. Munich: De Gruyter, 2014.
Semmel, Bernhard. *The Rise of Free Trade Imperialism: Classical Political Economy, the Empire of Free Trade, and Imperialism 1750–1850*. Cambridge: Cambridge University Press, 1970.
Senghor, L.S. *Nation et voie africaine du socialisme*. Paris: Présence Africaine, 1961.
Senghor, L.S. *Liberté 1: Négritude et humanisme*. Paris: Éditions du Seuil, 1964.
Sewell, William H., Jr. *Work and Revolution in France*. Cambridge: Cambridge University Press, 1980.
Shin, Jong-Hwa. 'The historical formation of modernity in Korea: Events, issues and actors'. PhD thesis, University of Warwick, 2002.
Sismondi, Jean-Charles-Léonard Simonde de. *Nouveaux principes d'économie*. Paris: Delaunay, 1819.
Skidelsky, Robert. *The Return of the Master*. London: Allen Lane, 2009.
Skinner, Quentin. 'Some problems in the analysis of political thought and action'. *Political Theory* 2, no. 3 (Aug 1974): 277–303.
Skinner, Quentin. *Liberty before Liberalism*. Cambridge: Cambridge University Press, 1998.
Skirrbek, Gunnar. 'Alternative processes of modernization?' In *Nordic Paths to Modernity*, edited by Johann P. Arnason and Björn Wittrock, 167–189. Oxford: Berghahn, 2012.
Sloterdijk, Peter. *God's Zeal: The Battle of the Three Monotheisms*. Cambridge: Polity Press, 2009.
Smith, Barry, and David Woodruff Smith, eds. *The Cambridge Companion to Husserl*. Cambridge: Cambridge University Press, 1995.
Spengler, Oswald. *The Decline of the West*, 2 vols. London: Allen & Unwin, 1922. Originally published as *Der Untergang des Abendlandes* (Leipzig: Wilhelm Braumuller, 1918–1923).
Stedman Jones, Gareth. 'Introduction'. In Karl Marx and Friedrich Engels, *The Communist Manifesto*, edited by Gareth Stedman Jones. London: Penguin Classics, 2002.
Stedman Jones, Gareth. *An End to Poverty? A Historical Debate*. London: Profile, 2004.
Stedman Jones, Gareth. 'The young Hegelians, Marx and Engels'. In *The Cambridge History of Nineteenth Century Political Thought*, edited by Gareth Stedman Jones and Gregory Clayes, 556–600. Cambridge: Cambridge University Press, 2011.
Stein, Lorenz. *Das Königtum, die Republik und die Souveränität der französischen Gesellschaft seit der Februarrevolution 1848*. Vol. 3 of *Geschichte der Sozialen Bewegung in Frankreich von 1789 bis auf unsere Tage*, 2nd edn. Leipzig: Wiegand, 1855.
Stråth, Bo. *The Politics of Deindustrialization*. London: Croom Helm, 1987.
Stråth, Bo. *The Organisation of Labour Markets: Governance, Culture and Modernity in Germany, Sweden, Britain and Japan*. London: Routledge, 1996.
Stråth, Bo. 'Introduction: Myth, memory and history in the construction of community'. In *Myth and Memory in the Construction of Community, Historical Patterns in Europe and Beyond*, edited by Bo Stråth. Brussels: P.I.E.-Peter Lang, 2000.

Stråth, Bo. 'The concept of work in the construction of community'. In *After Full Employment: European Discourses on Work and Flexibility*, edited by Bo Stråth. Brussels, P.I.E.-Peter Lang, 2000.
Stråth, Bo. 'A European identity: To the historical limits of a concept'. *European Journal of Social Theory* 5, no. 4 (Nov 2002): 387–401.
Stråth, Bo. 'Introduction: Europe as a discourse'. In *Europe and the Other and Europe as the Other*, edited by Bo Stråth. Brussels: P.I.E.-Peter Lang, 2010.
Stråth, Bo. 'Multiple Europes: Integration, identity and demarcation to the other'. In *Europe and the Other and Europe as the Other*, edited by Bo Stråth. Brussels: P.I.E.-Peter Lang, 2010.
Stråth, Bo. '*Ujamaa*: The evasive translation of an elusive concept'. In *Doing Conceptual History in Africa*, edited by Axel Fleisch and Rhiannon Stephens. New York and Oxford: Berghahn, 2016.
Stråth, Bo. *Europe's Utopias of Peace*. London: Bloomsbury, 2016.
Stråth, Bo. 'Identity and social solidarity: An ignored connection. A historical perspective on the state of Europe and its nations'. *Nations and Nationalism* 1 (2017).
Stråth, Bo, and Øystein Sørensen, eds. *The Cultural Construction of Norden*. Oslo: Universitetsforlaget, 1995.
Streeck, Wolfgang. 'Was nun, Europa?' *Blätter für deutsche und internationale Politik* (April 2013): 97–132.
Streeck, Wolfgang. *Gekaufte Zeit. Die vertagte Krise des demokratischen Kapitalismus*. Berlin: Suhrkamp, 2013.
Strong, Tracy B. *Politics Without Vision: Thinking Without a Banister in the Twentieth Century*. Chicago, IL: University of Chicago Press, 2012.
Studer, Roman. *The Great Divergence Reconsidered: Europe, India, and the Rise of Global Economic Power*. Cambridge: Cambridge University Press, 2015.
Tängerstad, Erik. '"The Third World" as an element in the collective construction of a post-colonial European identity'. In *Europe and the Other and Europe as the Other*, edited by Bo Stråth, 157–193. Brussels: P.I.E.-Peter Lang, 2000.
Taylor, Charles. *Sources of the Self*. Cambridge, MA: Harvard University Press, 1989.
Taylor, Charles. 'Cross-purposes: The Liberal-Communitarian debate'. In *Philosophical Arguments*. Cambridge, MA: Harvard University Press, 1995.
Taylor, Charles. *A Secular Age*. Cambridge, MA: Harvard University Press, 2007.
Therborn, Göran. *European Modernity and Beyond*. London: Sage, 1995.
Tocqueville, Alexis de. *De la démocratie en Amérique,* 2 vols. Paris: Gallimard, 1951. First published 1835, 1840.
Tönnies, Ferdinand. *Gemeinschaft und Gesellschaft. Grundbegriffe der Reinen Soziologie*. Darmstadt: Wissenschafliches Buchgesellschaft, 1991. First published 1887.
Topalov, Christian. *Naissance du chômeur 1890–1940*. Paris: Albin Michel, 1994.
Toulmin, Stephen. *Cosmopolis: The Hidden Agenda of Modernity*. Chicago, IL: University of Chicago Press, 1990.
Touraine, Alain. *Critique de la modernité*. Paris: Fayard, 1992.
Trüper, Henning, Dipesh Chakrabarty, and Sanjay Subrahmanyan, eds. *Historical Teleologies in the Modern World*. London: Bloomsbury, 2015.
Urbinati, Nadia. *Mill on Democracy: From the Athenian Polis to Representative Government*. Chicago, IL: University of Chicago Press, 2002.

Vidal-Naquet, Pierre. 'Tradition de la démocratie grecque'. Introduction to M.I. Finley, *Démocratie antique et démocratie moderne*, 9–44. Paris: Payot, 2009.
Vidal-Naquet, Pierre. *La démocratie grecque vue d'ailleurs*. Paris: Flammarion, 2009.
Viroli, Maurizio. *From Politics to Reason of State: The Acquisition and Transformation of the Language of Politics, 1250–1600*. Cambridge: Cambridge University Press, 1992.
Voegelin, Eric. *In Search of Order*. Vol. 5 of *Order and History*. Baton Rouge, LA: Louisiana State University Press, 1987.
Vries, Jan de. *The Dutch Rural Economy in the Golden Age, 1500–1700*. New Haven, CT: Yale University Press, 1974.
Vries, Peer. 'The California School and beyond: How to study the great divergence'. *History Compass* 8, no. 7 (2010): 730–751.
Wagner, Peter. *Sozialwissenschaften und Staat. Frankreich, Italien, Deutschland 1870–1980*. Frankfurt/Main: Campus, 1990.
Wagner, Peter. *A Sociology of Modernity*. London: Routledge, 1994.
Wagner, Peter. 'Crises of modernity: Political sociology in historical contexts'. In *Social Theory and Sociology: The Classics and Beyond*, edited by Stephen P. Turner, 97–115. Cambridge, MA: Basil Blackwell, 1996.
Wagner, Peter. 'The resistance that modernity constantly provokes: Europe, America and social theory'. *Thesis Eleven* 58 (Aug 1999): 35–58.
Wagner, Peter. 'The exit from organised modernity: "Flexibility" in social thought and in historical perspective'. In *After Full Employment: European Discourses on Work and Flexibility*, edited by Bo Stråth. Brussels: P.I.E.-Peter Lang, 2000.
Wagner, Peter. *Theorizing Modernity*. London: Sage, 2001.
Wagner, Peter. *A History and Theory of the Social Sciences*. London: Sage, 2001.
Wagner, Peter. 'The project of emancipation and the possibility of politics, or, what's wrong with post-1968 individualism?' *Thesis Eleven* 68 (2002): 31–45.
Wagner, Peter. 'As intellectual history meets historical sociology: Historical sociology after the linguistic turn'. In *Handbook of Historical Sociology*, edited by Gerard Delanty and Engin Isin, 168–179. London: Sage, 2003.
Wagner, Peter. 'Introduction: The political constitutions of contemporary capitalism'. In *The Economy as a Polity: The Political Constitution of Contemporary Capitalism*, edited by Peter Wagner, Bo Stråth and Christian Joerges. London: Cavendish Press, 2005.
Wagner, Peter. 'Freedom and solidarity: Retrieving the European political tradition of non-individualist liberalism'. In *European Solidarity*, edited by Nathalie Karagiannis. Liverpool: Liverpool University Press, 2007.
Wagner, Peter. *Modernity as Experience and Interpretation*. Cambridge: Polity Press, 2008.
Wagner, Peter. *Progress: A Reconstruction*. Cambridge: Polity Press, 2016.
Wallerstein, Immanuel. *The Modern World System*, 3 vols. New York: Academic Press, 1974, 1980, 1989.
Walzer, Michael. *Thick and Thin*. Notre Dame: University of Notre Dame Press, 1994.
Weber, Max. *Wirtschaft und Gesellschaft. Grundrisse der verstehenden Soziologie*, 5th rev. ed. Tübingen: J.C.B. Mohr, 1980. First published 1922.
Weber, Max. 'Die protestantische Ethik und der Geist des Kapitalismus'. In *Gesammelte Aufsätze zur Religionssoziologie*, vol. 1. Tübingen: J.C.B. Mohr, 1988. First published 1920.

Weber, Max. 'Die protestantischen Sekten und der Geist des Kapitalismus'. In *Gesammelte Aufsätze zur Religionssoziologie*, vol. 1. Tübingen: J.C.B. Mohr, 1988. First published 1920.

Weidner, Daniel. 'Thinking beyond secularization: Walter Benjamin, the "religious turn," and the poetics of theory'. *New German Critique* 111, vol. 37, no. 3 (Autumn 2010): 131–148.

Weinstein, Donald. *Savonarola: The Rise and Fall of a Renaissance Prophet*. New Haven, CT: Yale University Press, 2012.

Williams, Eric. *Capitalism and Slavery*. Chapel Hill, NC: University of North Carolina Press, 1994. First published 1944 by University of North Carolina Press.

Winkel, Harald. *Die deutsche Nationalokonomie im 19. Jahrhundert*. Darmstadt: Wissenschaftliche Buchgesellschaft, 1977.

Wittgenstein, Ludwig. *Philosophische Untersuchungen*. In *Tractatus logicus-philosophicus*. Vol. 1 of *Werkausgabe*. Frankfurt/Main: Suhrkamp, 1969.

Wolff, Larry. 'British travellers and Russian orthodoxy in the age of Enlightenment: The religious features of philosophic geography'. In *Unravelling Civilisation: European Travel and Travel Writing*, edited by Hagen Schulz-Forberg, 129–142. Brussels: P.I.E.-Peter Lang, 2005.

Wolff, Larry. *Inventing Eastern Europe: The Map of Civilisation on the Mind of the Enlightenment*. Stanford, CA: Stanford University Press, 1994.

INDEX

absolutism 128
activism, foreign 156
Adorno, Theodor W. 2
Africa, and Europe 51, 56–7
African labour, legacy of 89–98
agency, and the First World War 159
Albigensians 132
Alexander I 45
Algeria, and France 51
Algerian War (1954) 51
alienation 125
ambiguity 143
America
    African labour in 89–98
    and colonialism 49
    democracy in 53, 55, 78
    dollar collapse 175
    and Europe 52–5, 58
    migration to 54, 99, 100
    neoconservative politics 142
    political culture 54
    rise of 172
American Civil War (1861–1865) 100
American Revolution 52, 53
Andalusia 144
Anti-Corn Law League 107
anti-modernity 64
apathy of citizens 80, 85, 167, 171
Arendt, Hannah 10, 52, 79
Aristotle 75, 80, 81, 84
armaments race 1890s 152, 156
Arnason, Johann 41, 127
Asia, and Europe 55–7
Asian exodus 100
Assmann, Aleida 35
Assmann, Jan 33, 35, 128
Association of the Tax and Economy Reformers, Germany 153
Atlantic trade regime 7

Augsburg Treaty (1555) 129–30, 135, 136
austerity 165
Austria, social legislation 149–50
authoritarian conservatism 157
authoritarian government styles 61
authoritarianism, Europe 46, 163
authority, religion as 131–3
autonomy
    autonomous societies 82
    exclusions to 84
    idea of 15–16
    individual. *See* individual autonomy
    radical concept of 79, 144
    undermining of 17
Axial Age
    Axial Age debate 28–34
    axial transformations 17–18, 33–4, 35, 38, 39
    and civilizational patterns 34–6
    and Europe 36–8
    key contentions of 197n.10
    and modernity 38–9, 187
    as a turning point in history 25–6

Bandung conference (1955) 182
Bauman, Zygmunt 65
Bayly, Christopher 98
Beckert, Sven 95, 97
Begriffsgeschichte 70
Benjamin, Walter 129
Berger, Peter L. 140, 141
Berlin, Isaiah 62, 76, 121, 123
Bibliothèque orientale 56
bilateral free-trade agreements 108 (*see also* free trade)
Bismarck, Otto von 148, 149, 150, 154, 155
Bonaparte, Napoleon 46–7

bourgeois civilization 97
Bourgeois, Léon 150
Brague, Rémi 37, 41–3
Brandt, Willy 59
Brave New World 162
Brazil, Russia, India, China and South Africa (BRICS) 182
Bretton Woods order, collapse of 175
Bright, John 107, 108
Britain
   decolonization 164
   facism 163
   free trade 153
   leaving the European Union 184–5
   social reform 149
   unemployment 151
British Empire 157
British Union of Fascists 163
Buddhism 56
bureaucratization 139, 153
Bush, George W. 63

Calhoun, Craig 142
California School 91, 92, 93
Calvin, John 135
Cambridge contextual history, political thought 70
Capital 105, 151
capital
   and labour 102, 152–7
   reaction to the Great Depression 153
capitalism
   capitalist society 85
   and democracy 62, 87
   development of 90
   and economic growth 91
   and exploitation 105
   global cotton 95
   and imperialism 10, 49–50, 156
   industrial. *See* industrial capitalism
   laissez-faire/developmental 108
   and religion 138–9
   and social problems 102
   war capitalism 95
'Capitalism and Religion' 129
cartels, internationalization of 161
Casassas, David 85
Cassirer, Ernst 162

Castoriadis, Cornelius 14, 15, 32, 71, 79, 82
Cathars 132
Catholic Reformation 136
Central Federation of German Industrialists (CdI) 153
Centralverband deutscher Industrieller. *See* Central Federation of German Industrialists (CdI)
Chakrabarty, Dipesh 57
change
   social 170
   socio-political 10, 16, 174
Charles V 117
Charter of Fundamental Rights of the European Union 2009 124, 188
Chevalier, Michel 108
Christian Roman Empire 37
Christianity
   Christian civilizing mission 143
   Christian fundamentalism 142
   and the Enlightenment 42–3
   and Islam 56
   and origins of Europe 42, 45
Churchill, Winston 171
citizen apathy 80, 85, 167, 171
citizenship, and personal freedom 84–5
Civil War in France, The 105
civil wars, twentieth century 63
civilization, Europe as home of 48
civilizing mission
   in Africa 56
   Christian 143
   of colonialism 52, 54
   European 46, 49, 57, 63
class
   class conflict 158
   class-divided societies 4
   class formation of workers 106–7
   class question 148
   class solidarity 177
   class struggle 104, 148, 149, 154
   'new' industrial capitalist 158
   working classes 107, 149
Clausewitz, Carl von 159
Cleisthenes 77
Cobden-Chevalier Treaty 108
Cobden, Richard 107, 108

INDEX

Cold War 47, 50, 51, 52, 58–9, 62, 163–7
collective bargaining 154
collective self-determination 78, 81, 82, 190–1
collectivism, weakening of 173–4, 179
colonialism (*see also* decolonialization)
   civilizing mission of 52, 54
   colonial empires 3
   and economic growth 92, 93
   and European unification 46, 48–52
   global 95–7
   legacy of 63
   and missionaries 143
   and modernity 12
   and overpopulation 99
   and resistance 57
commerce, African-American-European 89
commercial freedom, and late-Enlightenment revolutions 75
commercial relations, nineteenth century 6, 7
commodification
   ideology of 10
   of labour 102, 209n.39
communication, new forms of 136
Communist Manifesto, The 7, 8, 125
Comte, Auguste 138
conceptuality, and historicity 14–15, 32
Condition of the Working Class in England, The 151
conservatism
   authoritarian 157
   conservative modernity 157
   paternalist 155
Constant, Benjamin 62, 74, 123, 124
Constitution of the European Union 60, 82, 184
contingency, and economic growth 92
control, and organized modernity 170–2
Coudenhove-Kalergi, Richard 47
Counter-Reformation 135
Crimean War (1853–1856) 100, 129
crisis
   and critique 137
   of economic liberalism 148

crisis politics 165
critical self-reflection 42
Critique and Crisis 64
critique, and crisis 137
crystallization 26, 28
cultural relativism 144
cultural representation, of the Orient 56
cultural superiority, of Europe 48
cultural transformations 26
cultural value, Europe as a 48
culture
   American political 54
   European 42
   Greek 42
   of individual autonomy 113, 114, 116, 122
   and politics 35–6
   and religion 46

Davignon Plan 59
debts
   European debt crisis 184
   state 176
Declaration of the Rights of Man and Citizen in France (1789) 117–18, 124
Decline of the West, The 162
decolonialization 50, 57, 164–7, 174, 191
de Gaulle, Charles 58–9
de-institutionalization 178–9, 182, 190
Delors, Jacques 183
democracy
   action and representation/size and self-understanding of 79–81
   American 53, 55, 78
   ancient/modern 82
   and capitalism 62, 87
   and conformism 125
   democratic political imaginary 71–3
   democratic revolutions 26, 69, 75, 76
   democratic self-understanding 76, 81, 141
   economic 175
   and elites 191
   in Europe, 1789–1960s 73–9
   European 189, 192–3

European attitude to 70
evolutionary thinking 77
and exclusion/inclusion 83–6
Germany 77
Greece 73, 77, 79, 82, 83–4, 205n.41
and human rights 190
and individual autonomy 124
liberal 77, 85
and Marx 106
nineteenth-century 76–8
participation in 76
and politico-institutional change 10
postwar 191
and representation 80
and republic 77–8
risks of 79
social preconditions for 86
stability and change in 81–3, 86
and technocracy 166–7
term 77–8, 205n.35
transformations of/key tensions up to the 1960s 78, 79–86
twentieth-century 78–9
and war 160
and welfare economies 165
West European model 166
and world wars 45
democratization 82
demography
  of Europe 50–1
  and industrial capitalism 98
Derrida, Jacques 57
Descartes, René 1, 118, 120, 121
Detienne, Marcel 69, 72
developmental capitalism 108
devotio moderna 136
Dewey, John 119
d'Herbelot, Bartélemy 56
Dialectic of Enlightenment 2
difference, and individual autonomy 116
discourse formations, analysis of 70
Discourse on Method 118
discourses, of the New Great Transformation 179–81
disenchantment 139, 140, 142
Disraeli, Benjamin 149
division of labour, global 151–2

Division of Labour in Society, The 150
domination
  and autonomy 17
  European 12, 94
  and modernity 12, 16
  and suffrage 80
Durkheim, Émile 8, 85, 140, 150

East-West division, Europe 46, 58
Eccentric Culture 42
eccentrism, European 42
economic, and the social 105
economic change, and instability 10
economic crises 47, 78, 175–9, 184
  (*see also* financial crises)
economic democracy 175
economic depression (1950s) 100 (*see also* Great Depression)
economic development
  European 193
  of Japan 157
Economic Ethics of the World Religions, The 139
economic expansion, sustained by naval/military force 94
economic freedom 179
economic growth
  and colonialism 92, 93
  postwar 166
  Western Europe 90, 91
economic integration 60
economic involvement, and political citizenship 83–6
economic market integration, and social disintegration 109
economic modernity
  of Europe 3–4, 109–10
  global dimension of 93, 100
economic progress 170–1
economic stagnation 148, 151, 152, 153, 175, 176
Economic Theory and Under-developed Regions 51
economic theory, classical 103
economics, Keynesian 166, 176
economy(ies)
  global 48
  political 7
  and politics 158, 165–6

Eisenstadt, Shmuel N. 17–18, 25–6, 27, 28, 29, 30, 131–2
elites
  and democracy 191
  economic 159
  and Enlightenment thinking 189
  European 3, 17
  fear of social unrest 103
  government by 173
  new forms of 107
  non-European 4, 6
  and the Paris Commune 148
  and polities 75
  power of 7
  and universal suffrage 81, 85
emancipation
  human/political 77
  and modernity 12
Employers and Workmen Act 1875, UK 149
employment (*see also* unemployment)
  labour without 106
  postwar 166
Engels, Friedrich 7, 105–6, 109–10, 125, 151
Enlightenment
  and autonomy 16
  and Christianity 42–3
  Enlightenment thinking 2, 14, 57, 61, 76, 189
  Enlightenment values 61
  era of 38, 39, 46
  and modernity 1, 11, 13, 26, 64, 186
  and religion 131
Euro crisis. *See* financial crises
Eurocentrism 42, 43, 46, 87–9
Europe
  and Africa 51, 56–7
  and America 52–5, 58
  and Asia 55–7
  authoritarianism 46, 163
  and Axial Age hypothesis 36–8
  as a cultural value 48
  culture of 42
  defining 44–8, 62
  demography of 50–1
  East–West division 46, 58

European integration project 58, 165, 183–4, 191 (*see also* European unification)
  nineteenth-century 6–7
  and organized modernity 183
  origins of 40–3
  post-axial Europe 37
  rise of 3, 192
  as a value community 61–5
Europe of the nations 58–9
European Coal and Steel Community 1951 58
European Communities 1957 58
European eccentrism 42
European exodus 100
European expansion 89
European federation 58
European integration 58, 165, 183–4, 191 (*see also* European unification)
European modernity, derailment of 186–93
European Monetary Union 59
European unification 46–7, 48–52, 58–61 (*see also* European integration)
European Union
  Constitution of the European Union 60, 82, 184
  enlargement of 60
evolutionary thinking, democracy 77
exceptionalism, radical Western 29–30
exchange, new patterns of 95
exclusion
  and democracy 83–6
  social 178
explicitness 13–14
exploitation
  European 49, 97
  of labour by capital 151
  of raw materials 96
  Western 89, 93
  of workers 105
expropriations, of land and labour 95

Fanon, Frantz 51, 57
fascism 45, 64, 160, 162, 163
federalism 59

INDEX

financial crises 60–1, 184 (*see also* economic crises)
First World War (1914–1918) 47, 78, 159
First Worlds 170, 173
flexibility, and neoliberalism 178
Foucault, Michel 39, 40, 70, 190
Fowden, Garth 43
France
  and Algeria 51
  decolonialization 164
  religious wars 118
  solidarisme 150
Frank, Andre Gunder 91
free trade
  Britain 153
  and peace 107–8, 110
  and protectionism 107–9, 152
  and socialism 125
freedom
  economic 179
  individual 63, 193
  individual/collective 77
  and late-Enlightenment revolutions 75
  liberal concept of 76
  and modernity 12, 16
  personal and citizenship 84–5
freedom of speech 72
Freedom's Right 123
French Revolution 1, 8, 46, 47, 51, 64
frontier myth 54–5
functionalism 58
fundamentalism
  American political culture 54
  religious 141, 142, 143–4
  religious/political 130–1

Gandhi, Mahatma 161
Gemeinschaft 150
General Theory of Employment, Interest and Money, The 165
genocides 63
Germany
  democracy 77
  German Association for Social Policy 148, 149
  Great Depression 162
  protectionism 150–1, 152–3

social democrats 154
social integration 148–9
social reform 149
Gesellschaft society 150
global capital regime 161
global financial crisis 60–1 (*see also* financial crises)
global modernity 161
global movement of labour 98–101
global South 182
global trade 89
globalization 2, 142, 174, 182
government
  authoritarian styles of 61
  by elites 173
Great Depression 147, 153, 161–2
Great Divergence 6, 91
Great Society programme 171
Great Transformation 6, 152, 157–9, 169, 174, 181, 188
  New Great Transformation 169, 174, 179–85, 188
Great Transformation, The 10, 158
Greece
  culture 42
  debt crisis 184
  democracy 73, 77, 79, 82, 83–4, 205n.41
  and freedom/self-determination 75
  institutional reform 77
  nineteenth century political view of 76–7
  and origins of Europe 40–1
  political thought 72, 73–4, 79
  politico-cultural transformation 71
Grote, George 77, 83

Halperin, Sandra 158–9
Hegel, G.W.F. 53, 61
Heidegger, Martin 41, 162
Hellenism 40
Herzen, Alexander 131
Hilferding, Rudolf 157
Hirschman, Albert 122
historical materialism 30, 196n.4
historical reflexivity 29, 31, 32–3
historical sociology 28, 31
historicity
  Axial Age hypothesis 197n.10

and conceptuality 14–15, 32
historico-philosophical perspective, of modernity 1, 2–3, 10–14
historico-sociological perspective, of modernity 1, 2–3, 4–6, 8–10
historiography of concepts 32
history
  legacy of Europe 65
  modernity in 15–17
  origins and goals of 25–7, 31
  philosophy of 28, 29, 31
History of Greece 77
Hitler, Adolf 47, 162
Hobbes, Thomas 1, 120, 136
Hobsbawm, Eric 97
Hobson, J.A. 49–50, 156
Holocaust 65
Holy Alliance 45–6
Holy Wars 130, 144
Homer 41
Honneth, Axel 62, 123, 124
Horkheimer, Max 2
Hountondji, Paulin 57
Huizinga, Johan 162
human action, temporality of 15
human agency, and First World War 159
human beings
  relations between 112
  as self-interpreting animals 14
human/political emancipation 77
human rights
  and democracy 190
  and Europe 189
  origins of 117–18
  universal 78–9
Hus, Jan 132–3
Husserl, Edmund 162
Hussite Wars (1420–1431) 133
Huxley, Aldous 162
hypocrisy 63, 64

identification, company-related habits of 177
identity 36, 36–7
immigration, European 100–1 (*see also* migration)
imperialism 10, 49–50, 89, 95–6, 156, 157
Imperialism. A Study 49

In the Shadow of Tomorrow 162
inclusion, social 171
inclusiveness, of democracy 83–6
Indian National Congress Movement 161
individual autonomy
  culture of 113, 114, 116, 122
  and democracy 124
  and difference 116
  European discovery of 113–18
  and European self-understanding 111
  and individualization 124–6
  individuals as source of legitimation 120–1
  knowledge-seeking subjects 118–20
  passions and interests 121–3
  as sole core value 123–4
individual freedom 63, 77, 193
individual rights 76, 179
individualism 187
individualist liberalism 124
individualization
  as the direction of European history 124–6
  negative consequences of 125, 189–90
individuals, as rights-holders 116–18
industrial capitalism
  and labour/raw materials/capital markets 95–6
  and overpopulation 98–9
  and poverty 148
  production relationships of 56
  and property 101
  and social problems 102–3
  and the social question 47, 109
  spread of 44, 90
industrial development 155
industrial relationships 155–6
industrial reserve army 106, 110, 151
Industrial Revolution 26, 87–8, 91, 94, 97, 99, 101–7
industrialization 4, 44, 48, 49, 92–3
industry, knowledge-based 155
inequalities
  international 51–2
  social 103–4
inflationary politics 176

injustice, and modernity 16, 190–1
Innocent III 132
instability, and economic change 10
instituting/instituted moments in society 82
institutional reform, Greece 77
institutional transformations 112
institutionalization 76, 91
institutions, dismantling of 178–9, 182, 190
instrumentalism 187
integration project, European 58, 165, 183–4, 191
intellectual change, and socio-political change 16
interest conflicts 155
interests, organization of 155
international cartels 161
International, the 105
Iranian Revolution 182
Iraq War 63, 142, 143–4
Irenaeus, Saint 43
Islam
  and Christianity 56
  and origins of Europe 43
Islamic State (IS) 130
Italy, fascism 160

Japan, economic development of 157
Jaspers, Karl 11, 25, 27, 28, 29, 30, 40, 41, 155
jihad 144
Johnson, Lyndon B. 171
justice 12, 16

Kafka, Franz 163
Kant, Immanuel 14, 39, 75
Keynes, John Maynard 156, 165–6
  Keynesian economics 166, 176
  Keynesian welfare states 173, 188
Kipling, Rudyard 49
Kjellén, Rudolf 150
knowledge-based industry 155
knowledge, progress of 170
knowledge-seeking subjects 118–20
Koselleck, Reinhart 39, 53, 64–5, 70, 78, 136, 137, 158, 210n.6
Kritik der politischen Ökonomie 106

La Convivencia 144
labour
  African 89–98
  and capital 102, 151, 152–7
  commodification of 102, 209n.39
  expropriations of 95
  global division of 151–2
  global movement of 98–101
  labour markets 177
  labour movements 107, 154
  labour relations 153–4
  without employment 106
  and work 105
laissez-faire 150, 152
laissez-faire capitalism 108
laissez-faire liberalism 147–8
land, expropriations of 95
Landes, David 87–8, 89, 90
las Casas, Bartolomé de 117, 118
law, de-sacralization of 139
League of Nations 47, 48, 161
Lefort, Claude 124
legitimacy, individuals as source of 120–1
Lenin, Vladimir 64
Leo XIII 138
Les damnés de la terre 51
Leviathan 136
liberal democracies 77, 85
liberal enlightenment, crisis of 63
liberal modernity, restricted 80
liberal oligarchies 80
liberalism
  crisis of 156
  laissez-faire 147–8
  market 151–2
  political 76, 123–4
  and universal values 62
liberation, and modernity 12
liberty
  concept of 14–15
  equality of 84
  individual 76
  as a universal right 102
Lisbon Treaty (2009) 124, 188
List, Friedrich 108–9
Locarno spirit 161
Locarno Treaty (1925) 160
Locke, John 1, 52, 102, 120

Lollards 132
Loyola, Ignatius 136
Luther, Martin 133, 134–5
Lutheranism 135, 137

Maastricht Treaty 1992 59, 184
MacMillan, Harold 163
Mair, Peter 167
Malthus, Thomas 98, 105–6
Man and Society in an Age of Reconstruction 9–10
Manchester School 107
Mannheim, Karl 9–10, 78
Marcionism 42–3
market economies, social 166
market freedom 7, 176 (*see also* free trade)
market-industrial revolution 1, 74
market integration, and social disintegration 109
market liberalism 151–2
market nations 177
market self-regulation 10
market society 63, 85
Marshall Plan 58–9
Marx, Karl 7, 8, 9, 56, 77, 104–7, 109–10, 125, 138, 148, 150, 151, 154, 155
Marxism 106, 131, 152
Marxist narratives 88
mass consumption 92
masses, rise of 160
mastery 15, 16, 119
Mazower, Mark 2
Mazzini, Giuseppe 47
mechanical solidarity 150
Meier, Christian 41, 69, 71
Mignolo, Walter 2
migration
  to America 54, 99, 100
  business of 101
  triggers for 99–101
military/naval power 94, 95, 97, 107
Mill, James 104
Mill, James Stuart 123
Mill, John Stuart 77
missionaries, and colonialism 143

modernity
  core model of 187–8
  derailment of European 186–93
  early modernity 188
  in history 15–17
  onset of 27, 38–9
  organized global 161
  origins of 26–7
  term 3
modernization theory 2, 30
monarchies 75
monasticism, Western 132
monotheistic religions, violence between 128
Moore, Barrington 141
Mosley, Oswald 163
most-favoured-nation clause 108
multiculturalism, and modernity 142–3
multiple modernities 26, 27, 28, 30, 35, 39
mundane, and the transcendental 34
Murphy, Peter 41
Mussolini, Benito 162
Myrdal, Gunnar 51–2

Napoleonic Wars (1792–1815) 47
nation, and state 151
nation building, nineteenth-century 45
nation-states
  establishment of 37
  fiction of 151
  Keynesian 188
  and organized modernity 183
national integration, academic-political approach to 149
national socialism 163
nationalism
  ethnic and social 61
  and imperialism 50
  nineteenth-century 45, 47
  and protectionism 151, 152–3, 161
  social 61, 156, 157
  for social integration 150
  in the under-developed world 52
Nationalökonomie 148
native Americans 52, 54, 120
native populations 100
naval/military power 94, 95, 97, 107

Nazism 45, 64, 162
négritude 57
neo-classicism, eighteenth/nineteenth century 41
neo-Roman political thought 75
neoconservative politics, America 142
neoliberalism 173, 175–9
New Age spirituality 141
New Great Transformation 169, 174, 179–85, 188
New Religious Movements 141
Nietzsche, Friedrich 44, 56
nihilism 56
9/11 63, 142, 143
normative project of modernity 12
Nouveaux principes d'économie politique 104

occidental rationalism 5
oil price shocks 175
Old Europe/Young Europe 63
Old World/New World 53–4
oligarchies, liberal 80
onset of modernity 27, 38–9
oppression, and modernity 12, 16
organic solidarity 85, 150
organized capital, and organized labour 152–7, 153–4
organized modernity
 challenging the conventions of 172–5
 demise of 168–70, 174
 and Europe 183
 hierarchization of 156–7
 and nation-states 183
 organized global modernity 161
 and protectionism 152–3
 and the Second Thirty Years War 159–63
 self-image of 170–2
Orient 56–7
Orientalism 56–7
Origin and Goal of History, The 11
origins of modernity 26–7
Origins of Totalitarianism, The 10
Ortega y Gasset, José 162
otherness 13
Others
 demarcation of 48, 49
 and demography 50–1

native Americans 52
 stereotypes of 56
 treatment of 117
overpopulation, and industrial capitalism 98–9

Palmer, R.R. 75
Pan-Europe 47
Paris Commune 105, 148, 149
Parsons, Talcott 8, 140
participation, political 75, 78–9
particularism, European 61
paternalist conservatism 155
peace
 Cold War as 163
 domestic/international 156, 157
 and free trade 107–8, 110
 nineteenth century 158
Peace of Westphalia 46
philhellenism 40
philosophy of history 28, 29, 31
Pius XI 138
Plato 75, 119, 203n.11
Polanyi, Karl 10, 157–9, 181, 188
policies, social/labour market 154
polis
 Greek 41
 size of 80
political apathy 171 (*see also* apathy of citizens)
political capacity, abandoning of 193
political citizenship, and economic involvement 83–6
political culture, American 54
political economy 7
political fundamentalism 130–1
political/human emancipation 77
political imaginary, democratic 71–3
political integration, European 183–4 (*see also* integration project, European)
political liberalism 76, 123–4
political modernity 3, 37, 44–5, 76, 81
political participation 75, 78–9
political philosophy, individualist 116
political problems, perennial nature of 73
political progress 171
political radicalization 176–7

political thought 69–70, 72, 73–4, 75, 79
politico-institutional change 10
politics
    absolute 128–9
    bottom-up approaches to 137
    crisis 165
    and culture 35–6
    of decolonization 57
    of development aid 143
    and the economy 158, 165–6
    European 192
    inflationary 176
    invented by the Greeks 71–3
    neoconservative American 142
    and the political 71
    professionalization of 167
    and religion 4, 34, 112–13, 127–31, 137
    Schumpeterian model of 79
    social politics 157
polities 39, 75, 80
Pomeranz, Kenneth 90, 91, 92
Poor Men of Lyons 132
population theory 105–6
positivism 138
post-modernity 143
post-secularization 141, 142
postcolonialism 57
postwar reconstruction boom 165–7
poverty
    capitalist market economy 103
    and industrial capitalism 148
    and migration 99, 100
    and population growth 98
power
    and the American Revolution 53
    and democracy 81
    differentials of 98
    of elites 7
    global economic/military 49
    illegitimate and unjustified 120–1
    naval/military 94, 95, 97, 109
    state and social politics 157
power relationships
    and colonialism 46
    and cultural representations of the Other 57
    social 38
    and the state 106

Prague Spring 175
private property 106 (*see also* property ownership)
private sphere, religion in 141
production
    American methods of 55
    capacity, and competition 148
    capitalist European/Asian 56
    capitalist mode of 106
    international cartels 161
    ownership of the means of 103, 104
    science-based management of 55
progress, and organized modernity 170–2
property ownership
    and Marx 106
    new forms of 101
    and republicanism 84
property rights 96, 102
protectionism
    and free trade 107–9, 152
    Germany 150–1, 152–3
    and nationalism 151, 152–3, 161
protest, religion as 131–3
Protestant Ethics 139
protestant movement 135
protests
    1960s/1970s 173
    social protest 159–60
    socio-religious protest 137

Quadragesimo Anno 138

Raaflaub, Kurt 34
radical criticism 13
radicality 13–14, 72
radicalization, political 176–7
Ranke, Leopold von 53
rational subjects 14
raw materials, exploitation of 96
Rawls, John 121
reflexivity
    Axial Age hypothesis 197n.10
    historical 29, 31, 32–3
Reformation 133–6
refugees 184
regions, spatio-temporal envelopes of 183

regulation
  and economic growth 91
  self-regulation 122
religion
  as authority and as protest 131–3
  bottom-up approaches to 137
  and capitalism 138–9
  and culture 46
  and the emergence of modernity 133–8
  and the Enlightenment 131
  as European value 143–4
  and politics 4, 34, 112–13, 127–31, 137
  public 193
  religio-political nexus 127–8
  religious conflicts/wars 118, 132–3, 142, 144
  religious diversity 144
  religious fundamentalism 130–1, 141, 142, 143–4
  religious rationalization 139
  rise of religiosity 142
  and violence 128
Renaissance era 38, 114
representation, and democracy 80
republic
  and democracy 77–8
  term 75
republicanism 53, 84, 85
Rerum Novarum 138
reserve army of workers 106, 110, 151
resistance
  and colonialism 57
  to domination 16
  to socio-political transformations 14
resources, exploitation of 93
restricted liberal modernity 80
revolutionary moments 1, 16, 27, 160
revolutionary threats 160
Ricardo, David 104, 106
rights
  individual 76, 179
  liberty as a universal right 102
  property rights 96, 102
rights-holders, individuals as 116–18
risk-taking, and shareholding 101

risks
  of democracy 79
  of self-understanding 81
Romans, and origins of Europe 41–3
Romantic poets 40
Roosevelt, Franklin D. 162
Rousseau, Jean-Jacques 74, 120
Roy, Olivier 142
Ruge, Arnold 77
rule of law 96
Russian Revolution 45, 78

Sacred Canopy, The 140
Saïd, Edward 56
Sauvy, Alfred 50–1
Savonarola, Girolamo 133
Say, Jean-Baptiste 104, 108
Schiller, Friedrich 139
Schmidt, Helmut 176
Schmoller, Gustav 107
Schreiner, Olive 115–16
Schumpeterian model, of politics 79
science-based management, of production 55
Scientific Revolution 7, 26
scientific socialism 148
sea travel, steamships 100–1
Second World 170
Second World War (1939–1945) 47, 78, 82, 163
Secular Age, A 142
secularization, and modernity 111, 127, 138–43
self-critical view, of Europe 30
self-defence of society 10
self-determination
  collective 78, 81, 82, 190–1
  and individual autonomy 113
  and late-Enlightenment revolutions 75
  of the rules for communal life 73
self-government 80
self-reflection 42
self-regulation 10, 122
self-understanding
  democratic 76, 81, 141
  of Europe 63
  modern European 111
  political 72, 182

Senghor, Léopold 57
Sepùlveda, Ginés de 117
Seven Years War (1756–1763) 47
shareholdings 101
shipping companies 101
Sismondi, Sismonde de 104, 108
Skinner, Quentin 70
slave trade 49, 93–4, 95, 99–100, 207–8n.15, 209n.39
slavery 76, 83, 93, 95
Smith, Adam 1, 85, 89, 101–2, 103, 108
social, and the economic 105
social bond, thick theories of 121
social change 170
social conflicts 158
social-contract theory 120–1
social democrats 107, 154
social disintegration, and economic market integration 109
social engineering 64
social exclusion 178
social imperialism 156
social inclusion 171
social inequalities 103–4
social integration
    Germany 148–9
    and modernity 138–43
    nationalism for 150
    as a responsibility of the state 150–1, 159
    welfare for 149
social issue, and European unification 60
social labour, division of 85
social legislation, Austria 149–50
social life, and the market 101
social marginalization 177
social market economies 166
social movements 85
social nationalism 61, 156, 157
social politics 148–9, 157
social power relationships 38
social problems, and capitalist market economies 102–3
social progress 171
social protest 148, 159–60
social reform, United Kingdom/Germany 149

social relations, nineteenth century 5–6, 8
social revolutions 160
social transformations 9, 10, 126, 131, 174–5
social unrest, fear of 102–3
socialism 78, 125, 148, 149, 150, 163
societal transformations, character of 39
socio-cultural transformations 27
socio-historical investigation 29
socio-political change 10, 16, 174
socio-political concepts, ambivalence of 15
socio-political organization 169
socio-political transformations 7, 13, 14
socio-religious protest 137
sociological account, of modernization 2
sociological thought 125
sociology, early European 5
sociology of modern societies 8, 26
sociology of modernity 8–9
Socrates 14
solidarisme 150
solidarity 85, 124, 150, 177
Sources of the Self 113
South African Native National Congress 161
sovereignty, popular 3
Soviet Union, spirituality of 55
space, erasure of 180, 181
spectator theory of knowing 119
speculation bubbles 161–2
Spengler, Oswald 162
Stalinism 163
state of nature 120
state(s)
    and nations 151
    power of and social politics 157
    social integration as a responsibility of 150–1, 159
    state socialism 150
steamships, impact of 101
Stein, Lorenz von 8
stereotypes, of the Other 56
stock markets 101
Story of an African Farm, The 115–16

Streeck, Wolfgang 177
suffrage 78, 80, 81, 85
super-powers 183
superiority, European sense of 4–5
Sweden, national socialism 150
sweet commerce 122
Sybil, or the Two Nations 149

Taaffe, Eduard 149
tariffs, trade 108
Taylor, Charles 14, 113, 142
techno-economic transformation 7
technocracy, and democracy 166–7
Thatcher, Margaret 183
Thatcherism 178
Theory of Justice 121
Third World 170, 171, 182
Thirty Years War (1618–1648) 45, 129, 130
Thirty Years War, second European 159–63
Thousand and One Nights, A 56
three-worlds imagery 170, 182
throne-altar compacts 45
Tiers Monde 50–1
time, erasure of 180, 181
'To a foil'd European revolutionaire' 123
Tocqueville, Alexis de 8, 10, 53, 55, 78, 124, 125, 188
Tönnies, Ferdinand 150
totalitarianism 10, 63
trade
  British 93
  global 89
  trade tariffs 108
trade unions 153, 177, 178
Traité d'économie politique 104
Transatlantic Trade and Investment Partnership (TTIP) 189
transcendental, and the mundane 34
transcendental reflection 138
transformations (*see also* Great Transformation)
  eighth to second centuries BCE 29
  institutionalized 33
  social transformations 9, 10, 126, 131, 174–5

socio-political transformations 7, 13, 14
transport markets 101
travel, steamships 100–1
Treaty of Westphalia 37
Trilateral Commission 182
Turner, Frederick Jackson 54
'Two Concepts of Liberty' 121
tyranny of the majority 81

Unbound Prometheus, The 87
under-developed regions 52
unemployment 148, 151, 162, 176, 177 (*see also* employment)
unification of Europe 46–7, 48–52, 58–61 (*see also* European integration)
United Kingdom. *See* Britain
United Nations Universal Declaration of Human Rights 1948 78, 81, 117, 118
United States. *See* America
United States of Europe (USE) 58
unity in diversity, European Union 60–1
universal modernization 52
universal right, liberty as 102
universal suffrage 78, 80, 81, 85
universal values, and liberalism 62 (*see also* values)
universalism, European 61–2
unpolitical moment 136

Valladolid-Salamanca debates 117
value community, Europe as a 61–5
values
  Enlightenment values 61
  European 63
  individual autonomy as sole core value 123–4
  religion as a European value 143–4
  universal 62
veil of ignorance 121
Verein für Sozialpolitik. *See* Association for Social Policy, Germany
Vereinigung der Steuer- und Wirtschaftsreformer. *See* Association of the Tax and Economy Reformers, Germany

Versailles Peace Treaty (1919) 7, 48, 160, 161
Vienna Congress 1815 7, 16, 47
Vietnam War 175
violence, and religion 128
violent European conflicts 47–8
Voegelin, Eric 27, 28, 29, 30
Voltaire 56
Vries, Peer 93

Waldensians 132
Wallerstein, Immanuel 90
Walzer, Michael 121
war(s) (*see also* names of individual wars; world wars)
   and democracy 160
   war capitalism 95
   War on Poverty 171
   wars on terror 63, 143
Wealth of Nations, The 102
Weber, Alfred 27, 28
Weber, Max 5, 8, 9, 27, 28, 29–30, 37, 64, 78, 88, 125, 127, 131, 138–40, 152, 167
Weimar Republic 160, 162
welfare
   government-supported 98–9
   for social integration 149
welfare economies 165, 175
welfare states 63, 149, 171, 173, 178, 188
Werner Plan 59
Western Europe
   and Eastern Europe 58
   economic growth 90, 91
   rise of 91
   superiority of 46
Western supremacy 63
white man's burden 54 (*see also* civilizing mission)
white supremacy 49
Whitman, Walt 123
Wilhelm II 156
Winckelmann, Johann Joachim 40
Wittgenstein, Ludwig 120
women, and democracy 76, 83
women's movement 174
work, and labour 105
workers
   radicalization of 176–7
   reserve army of 106, 110, 151
   worker representation 153
working classes 107, 149
world-domination, European 3, 6, 7, 11
World Economic Forum 182
World Social Forum 182
world wars 45, 47 (*see also* First World War (1914–1918); Second World War (1939–1945))
Wycliffe, John 132

Young Europe/Old Europe 63

Zwingli, Huldrych 135

www.ingramcontent.com/pod-product-compliance
Lightning Source LLC
Chambersburg PA
CBHW050137240426
43673CB00043B/1698